Liturgical Semiotics
from Below

Liturgical Semiotics from Below

Breathing Up the Holy Eucharist

KEVIN O. OLDS

PICKWICK *Publications* · Eugene, Oregon

LITURGICAL SEMIOTICS FROM BELOW
Breathing Up the Holy Eucharist

Pickwick Publications
An Imprint of Wipf and Stock Publishers
199 W. 8th Ave., Suite 3
Eugene, OR 97401

www.wipfandstock.com

PAPERBACK ISBN: 978-1-6667-8302-5
HARDCOVER ISBN: 978-1-6667-8303-2
EBOOK ISBN: 978-1-6667-8304-9

Cataloguing-in-Publication data:

Names: Olds, Kevin O., author.

Title: Liturgical semiotics from below : breathing up the holy eucharist / Kevin O. Olds.

Description: Eugene, OR : Pickwick Publications, 2023 | Includes bibliographical references and index.

Identifiers: ISBN 978-1-6667-8302-5 (paperback) | ISBN 978-1-6667-8303-2 (hardcover) | ISBN 978-1-6667-8304-9 (ebook)

Subjects: LCSH: Sacraments (Liturgy). | Semiotics—Religious aspects.

Classification: BV170 .O53 2023 (paperback) | BV170 .O53 (ebook)

12/06/23

This book is dedicated to my sons, Zack and Tommy. Boys, you can accomplish things in this life that you never dreamed possible. Just trust in the story of God's love for you, read the signs of that love in the world around you and in your lives, and connect the dots.

Contents

Introduction

"Take a deep breath and focus on what's really important."

~WAYNE DYER[1]

THE SUPER BOWL AS AMERICAN RITUAL

IT IS ESTIMATED THAT over 112 million people watched the NFL's Super Bowl on February 13, 2022.[2] This is about six and a half times higher than the average NFL viewership of 17.1 million.[3] The meaning inherent in these data is that a lot of people watch the Super Bowl who do not usually watch football.

This should come as no surprise. Simple observation tells us that, every February, millions of people who are not football fans watch the Super Bowl. They often participate in any number of associated activities: attending Super Bowl parties, spotting celebrities and dignitaries in the stands, watching the oft-hyped commercials during the broadcast, making a parlay in an office pool, or becoming at least dimly aware of the storylines that are ballyhooed for a full two weeks before the event.

The Super Bowl, and everything that comes with it, is an example of American ritual par excellence.

THE IMPORTANCE AND UBIQUITY OF RITUAL

At its most basic, ritual is "an act or series of acts regularly repeated in a set precise manner."[4] In a secular sense, one could define rituals as "symbolic

1. Dyer, "Go with the Love," para. 1.
2. NBC Sports Group Press Box, "NBC Sports' Coverage," para. 1.
3. Jones, "NFL," para. 1.
4. *Merriam-Webster*, s.v. "Ritual," https://www.merriam-webster.com/dictionary/ritual.

techniques of making oneself at home in the world."[5] For Christians, a natural definition of ritual might be a "customary practice relating to a religion that is often an expression of worship."[6]

Yet ritual does not exist exclusively within the purview of religion, of course. In addition to the Super Bowl, think about the inauguration of the president of the United States. It is a series of acts regularly repeated in a precise manner. It even includes an oath.

In a less grandiose manner, parents understand the importance and prominence of ritual when it comes to their children. There are any number of bedtime rituals, for example, from teeth brushing to story reading to prayers, that are designed to foster restful sleep and keep at bay whatever is perceived to lurk under the bed or in the closet.

Not only are rituals everywhere, but they have been everywhen. Ritual has been engaged in by cultures around the world and throughout history. While their form and content vary, rituals are a universal aspect of human civilization.

Victor Turner, a pioneer of ritual study in the twentieth century, noted that ritual "might be said to 'create' society, in much the same way as Oscar Wilde held life to be 'an imitation of art.'"[7] These rituals can pertain to the individual as they mark various status changes ("life-crisis rites") or pertain to groups, or society as a whole, at various appointed times ("calendrical rites"). In either case, it is the performance of the rituals themselves that help to create true community, something Turner referred to as "communitas."

Further, according to Matt Rossano, ritual was critical to the very formation of the modern human. Rossano's argument rests on four premises: "(1) Humanity is defined by cooperative communities, (2) cooperative communities are defined by shared values, (3) shared values are defined by ritual, and (4) religious ritual elevates shared values to sacred status."[8]

While religious ritual once elevated shared values to sacred status, the intersection of institutional religious ritual with postmodern American society is fading. More and more, funeral services are being held in funeral homes rather than churches, and sometimes without clergy present. More and more, weddings are happening at "destinations" rather than churches, with civic rather than clerical officiants.

---

5. Han, *Disappearance of Rituals*, 2.

6. Witthoff, *Lexham Cultural Ontology Glossary*, s.v. "ritual."

7. Turner, *Ritual Process*, 117.

8. Rossano, "Ritual Origins of Humanity," 3.

This fading of religious ritual in society has contributed to what Byung-Chul Han has described as the "communication without community"[9] which prevails today in Western culture. While there are still rituals, they "do not exert the symbolic force which directs life towards something higher and thus provides meaning and orientation."[10]

ANXIETY AND INSTITUTIONAL DIMINISHMENT

If ritual has not only existed as a part of human culture since our beginning, but was actually central to our becoming human, then it is a far more crucial aspect of our common life than one might first think. Its dissociation from religious institutions is both worrisome and important to keep in mind as we take stock of our situation.

In many ways, our world is not in a good way in this year of our Lord, 2023. Even before the COVID-19 pandemic, "mental disorders were leading causes of the global health-related burden, with depressive and anxiety disorders being leading contributors to this burden."[11] All the pandemic related stress and pressure of what we have been under as the human family since the beginning of 2020 has only exacerbated our collective depression and anxiety. It is up at least 26 percent according to one study.[12]

On top of that, consider the political discourse in the United States. The events of the last few years suggest that it is the most divisive that it has been in generations.

Also, let us not forget the state of racial relations in this country. From the disproportionate level of incarceration for people of color to the fact that too many of our brothers and sisters "can't breathe," it can be argued that something is systemically, and dreadfully, wrong in our society.

After moving from the global to the national, let us now get even more granular. Before the COVID-19 crisis, there was a lot of anxiety among American Christians about the steady decline of the institutional church, particularly among mainline denominations. That anxiety has also heightened with not only the impact of the virus, but with the great uncertainty about what the near future holds for the church.

9. Han, *Disappearance of Rituals*, 1.
10. Han, *Disappearance of Rituals*, 91.
11. COVID-19 Mental Disorders Collaborators, "Global Prevalence," 1700.
12. COVID-19 Mental Disorders Collaborators, "Global Prevalence," 1700.

To wit, in 2021 a blog post entitled "The Death of the Episcopal Church Is Near"[13] caused a bit of clamor in digital Episcopal circles. The post, after presenting a variety of data, boldly suggested the demise of the denomination by 2040.

Broadening the perspective, consider that as of 2021, about 30 percent of Americans consider themselves to be religiously unaffiliated.[14] This statistic is up ten points in the last decade. Professed Christians make up 63 percent of the population, down from 75 percent a decade ago.

This is the religious and social zeitgeist into which my work is being birthed. The mainline denominations are beset by anxiety and fear over the graying of their congregations and the closing of their churches. Indeed, they have existed in this state of vexation for an entire generation, ever since the post-WWII church boom began to fade.

Now add to that all that the pandemic has brought the institutional church in America. There are no two ways about it, things look dour. As people of faith, Christians can be assured that in the end (at the eschaton, as the theologians say) everything will be okay. The near future, however, is much more in question.

A DIFFERENT INTERPRETATION

The conventional wisdom in interpreting this long-standing trend is to suggest that America is becoming more and more secular. Tara Isabella Burton, in her book *Strange Rites: New Religions for a Godless World*, suggests a different interpretation.

Instead of a societal shift from religious to secular, Burton sees a rise in what she calls Remix culture. The remixing of culture is the result of the interweaving of all areas of life and thought, due to the rise of the Internet, combined with a belief that everything can be customized to the individual (including belief systems). She sketches out three segments of Remixed Americans, which taken together make up over half of the adult population in the United States.[15]

The first group is those who are spiritual but not religious. These people, while identifying as not religious, may or may not have a religious affiliation. Even if they identify with a religion, however, "their primary source of

13. Burge, "Death of the Episcopal Church Is Near."

14. Smith, "About Three-in-Ten U.S. Adults."

15. Burton looks primarily to the Pew Research Center and the Public Religion Research Institute for her data. She then aggregates and approximates both sets of data (Burton, *Strange Rites*, 250).

what we might call meaning-making, their sense of purpose, their source of wonder at the world, come from outside their religious traditions."[16]

The second group are faithful Nones. These are people who are religiously unaffiliated yet have a belief in something beyond science alone (e.g., a higher power, God, or something else). They do not subscribe to the institutions of organized religion, but they often "seek out other forms of community life, finding and creating rituals with a chosen family of like-minded people who may or may not share their metaphysical example."[17]

The third group are religious hybrids. These are people that do identify with a given religion, but take a buffet style approach to it. They feel free to believe and practice certain parts of the religion they identify with, but eschew other parts of it. They may also "supplement their official practice with spiritual or ritualistic elements, not to mention beliefs, from other traditions."[18]

These three distinct segments of Remixers appear to share certain qualities. One, they are all searching for meaning. This is common to all of humanity, if the truth be told. We as a species are hungry for meaning. Yet those who identify as spiritual or religious tend to be more vigilant about that quest.

Two, they find ritual to be important. Whether an official part of a religion or not, Remixed Americans have certain rites that they intentionally engage in to their betterment. If one is not available that meets their needs, they create one.[19]

Three, they see individual experience as more important than corporate belief. If a doctrine or creedal statement does not match with their lived experience, then that doctrine or creedal statement can be devalued. Identities, including beliefs, are formed inside-out rather than outside-in.

Together these three groups, and these three characteristics, make up a majority of Americans.

16. Burton, *Strange Rites*, 19.

17. Burton, *Strange Rites*, 21.

18. Burton, *Strange Rites*, 22.

19. One example might be the actions or activities that have cropped up around someone taking a new name following gender transition. While some churches have now entered this ritual space with liturgies, the desire for an intentional gathering to find meaning in this event was born out of the transgender community and met by that community. The trend of which this is an example has even birthed a new industry: nonreligious ritual design.

THE RESPONSE: LITURGICAL SEMIOTICS

How ought the church in America respond to the situation it finds itself in? The institutional church is in decline. Ritual, historically a crucial point of intersection between the church and the wider culture, appears to be losing its intersectionality. How are we as the body of Christ, the church, to respond?

I suggest that we follow the advice of the quote at the beginning of this introduction: let's take a deep breath and focus on what's really important. For us as Christians, I identify worship as what is really important. Further, I submit that the means of focus is something called *liturgical semiotics.*

Remixers, in their search for meaning through the personal experience of ritual, are sending a strong signal to the institutional church. The signal is that this concept, liturgical semiotics, occupies a place of importance in the twenty-first-century human condition.

Semiotics is the study of signs and their ability to transmit meaning. When people are searching for meaning, they are doing semiotics. Their finding of that meaning is grounded in their personal experience.

Liturgy, which is often loosely translated from its Greek origin as *the work of the People,* can be understood to be Christian worship. This also can be considered to encompass ritual, and when interpreted broadly, even many kinds of ritualized activities.

A Trinitarian Approach

My vision of liturgical semiotics is threefold. I advocate a trinitarian approach, if you will.

First, liturgical semiotics can lead to the uncovering of new meaning in worship. By reading the signs of our liturgy, and connecting the dots of the stories it tells, new insights can be gained.

Second, liturgical semiotics can lead to more evocative worship. As we progress through the church year, certain days or seasons call for particular emphases in our corporate worship. Enacting our worship with intentionality can make those liturgical events more redolent of the day's focus.

Three, liturgical semiotics can make our worship more resonant with the current culture. The cultural significance that various objects carry changes over time. The church finds itself in a time when how it understands the artifacts it uses in worship differs greatly from how the culture of the day understands them. Liturgical semiotics can help bridge that gap.

The Hope

There are multiple hopes implicit in this triadic approach to liturgical semiotics.

Perhaps least importantly, there is the hope that, by making our worship more resonant with the current culture, more people will join the church. While this would indeed be welcome, it is best seen as a by-product of the primary aim, rather than the aim itself.

A better hope to name is that there will be a quickening, a vivification, of our worship as Christians. We will find more meaning in our worship, and we will discover how to worship more meaningfully.

The hope in bringing our use of worship artifacts more in line with how the wider society understands them is twofold. Yes, there is the hope that denizens of the current culture, the Remixers and others, will be better able to understand Christian worship. Yet there is also the hope that we will understand the natives of the current culture better by grasping a bit more how they experience and interpret the world around them.

Most importantly, the hope in liturgical semiotics is that, as followers of Christ, we will be more truly ourselves. To focus on worship by undertaking liturgical semiotics is to get back to the heart and soul of who we are. If we are doing what is most important to us as Christians (i.e., worship), and endeavoring to do it better, then we are living out of our core identity as followers of Christ. Come what may, we are being true to ourselves.

Will liturgical semiotics solve the problem of institutional decline? It seems doubtful. The factors that have contributed to the decline are numerous and intertwined, and there is no magic bullet that will reverse it. Liturgical semiotics is no panacea.

Will liturgical semiotics enrich our lives as Christians and perhaps come with benefits heretofore undiscovered? Almost certainly. Who knows, it may even provide a path forward toward the church that will be.

A Kindness

As Brené Brown has written, "clear is kind."[20] So let me be kind: the thesis of this book is that the doing of liturgical semiotics will lead to the discovery of new meanings in existing liturgies, improvements in the enacting of those liturgies by making them more evocative of the intended emphasis of the event, and bring the use of worship artifacts more in line with current

---

20. Brown, "Clear Is Kind. Unclear Is Unkind."

cultural understandings. This statement encompasses the threefold approach described above. This kindness is revisited in the book's conclusion.

The Form of What Follows

This is the journey of liturgical semiotics, and that is what this book is about. The journey is taken over five parts. By its end, those who have walked this path will be equipped to begin their own unique journeys into liturgical semiotics.

Part One ("With Bated Breath") is broken into two chapters. Chapter 1 makes an argument for the importance of worship as the central act of the church. Chapter 2 introduces the narraphor[21] of breathing as an apt one for exploring worship.[22]

This part lays the foundation for what is to follow. It is preparatory work that situates us to then delve more deeply. If worship is not understood as critically important to the Christian identity, then exploring liturgical semiotics carries little weight. Exploring the concept of a narraphor as an excellent transmitter of meaning will bolster the later discussion. Choosing a narraphor to apply to this work aids in its own meaning transmission.

Part Two ("A Breath of Fresh Air") is broken into two chapters. Chapter 3 gives a foundational understanding of the two parts that make up liturgical semiotics: semiotics and liturgy. Chapter 4 lays out my approach to liturgical semiotics as captured in the acronyms BREATHE, GASP, and RASP.

Chapter 5 reviews the kind of work done in liturgical semiotics until now, with an eye toward how that work differs from my approach. This chapter provides a window into what the academy has had to say about the subject, and so the language is rather academic. It sounds different from the rest of the book because it is different from the rest of the book. While it can be skimmed or skipped without losing sight of what I am saying about liturgical semiotics, it is fertile ground for those wanting to know more about what others have had to say about this subject, and where my work stands in relation to it.

Having begun with general preparatory work in the last part, this part introduces the concept of liturgical semiotics and sketches out its landscape. While searching for meaning in worship is not novel, my approach to that search is. In a general sense, I bring the story-based semiotics of Leonard

21. If unfamiliar with this term, for the moment think of a narraphor as a narrative plus a metaphor, a story wrapped around an image.

22. This is why every part and chapter has idioms or quotes that are breath related.

Sweet into conversation with liturgy. I also, however, include elements of other semioticians, such as Charles Sanders Peirce and Crystal Downing.

Part Three ("Breathe In through Nose, and Out through the Mouth") is also broken into three chapters. Chapter 6 provides a practical application of the BREATHE process by looking at the actions taken with the bread and wine at the altar. Chapter 7 gives a practical application of the GASP tools, making the fraction of the bread more evocative of particular celebrations. Chapter 8 is a practical application of the RASP task, (re)signing the bread and wine to generate fresh signs for the current culture.

I see semiotics as a discipline that is always applied to other disciplines. As one seeks meaning, they are seeking meaning in *something*. That something could be anything, but it always has specificity. This means semiotics is an inherently practical, rather than an abstract, task. Hence the importance of having chapters of practica that demonstrate the approaches to liturgical semiotics developed in chapter 4.

Part Four ("Breathing Space . . . and Time") is divided into two chapters. Chapter 9 explores the semiotics of liturgical space. Chapter 10 delves into the semiotics of liturgical time.

Every liturgical event shares at least two characteristics. It happens in a particular place and at a particular time. Everything we do, including worship, happens within the confines of space and time. This part allows the broadening of semiotic perspective to consider that which is ubiquitous and therefore often becomes invisible to us: space and time.

Part Five ("Deep Breathing Exercises") is broken into two chapters and looks at how liturgical semiotics can be more broadly applied than to just the Rite II Holy Eucharist from the Episcopal Church's Book of Common Prayer. As an Episcopal priest, the Holy Eucharist is inexorably bound up with my understanding of my vocation. Thus it is where I have focused my journey into liturgical semiotics. But liturgical semiotics is not solely a eucharistic endeavor, or an Episcopal one for that matter.

Chapter 11 is about the semiotician finding their unique identity. It helps someone to develop their own approach and practice of liturgical semiotics. Chapter 12 is about providing jumping off points for further semiotic engagement. Various worship services are presented, and a point of semiosis is introduced for each.

Liturgical semiotics as I present it has a decidedly Episcopal bent. This part broadens the perspective so that non-Episcopalians may feel prepared to engage liturgical semiotics in their own contexts. It also provides some points of engagement and a few thoughts on how to go about doing liturgical semiotics in the places they find themselves.

WHAT'S IN A NAME?

"What's in a name? That which we call a rose by any other word would smell as sweet."[23]

In his play *Romeo and Juliet*, William Shakespeare suggests that the naming of things is irrelevant. While this sentiment is on point for the purposes of the play, I offer that the names we give things can be quite relevant. Before concluding this introduction, the name given to this book, *Liturgical Semiotics from Below: Breathing Up the Holy Eucharist*, needs to be addressed. Delving into what is meant by this title constitutes a brief foray into the bounty of semiotics.

Taken in pieces, one may find that most of the title makes eminent sense. Above, the notion of *liturgical semiotics* was broached. For the majority of Christians, *the Holy Eucharist* is a familiar phrase.

Likewise, the phrase *from below* likely carries some basic connotation: something is ascending, having started lower and is now rising higher. It may well conjure up images of underwater vistas, underground scenes, or aerial maneuvers. It may even bring to mind a value judgment where being *from below* is less desirable than being *from above*.

The phrase *breathing up*, however, may resist easy interpretation. One might breathe quickly or slowly, deeply or shallowly. But does one breathe down or up? How to make sense of this phrase, much less apply it to the Holy Eucharist?

The interpretive key lies in a specific field of endeavor called freediving. Instead of using underwater breathing apparatus, such as scuba tanks, freedivers hold their breath while underwater. There are many ways to engage in freediving, but to give an example of the undertaking, the deepest that someone has gone while holding their breath is 830.[24]

In freediving parlance, the breathe up is "a series of breaths that are aimed at relaxing the body and mind, and getting [divers] into a good place to begin."[25] It is part of the preparation for making a freedive. To put it simply, to engage in a breathe up leads to better freediving.

With all the pieces of the full title examined, we next turn to how those pieces have been put together, beginning with the title proper: *Liturgical Semiotics from Below*. This might well also offer interpretive difficulty, as one might be hard pressed to imagine how to apply directionality to liturgical semiotics.

---

23. Shakespeare, *Tragedy of Romeo and Juliet*, 2.2.43–44.

24. Guinness World Records, "Deepest No-limit Freedive (Male)."

25. Blue Corner Dive, "How to Relax," para. 1.

Yet there is another meaning for *from below* which comes to us from theological discourse. Chapter 5 dives into these waters in more detail, including how that terminology finds expression. For our introductory purposes, however, from below can be considered to be more practical and pragmatic rather than conceptual and abstract. Thus, liturgical semiotics from below is more focused on praxis than it is on theory.

In contemplating the subtitle, *Breathing Up the Holy Eucharist*, the theme of preparation comes through. As one breathes up to prepare themselves for a freedive, one breathes up to prepare themselves to celebrate the Holy Eucharist. Doing so will lead to better worship.

Beyond these specific meanings laid out in the construction of the title, there are several ancillary meanings that might come to the fore as one continues to ponder. Here are four:

- The Holy Eucharist is the liturgy that is used as the primary example in the book.

- *From below* in the title and *up* in the subtitle are either juxtaposed or complementary, depending on how one interprets them.

- Breathing is a metaphor that is carried throughout the book.

- One breathes up in order to go down, to plumb the depths—either of the water or of the liturgy.

More meanings are available, depending on the interpreter's (i.e., the semiotician's) knowledge base and cultural context. The full title is one that is semiotically rich, and provides a glimpse into the world of meaning-making. Yet, this exercise of finding out what's in the name of this book is just scratching the surface of semiotics. Much more lies ahead—or perhaps below.

CONCLUSION

This book is about getting back to what is at the core of the Christian identity, worship, and exploring how to find and make meaning in it. In doing so, we will find out not only more about our worship, but about ourselves. Liturgical semiotics is not only about the liturgical event, but about the semiotician as well. In this time of crisis—in the world, in the country, in the church, and perhaps even in ourselves—returning to the fountainhead of our faith and taking a few deep breaths might be just what the doctor ordered.

PART ONE

"With Bated Breath"

THE WHAT

The idiom that titles the first part of this work is something of a relic. Running across this turn of phrase is sort of like stumbling upon the ruins of an ancient temple. You recognize that you have encountered something that was important in olden times. Yet, at the same time, all that is left of it today is the merest echo of what once was.

We only see the term *bated breath* anymore in the context of waiting: to wait with bated breath. So remote is the meaning to us today that half the time you might see it instead spelled incorrectly as *baited breath*. In fact, over four hundred years have passed since this phrase first appeared in print in William Shakespeare's *Merchant of Venice*:

> Or
> Shall I bend low, and in a bondman's key,
> With bated breath and whisp'ring humbleness.[1]

It is apt for our purposes that the phrase persists within the context of waiting. The word bate was originally abate, as in "to decrease in force or intensity."[2] Over time the unstressed vowel at the beginning of the word faded away in a process called aphesis.

Thus we find ourselves in the position of waiting with abated breath. This would be with breath that is decreased, restrained, or, as one dictionary

---

1. Shakespeare, *Merchant of Venice*, 1.3.32–34.
2. *Merriam-Webster*, s.v. "abate," https://www.merriam-webster.com/dictionary/abate.

puts it, "in great suspense."[3] Hence, this is why characters at the crescendo of a mystery novel are waiting with bated breath for what is about to happen.

THE WHY

That is what the first part of this work is about—waiting in suspense for what is about to happen. Worshipers entering the church on Sunday morning wait with bated breath in anticipation of being nourished by God in the sacred meal that is Holy Eucharist. While the entire worship service is edifying, the reception of the sacrament is what the service builds toward, at least in many Christian circles.

Similarly, readers entering this book must wait with bated breath in anticipation of being nourished by the main argument of the text. The meat of this work is about liturgical semiotics. It does a deep dive into how meaning is found in corporate worship and what measures amplify the particular meanings that worship hopefully conveys.

Yet, as the parable of the wise and foolish builders (Matt 7:24–27) shows, one must build upon a firm foundation. Simply launching into a conversation about liturgical semiotics, without establishing the firm foundation of agreed upon tenants, risks the collapse of the building that is the shared endeavor of author and reader.

Part One is comprised of chapters 1 and 2. Chapter 1 makes the argument that worship is the primary activity that Christians engage in. It is the most important thing we do. If worship does not matter, then liturgical semiotics does not matter. If worship is critically important to the Christian endeavor, however, then the power and usefulness of liturgical semiotics becomes apparent.

Chapter 2 discusses the power of image, metaphor, and story in meaning-making. The kind of liturgical semiotics I am advocating is based on these things. This stands in contradistinction to how liturgical semiotics has been envisioned by others. Being versed in the importance and robustness of narraphor (narrative combined with metaphor) will prepare us to employ these tools as we move forward with the rest of the task at hand. Chapter 2 also explores the choice of breathing as the overarching narraphor for this entire text, thereby adding more reason to why this section is entitled *with bated breath* in the first place.

At the conclusion of Part One, a firm foundation will have been built. Worship will be understood as the primary act that Christians engage in, and the power of image, metaphor, and story in meaning-making will be clear.

3. Soanes and Stevenson, *Oxford Concise English Dictionary*, s.v. "bated."

I

The Primacy of Worship

"Our most basic common link is that we all inhabit this planet. We all breathe the same air."

~JOHN F. KENNEDY[1]

WORSHIP IS THE MOST important activity that we engage in as Christians. It is our primary act as followers of Jesus Christ. The church is "first and foremost a worshiping community. It is the synaxis, the gathering together of the people of God for corporate worship, which is the heart and soul of the church's life."[2] All other aspects of our lives as Christians flow from our worship. Those who already believe this are likely ready to proceed to chapter 2. Those who need some convincing about the primacy of worship in the lives of Christians, however, may wish to read on.

It is well established that not everyone learns in the same way. Some people are better visual learners than they are aural learners. Some people learn better individually than they do in groups. Some people learn best when they do something in a hands-on (kinesthetic) fashion. Learning is an example of *different strokes for different folks*, as the saying goes.

In a similar fashion, people are persuaded by different kinds of arguments. Some people are convinced by hard data, others by creativity and innovation. Some follow cold lines of logic. Others hear best the siren call of the artistic muse. In an effort to be as persuasive as possible to as broad an audience as possible, what follows is commentary on the primacy of

1. Kennedy, "Commencement Address."
2. Mitchell and Meyers, *Praying Shapes Believing*, 1.

worship incorporating several different hermeneutics. While some may see this as a patchwork approach, others will discern echoes of the apostle Paul: "I have become all things to all people, that I might by all means save some" (1 Cor 9:22).[3]

OUR NATURE (ONTOLOGY)

As a wise person once said, we see from where we stand. Our experience is what informs our understanding of the world we live in and how it functions. So let us begin with something that we can all clearly observe: human beings are the dominant species on Earth. There is really no doubt about it—we run the show on this planet.

A sobering reality is that our dominance is potentially being challenged by viruses. Yet, it is we who have crippled the climate's natural rhythm. It is we who shape the land as we see fit. It is we who cause the extinction of other species. Even if for ill rather than for good, we are the ascendant species on planet Earth.

This domination has come, anthropologically speaking, as a result of our greatest strengths: our sociability and adaptability. Our adaptability is evidenced by the fact that we have spread the world over and learned to thrive in almost any kind of natural environment. Our sociability, however, is what I want to focus on.

Consider our early days as a species, when *Homo sapiens* shared the earth with *Homo neanderthalensis*. There is a common misconception in our popular culture that Neanderthals were strong but stupid, the quintessential knuckle-dragging cavemen. The popular myth is that humans outwitted these hulking brutes by using their superior intellect, and so won the day and the planet.

The historically accurate narrative is quite different. Neanderthals were indeed stronger than their human counterparts. They were also bigger, including having larger brains. They put those large brains to good use as well, fashioning jewelry, musical instruments, and very useful tools. On an individual basis, the average Neanderthal was likely superior to the average human in several ways.

Where humans excelled, however, was in their ability to socialize and work together. As Rutger Bregman puts it in his book *Humankind: A Hopeful History*, "On his own, a *Homo neanderthalensis* may have been smarter than any one *Homo sapiens*, but the *sapiens* cohabited in larger groups,

---

3. Unless otherwise noted, all Bible quotations are from the New Revised Standard Version (NRSV).

migrated from one group to another more frequently and may also have been better imitators."[4]

Thus one can imagine a scenario where both a Neanderthal and a human had invented a new kind of tool. The Neanderthal's tool is actually better. He (or she) has created a superior product. The Neanderthal, however, may only share that invention with one other person. In the meantime, the human will have shared their inferior tool with ten other people. Very quickly you have a human group that has assimilated the use of this new technology into their lives and are reaping the benefits of it. Over the same span, you have a couple of Neanderthals who are living a better life, while most of them have not assimilated the new technology. Scale that example up, and it quickly becomes apparent that the sociability of humans won them the day, and the planet.

Human sociability is also a strength because it helps with self-knowledge. Consider this: A human cannot see their face. Their eyes are in their head, so they physically cannot see their own face. Without the help of a reflective surface, they do not know what they look like.

There is a catch, however. Reflective surfaces give a mirror image, not a true image. To illustrate the point, take a moment and think about what you look like. Picture yourself in your mind. Chances are, what you are picturing is not you as you truly are. Instead, you are picturing your reflection—the *you* that you see in the mirror every morning.

This idea, that what humans look like is a mirror image instead of the true self, runs deep. One of the effects of the pandemic is that most people became well acquainted with online meeting software, like Zoom. Someone can use Zoom quite often and not realize that the default setting on Zoom perpetuates an incorrect understanding of what the user looks like. When someone is on a Zoom call, they see everyone else as they really are. The user sees themselves on Zoom, however, as their mirror image. The makers of Zoom knew that the default understanding humans have of themselves is a mirror image, and they set the software up to show that as the default.

The point is that humans cannot know themselves in isolation. They know themselves in community. They know themselves in relationship with others. It is only through their sociability that they are able to grasp who they really are. Left to their own devices, they are unknowable to themselves. It is as the French poet Arthur Rimbaud wrote, "I is someone else."[5]

All this is to say that human beings, by their very nature, are meant to be together. They are meant to form community. They are meant to gather.

4. Bregman, *Humankind*, 70.
5. Rimbaud, "Seer Letter," para. 3.

OUR PURPOSE (TELEOLOGY)

While it is in humans' very nature to be together, what is their purpose once they are together? To get at this I want to engage in some daydreaming. Imagine that someone is going to invite someone they know to join them at the church for worship on Sunday morning. What word are they going to use to describe the gathering? Depending on their religious background, and their vocabulary of choice, they might invite their friend to *church*, or *worship*, or *mass*. Or, and this begins to point in a particular direction, they might invite them to *services*.

Worship is a form of service. There is an important distinction to be made here, however, between the kind of service being described and the common cultural understanding of service. In a country that is built on an economy of consumerism, the default thought about service is that something is being received by the consumer. Whether it is guest services in a hotel, getting one's car serviced at the dealership, or receiving bad service at a restaurant, the orientation of the term is that one is receiving something.

This is not the orientation of the service that worship is. God is not serving the worshipers. Rather, the worshipers are serving God. Those gathered definitely benefit from worship, they definitely receive something, but that is different from the service that is going on. Participating in worship is a form of divine service rendered to God.

It must be said that not all corners of the Christian family would agree with this sentiment. To some Protestants, understanding divine service in this way suggests that humans have something to offer God in worship. This, in turn, would contravene the utter fallenness (i.e., total depravity) of humanity. This is not the view that I subscribe to.

Instead, think of Christians' ancestors in the faith, the ancient Israelites. Their worship was structured around offerings and sacrifices. It was something that was done for YHWH, in order to achieve certain ends. These rituals, detailed in the book of Leviticus, were services that were rendered in order to accomplish various things in relation to God Almighty.

This theme is visible even in the antecedents of formalized religion—the ancestor worship engaged in by ancient families. Around the family hearth, "with the father tending its sacred fire, offering sacrifices, libations and incantations learned from his father—members of the family achieved union with their ancestors and prepared for the future."[6]

If one looks at religions from the past that used idols in their worship, then the theme of service was very much at play as well. The god (i.e., the

---

6. Siedentop, *Inventing the Individual*, 10.

idol) was fed, bathed, put to sleep, woken up, etc. It was very much that the god was being served by the worshiper.

This idea is carried in the ancient Greek and Hebrew words that are translated as *worship* in English bibles. Take Romans 9:4 as an example: "They are Israelites, and to them belong the adoption, the glory, the covenants, the giving of the law, the worship, and the promises." The word that is translated as *worship* is λατρεία. In ancient contexts, this word first meant "the state of a hired labourer, service"[7] and regarded engaging in "the business or duties of life." Secondarily this word took on the meaning of that service being to the gods, and hence became worship.

An example from the Hebrew Bible is Exodus 12:25, where we read the following: "When you come to the land that the Lord will give you, as he has promised, you shall keep this observance." The word translated as *observance*, which is λατρεία in the Septuagint, is עֲבֹדָה in Hebrew. This word took on several meanings, including work, slavery, ministerial duties, ceremony, military campaign, use, and farming.[8] Across these meanings, there is clearly a component of service being rendered.

We even see this play out when comparing some of our English translations of Scripture. Below is the beginning of Psalm 100, from the New Revised Standard Version and from the 1979 Book of Common Prayer. Note the difference:

Psalm 100:1–2 (NRSV)	Psalm 100:1 (BCP)
Make a joyful noise to the Lord, all the earth. Worship the Lord with gladness; come into his presence with singing.	Be joyful in the LORD, all you lands; * serve the LORD with gladness and come before his presence with a song.

That thread continues to this day. There continues to be a component of our worship that is very much service rendered to God. In the Episcopal Church's Book of Common Prayer,[9] the Holy Eucharist that we participate in is described as a "sacrifice of praise and thanksgiving."[10]

Human beings, by their very nature, gather. The purpose of that gathering, throughout the course of history, has included serving what is perceived as divine. The creation narrative of the Bible buttresses this idea when the first human, Adam, is tasked with serving God by tending the garden (Gen 2:15). Humanity's purpose has been to serve God, and that

7. Liddell et al., *Lexicon*, s.v. "λατρεία."

8. Swanson, *Dictionary of Biblical Languages*, s.v. "עֲבֹדָה."

9. This is true for the current prayer book, which received final authorization in 1979. For a large swath of Episcopal history, this sentiment was not present in the liturgy.

10. Episcopal Church, *Book of Common Prayer*, 369.

service is often formed as worship. Perhaps Jesus put it best when he said, "Away with you, Satan! for it is written, 'Worship the Lord your God, and serve only him'" (Matt 4:10).

WORDS MATTER (ETYMOLOGY)

Words matter. They make a difference. In order to say that worship is the primary act that Christians engage in, the word *worship* itself must be defined. Beyond the work with Greek and Hebrew above, some investigation of the English language is useful as well. The word *worship* "comes into our modern speech from the Anglo-Saxon *weorthscipe*. This later developed into *worthship*, and then into *worship*. It means, 'to attribute worth' to an object."[11]

To put it mundanely, the act of worship attributes worth to God. Of equal subtlety, the catechism found in the Book of Common Prayer states that corporate worship is done in part to "acknowledge the holiness of God."[12] To state it with more verve, "Ascribe to the Lord the glory due his name; bring an offering, and come before him. Worship the Lord in holy splendor" (1 Chr 16:29).

Worship is Christians' primary activity because, as created beings, Christians are ascribing glory to their creator. Without God humanity would not be. The very fact of existence makes glorifying God in the highest heaven, also known as worship, the primary human activity.

BECAUSE JESUS TOLD US TO (SACRAMENTOLOGY)

"Then he took a loaf of bread, and when he had given thanks, he broke it and gave it to them, saying, 'This is my body, which is given for you. Do this in remembrance of me'" (Luke 22:19). At the last supper with his disciples, Jesus told them to "do this" in remembrance of him. He did not say "go run a 5k in remembrance of me" or "protest in the streets in remembrance of me" or even "volunteer in a soup kitchen in remembrance of me." Rather, he said to "do this" in remembrance of him.

In discerning what the *this* was that Jesus referred to, it is worth remembering the words of Franciscan friar William of Ockham, "Plurality

---

11. Martin, *Worship in the Early Church*, 10.
12. Episcopal Church, *Book of Common Prayer*, 857.

must never be posited without necessity."[13] This sentiment is more often paraphrased as "the simplest explanation is usually the best one."

What is the *this* to which Jesus referred? Let us take the simplest and most straightforward possibility. He was gathered with his disciples, sharing a meal. At that meal, bread and wine were shared in a particular way. Those were the actions that Jesus was engaged in when he said to do something in remembrance of him. That was the context in which the sharing happened.

The *this* that his followers were to *do* was to gather together and share a meal in remembrance of him. This meal, quite naturally for them, involved the sharing of bread and wine. Over time, that gathering to eat and drink in remembrance of Jesus has become the Holy Eucharist (a.k.a. Holy Communion, a.k.a. The Lord's Supper). While it no longer resembles a meal in the way that it once did, the echoes are still there: Jesus' followers gather together and share a meal in remembrance of him. Now, however, the meal consists entirely of bread and wine, and is interspersed with everything else that one sees in a worship service.

Jesus told the disciples to share a meal. As disciples down through the ages have endeavored to do that, the result has become a celebration of the sacrament of Holy Eucharist. That is a form of worship. In fact, over half of the Christian family considers the Holy Eucharist to be the most important form of worship.

If that sounds off, then think of it this way: certain denominations believe[14] that Jesus is really and truly present in the celebration of the Holy Eucharist, including in the elements of the bread and the wine. These denominations typically celebrate the Eucharist weekly, or even daily. For these denominations, one might even use the metaphor that the celebration of Holy Eucharist is the heartbeat of the body of Christ. Denominations that hold this type of high regard for the sacrament of Holy Eucharist (e.g., various flavors of Catholicism, Orthodoxy, and Anglicanism) make up over half of the Christians in the world.

Why is worship the primary activity that Christians engage in? Because Jesus told us to celebrate the Holy Eucharist, demonstrated how to do it as he told us, and over half of Christians in the world see that act as the central act of faith.

---

13. William of Ockham, *Quaestiones et decisiones*, i, dist. 27, qu. 2, K.

14. In referring to the *beliefs* of denominations, I have in view the official stances of these organizations as evidenced by things like doctrine, dogma, canons, constitutions, and traditions. Through the gift of free will, individuals who self-identify as a member of a particular denomination can and often do hold any number of beliefs that stand in direct opposition to the official stance of the governing body.

IT'S HOW PASTORS TEND TO SPEND THEIR TIME (TIME-STUDY)

While a majority of the world's Christians see worship as the primary act of the faithful because of their high regard for Holy Eucharist, to end the argument there leaves a lot of very faithful folks out in the cold (so to speak). There are plenty of branches of the Christian family that are more focused on word than sacrament when it comes to worship.

I would suggest that worship could still be considered the primary act of Christians for many of these denominations because of how much time the pastor spends on preparing worship. With ministry professionals who identify as priests, the liturgy for worship tends to be less variable and the sermons tend to be shorter. I know I am painting here with a broad brush, but this generally holds true.

Ministry professionals who identify as pastors or ministers usually (although not universally) have to create more of the liturgy and prepare longer sermons. Both of those things are an investment of time. There is an old saw that preachers spend an hour of preparation for every minute of sermon time. I do not personally know anyone who lives that out, but it points toward a truth: the preached sermon is the visible tip of the iceberg of time that went into preparing it. One study found that Protestant pastors in the United States not only spend more time doing sermon preparation than they do in prayer, but time spent in sermon preparation is "also well above the time put into hospital, home, or witnessing visits (an average of 6.3 hours each week), personal devotions not related to preparing to teach (5.6 hours), meetings for church (4.8 hours), counseling others (4.7 hours), and handling email and other correspondence (4.5 hours)."[15] The upshot is that for denominations that are heavily word-focused, ministry professionals are spending more of their time on worship than any other part of their vocation.

The same holds true for ministry professionals who do not serve full-time. As the institutional church in America continues to erode, more and more ministry professionals are becoming either bi-vocational or they are working less than full-time. As ministers have less time to spend in their church work, not everything can be done the way that it once was. Worship, however, is typically the last thing that gets cut from the pastor's workload. A part-time pastor is still at church every Sunday.[16]

15. Earls, "How Do Most Pastors Plan Their Sermons?," para. 5.

16. It is important to note that this is changing in some places. In the Episcopal Church in Connecticut, for example, priests serve on Sundays in proportion to their employment level (a one-fourth time priest-in-charge, for example, only serves one Sunday a month). This change is recent, however, and is not the norm.

THE HORSE GOES BEFORE THE CART (*LEX ORANDI, LEX CREDENDI*)

Worship is the primary act that Christians engage in because *lex orandi, lex credendi*. This is traditionally rendered as "the law of prayer is the law of belief."[17] The intent behind the phrase is that our worship exhibits our beliefs. This has become a dictum within liturgical theology. What we do in worship is an expression of what we believe. If this is not true, then we who worship are frauds—and frauds before God.

The dictum as given above is actually shorthand for something written by Prosper of Aquataine (390–455), "legem credendi lex statuat supplicandi." This translates to "the law of praying is to establish the law of believing." The intent of Prosper's claim was to defend the doctrine of the church by showing that those beliefs were part of the church's worship. If that is how the church worshiped, and that worship had been handed down from our forerunners in the faith, then that worship justifies the beliefs espoused therein.

This gives a bit more precision to the concept. How we worship (i.e., what we pray) manifests, or *establishes*, what we believe.

When looking toward the sources of our belief as Christians, it is natural to look to the Bible. It is also natural for many Christians to look toward our ancient creeds. Yet, our worship predates both the formation of our creeds and the establishment of the biblical canon.

In the earliest expressions of the Christian church it "was the custom—presumably every Sunday—for the community to come together in the evenings for a common meal."[18] At this meal, followers of Jesus would eat, share stories about him, and pray. The meal also had a sacramental character to it. While eucharistic theology had not yet been fully worked out, we can be assured that "originally the appeasing of hunger also was joined with the observance of the sacrament."[19]

This gathering of the earliest followers of Jesus was clearly a form of worship. This nascent worship of the earliest Christians ultimately led to everything else that falls within the confines of what we call the church. How the first Christians worshiped established (that is to say, manifested) what they believed. The rest, as they say, is Christian history.

---

17. It is worth noting that, grammatically, it could also be rendered as "the law of belief is the law of prayer."

18. Dobschütz, *Christian Life in the Primitive Church*, 60–61.

19. Conzelmann, *History of Primitive Christianity*, 52.

A FORETASTE OF THE FUTURE (ESCHATOLOGY)

If not raised in it, it is not unusual for someone to experience highly liturgical worship, for example in a Roman Catholic, Eastern Orthodox, or Anglican church, and wonder "what in the world is going on!?" Sometimes the worship of the highly liturgical corners of the Christian family can seem abstruse and opaque to the casual observer.

Some of that opaqueness clears up when considering the roots of those rituals. Early Christians came to believe that they were truly encountering Jesus in their shared meals. In light of this, rites and rituals evolved. These rites and rituals grew out of, and drew upon, the cultural context in which the worshiping communities were situated. Given that these cultural contexts are increasingly foreign to most twenty-first-century people, what is encountered by unfamiliar worshipers can seem inscrutable.

Some of that opaqueness also clears up when one looks toward worship as it is described in the book of Revelation, chapters 4 and 5. The worship described therein is of a heavenly liturgy, eternally celebrated, with the Lamb (i.e., Jesus Christ) at its center. Highly liturgical churches believe that they are participating in that heavenly liturgy. As a result, they (each in their own way) enact in the temporal sphere what they believe is happening in the eternal sphere. This is a visual cue of their participation in that eternal worship. Joseph Ratzinger put it this way:

> With its vision of the cosmic liturgy, in the midst of which stands the Lamb who was sacrificed, the Apocalypse has presented the essential contents of the eucharistic sacrament in an impressive form that sets a standard for every local liturgy. From the point of view of the Apocalypse, the essential matter of all eucharistic liturgy is its participation in the heavenly liturgy; it is from thence that it necessarily derives its unity, its catholicity, and its universality.[20]

Why is worship the primary activity that Christians engage in? Because to do so transcends space and time and connects us with the ongoing, eternal worship in heaven.

---

20. Ratzinger, *Pilgrim Fellowship of Faith*, 10.

FOLLOWING THE SIGNS (SEMIOTICS)

Semiotics is the study of signs. We will get into this more deeply beginning in chapter 3. For our purposes here, however, a toe dipped into the semiotic waters will suffice.

To provide an example of semiotics in action, take a moment to think about coffee. Coffee is a brewed beverage containing caffeine. But it is also a sign that conveys meaning. What meaning does coffee convey? The answer will depend on who is answering, because their context will inform their understanding of the sign that coffee is. Yet the meaning that coffee conveys may well be things like comfort, morning, alertness, bitterness, and heat. In looking at an object (a cup of coffee), the observer has discerned meaning in it based on their context. That is semiotics at work, in an elementary fashion at least.

Armed with such an example, we can turn toward the issue of the primacy of worship to Christians. What is the most ubiquitous sign associated with Christianity? Unless there is something rather rare about how someone identifies as a Christian, an image of a cross comes to mind. Additionally, depending on what part of the Christian family someone hails from, that cross might have Jesus on it, either crucified or risen in the form of a Christus Rex. Regardless of whether it is filled or empty, however, a cross is there.

So what might be said about the cross? It is something that lifts up. Historically, it lifted up the condemned off the ground when it was used as an instrument of torturous execution. It lifted Jesus. Today, we lift it and hang it on the walls of our sanctuaries.

What effect does that have on us, physically? It causes us to look up. The story of the cross and humanity is that it lifts our eyes. It does this both historically and spiritually. Think about Mary and the disciple whom Jesus loved at the foot of the cross (John 19:2). When Jesus spoke to them, they must have lifted their gaze to him. Presented with the cross we lift our faces. We look up.

Next, another question: where is heaven? Our societal gut reaction is to think "up." This reaction is natural because, in the ancient cosmologies, heaven was indeed straight up. Jesus even said, "No one has ascended into heaven except the one who descended from heaven, the Son of Man" (John 3:13).

Even once modern scientific understanding rendered that an impossibility, the perception of heaven being up has persisted on some level. For instance, think of cartoons where a character dies and then are seen floating up to cloud-laden heaven while wearing a white robe, playing a harp, and sporting wings and a halo. Our rational minds know that heaven, while real to those of faith, is not physically above us. Yet there is something in the human condition that locates heaven as above.

The foundational sign of Christian faith, the cross, lifts our faces. It is in that lifting that someone encounters Jesus Christ. Mary and John did that at the crucifixion. We do that as well, seeking to encounter Jesus Christ not only crucified, but also risen, and ascended to the right hand of the Father.

Finally, is not lifting one's face to the Son, seeking to encounter the Father, a way to express what happens in worship?[21] Worship is the primary activity that Christians engage in because the sign of the cross points us there.

IT'S A NUMBERS GAME (STATISTICS)

Worship is the primary activity that Christians engage in because, frankly, that is the kind of data Christians are most interested in tracking. How many people were there on Sunday? What is our average Sunday attendance (ASA)? Did we have as many people for Christmas Eve and Easter this year as we did last year? The only statistic that might be of equal concern for most churches has to do with financial stability (e.g., pledging and planned giving).

The two areas, worship attendance and financial stability, are intertwined. The more people you have attending worship, the more people you have invested in the life of the faith community. The more people you have invested in the life of the faith community, the higher your pledging and planned giving.

In the Episcopal Church there is a form that all churches must fill out annually called the Parochial Report. While efforts are being made to soften and nuance what is tracked in the form, it still boils down to two things: the attendance at worship, and how much money you have in the bank. We keep track of that which is most important to us. To put it another way, we treasure what we measure. The evidence would suggest that what is most important to us (at least in mainline churches) is the number of people attending worship. This implies that worship is the primary activity we engage in.

---

21. The connection between lifting up the face and worshiping can be seen in 1 Esd 4:58–60: "When the young man went out, he lifted up his face to heaven toward Jerusalem, and praised the King of heaven, saying, 'From you comes the victory; from you comes wisdom, and yours is the glory. I am your servant. Blessed are you, who have given me wisdom; I give you thanks, O Lord of our ancestors.'"

IT'S WHAT WE DO ON SUNDAYS (PRIMA FACIE)

Worship is the primary activity that Christians engage in because it is what we do on the most important day of the week: Sunday. The identification of the Resurrection with Sunday is a strong sign of the day's importance to Christians.

The historical roots of Sunday becoming the gathering day for Christians, however, is more nuanced. It involved the confluence of several factors, Jewish, pagan, and Christian. Ultimately, however, the decision was made by ecclesiastical authority. Samuele Bacchiocchi, in *From Sabbath to Sunday: A Historical Investigation of the Rise of Sunday Observance in Early Christianity*, put it this way, "the adoption of Sunday observance in place of the Sabbath did not occur in the primitive Church of Jerusalem by virtue of the authority of Christ or of the Apostles, but rather took place several decades later, seemingly in the Church of Rome, solicited by external circumstances."[22]

Evidence of worship as the purpose of the Sunday gathering appears circa year 150 CE in Justin Martyr's *First Apology*:

> On the day which is called Sunday we have a common assembly of all who live in the cities or in the outlying districts, and the memoirs of the Apostles or the writings of the Prophets are read, as long as there is time. Then, when the reader has finished, the president of the assembly verbally admonishes and invites all to imitate such examples of virtue. Then we all stand up together and offer up our prayers, and, as we said before, after we finish our prayers, bread and wine and water are presented. He who presides likewise offers up prayers and thanksgivings, to the best of his ability, and the people express their approval by saying "Amen." The Eucharistic elements are distributed and consumed by those present, and to those who are absent they are sent through the deacons.[23]

Sunday is the most important day of the Christian week. It is the day we gather. The purpose of that gathering is, first and foremost, worship. We do other things that day as well. There may be formation activities like Church School, or fellowship activities like coffee hour or a meal. These, however, are structured around and attached to the primary activity of the day: worship.

---

22. Bacchiocchi, *From Sabbath to Sunday*, 313.
23. Justin Martyr, *First Apology*, ch. 67.

IT'S OUR FINGERPRINT (DERMATOGLYPHICS)

Fingerprints are unique identifiers. No two fingerprints are the same. It is of course true that DNA testing is the ultimate unique identifier these days—but the classic example is the fingerprint. It has even entered our idiomatic speech: if I say that someone's "fingerprints are all over" a press release, for example, it is clear that I mean that person was the instigator of the press release.

Worship is the fingerprint of religious folk, Christians included. There are other groups and organizations that do the other things Christians do. There are others who feed the hungry, welcome the stranger, clothe the naked, tend the sick, and visit the prisoner. There are others who protest injustice, raise funds for worthy causes, and attempt to form people in accordance with their values. In fact, those organizations often do their particular "other thing" better than Christians do because it is their primary thing. What sets Christians apart and identifies them uniquely, what their primary thing is as Christians, is worship.

There is another way that worship is the Christian fingerprint, by the way. The tiny ridges that form fingerprints also aid in someone's ability to grip things. Worship helps Christians maintain their grip in the midst of a world that they are in, but not of.

IT'S THE AIR WE BREATHE (PRACTICAL METAPHOR)

The next chapter explores the benefit of image, metaphor, and story in a more intense way. For the moment, suffice it to say that a metaphor is a great way to grasp the truth about something that otherwise might not be evident. To think about worship metaphorically: if the church is the body of Christ, then worship is like the breathing of that body. The various functions that the body does (e.g., moving muscles or even thinking) require oxygen. It is the act of breathing that gets the waste material (carbon dioxide) out of the blood and gets more oxygen into the blood. When Christians worship, they are getting fresh oxygen into the body of Christ. This image of breathing is explored much more robustly in the next chapter.

This also resonates if one simply thinks about it practically. During the rest of the week, Christians are expending themselves. Jobs, families, volunteering, and relationships: all of them take energy. That is not to say that these things do not also give to us in certain ways. But the danger of depletion is real. One of the benefits of serving God through worship is that it is a way to fill oneself up again. It is a way to re-oxygenate the blood, spiritually speaking.

CONCLUSION

Like a group of stars forming the shape of a constellation, the above arguments form the shape of a maxim for Christians: Worship is the primary act that is engaged in.

It is humans' very nature to gather. A discernible thread down through history is that human gathering has included serving what is perceived as divine. That service has often taken the form of worship. That is how humanity outwardly attributes worth to the One who created all there is.

Worship is also what Jesus told us to do. Worship related duties are where pastors spend the largest chunk of their time. Worship is what established the beliefs of the church at its beginning. Our worship joins those gathered with the eternal worship that goes on in heaven.

Practicality proclaims the primacy of worship as well: data about worship is what Christians take the time to track, and worship is what Christians have always done on the most important day of the week. Worship is what makes people of faith unique. Worship is also foundationally functional: it is the air that the body of Christ breathes.

If by this time someone does not believe that worship is the primary activity that Christians engage in, then there is clearly no persuading them. Sometimes it is best to agree to disagree and move on.

2

Choosing a Framework

"Remember to breathe. . . . It is, after all, the secret of life."

~GREGORY MAGUIRE[1]

IN THE FIRST CHAPTER, the primacy of worship was established. This chapter investigates various vehicles of meaning transmission, ultimately choosing one to be the framework and guide for delving into liturgical semiotics.

All writers or speakers want the same thing. They want the reader or listener to understand what was written or said. Not every jot and tittle, necessarily. But they want the receiver to get the crux of the message they were trying to send. They want their argument to be understood.

We can generalize this by saying that the goal of all communication is transmission of meaning. The point of communication is for a particular meaning or meanings (e.g., a message, idea, or feeling) to be successfully transmitted from the one sending the information to the one receiving the information.

The five interconnected vehicles for achieving successful communication that are examined are story, metaphor, proverb, image, and narraphor. The results provide a dictum: as the length of the communication diminishes, successful transmission of meaning requires a larger shared knowledge base.

---

1. Maguire, *Lion among Men*, 12.

STORY AND MEMORY

Stories are perhaps the oldest and best ways to communicate information. They stand the test of time by being passed down through the generations. They help us remember. They can heal us. They are highly effective transmitters of meaning.

One of the most powerful ways to remember something is to embed it in a story. There is an oft-recited statistic that states that messages delivered as stories are twenty-two times more memorable than if they are presented as just plain facts. This statistic is attributed to the late American psychologist Jerome Bruner. The problem is that no one has been able to verify that Bruner ever said that, or what research supported that conclusion.

Despite the number twenty-two being unverifiable and probably apocryphal, research does show that stories enhance our remembering. A study in 1969, for example, found that a list of words was remembered seven times better if the words were woven into a story than if the list was memorized.[2]

Beyond the research, however, the idea that stories help us remember is borne out by our lived experience. That is because humans interpret the world around them through the experiences they have had. Our lives have given us a database of stories in our brains (i.e., our lived experiences). When we encounter new facts we try to interpret them by fitting them into a narrative, a story, which we already know. Storyteller Annette Simmons puts it this way, "People interpret facts to mean what their story tells them they mean."[3] Since stories are our interpretive framework, they naturally help us remember things.

To illustrate the idea, think of a time when someone from an older generation tried to dispense advice to someone from a younger generation. Maybe it was a grandparent talking to a grandchild. Did the advice come in the form of facts and figures? Unlikely. Rather, the advice probably came in the form of a story.

Mary Schmich put it this way in a column for the Chicago Tribune: "Advice is a form of nostalgia. Dispensing it is a way of fishing the past from the disposal, wiping it off, painting over the ugly parts and recycling it for more than it's worth."[4] Our memories are vast repositories of stories, holding the accumulated wisdom of our lived experience.

2. Bower and Clark, "Narrative Stories," 181–82.

3. Simmons, *Story Factor*, 53.

4. Schmich, "Advice," para. 29.

Story and Physical Healing

Stories are powerful. They have the ability to heal us, physically. This is called the placebo effect. A placebo is a type of medicine or treatment that is devoid of therapeutic value. Examples would include things like sugar pills or saline injections. There is even something called *sham surgery* where the patient is anesthetized and cut open, but no other surgical intervention takes place.

The placebo effect is the positive effect that happens to the patient even though no appropriate medical treatment has actually taken place. In study after study, patients report an improvement when no real medicine has been taken and no legitimate treatment has been administered. Less pain, more energy, and relief from depression are all reported examples of the placebo effect. There is even research linking the placebo effect to improved motor function in patients with Parkinson's disease.

How is this possible? Because of the power of story. Patients are told the story that the medicine or treatment they are being given is real and beneficial. The patients who believe the story, who find it persuasive, can report actual improvement in their condition. With regards to patients with Parkinson's disease, one medical journal put it this way: "the magnitude of placebo-induced effects is modulated by an expectancy of improvement, which is in turn related to the release of dopamine within the ventral striatum."[5] Stories have the power to heal the body.

Story and Spiritual Healing

Stories also have the power to heal the spirit. This is because story is the building block of all relationships. You can only form a relationship with someone by sharing experiences with them. When you share an experience with someone, you have written a story together.

Think of someone that you have a strong, beneficial relationship with. When thinking of the arc of the relationship with that person, a bevy of stories are at the ready. Those stories are reservoirs of healing grace, a balm that can be applied to bind wounds of the spirit and effect healing.

Yet personal stories borne out of relational experiences are not the only way that stories can heal the spirit. The right story from a total stranger, which re-frames someone's spiritual woundedness, can be healing.

I have a story to illuminate my point. Years ago, my wife and I were very much looking forward to having kids. We had grand pictures in our

---

5. Quattrone et al., "Neurobiology," 1213.

minds of what the journey of parenthood would be like. We were not polly-annaish. We were sure that to be parents would be a calling with its share of challenges. But we also knew that it was our calling, and we looked forward to it.

Then we became the parents of a child with special needs. Our hopes and dreams were not matching up with our lived experience. It was a very hard reality to digest. We were in a place of spiritual woundedness and torpor.

One of the things that helped move us through that space was a story. It was written by Emily Perl Kingsley, and was entitled "Welcome to Holland." The story likens having kids to taking a vacation. You prepare to go to Italy. You plan out everything you want to see. You read all the best guidebooks. But when the plane lands, you find that you are in Holland rather than Italy. The story goes on to find the vacationer coming to terms with being in Holland and learning to appreciate what it offers, even though the pain of missing out on Italy never truly disappears.

That essay, that story, helped to bring spiritual and emotional healing to my wife and me. It helped us to see parenthood in a new light. We were able to move forward and find hope for the future again, even though our life circumstances had not changed.

I learned the potency of story before becoming a parent, however. I learned it in a special way as a hospital chaplain when I undertook a Clinical Pastoral Education (CPE) residency at a Level 1 trauma hospital.

One of the most important things that one does as a hospital chaplain is to listen to people's stories. The story of how they or their loved one wound up in the hospital. The story of the hopes they have for getting back home to where they live—or sometimes back home to God. The story of who is there for them, and who is not.

When the hospital chaplain walks into a patient's room, they are entering into the story of someone else. Furthermore, the chaplain usually enters the person's story at a time of heightened stress and anxiety.

Indeed, the chaplain may be walking into any of the five part dramatic structure laid out by German playwright and novelist Gustav Freytag.[6] From exposition to denouement, the patient's life is a story that the chaplain enters into and is for a time a character on the stage of.

My time at the hospital crystallized for me the notion that our lives *are* stories—and we inherently want them to be good ones. Our visualization of our lives as story is a vibrant example of the power that narrative holds

---

6. The five parts are exposition, rising action, climax, falling action, and resolution (or denouement).

for us as a species. It also makes sense of an anecdotal experience of many hospital chaplains: when someone takes the time to listen to the story of another, to show that they begin to understand it and accept it, it can be spiritually healing for the storyteller.

Healing Trumps Curing

A word of caution, lest story be painted as the fix for all that ails us. While stories can affect healing, they cannot cure. Yet, as it turns out, this is okay.

The placebo effect does not remove the underlying issue. The placebo effect cannot rid someone of cancer. It might, however, help ease the pain of someone with cancer.

The spiritual healing that a story brings is not synonymous with a spiritual cure. The parent who comes to appreciate the tulips and Rembrandts of Holland still feels the pain of knowing they will never see the ceiling of the Sistine Chapel.

In our current age, medical science gives humanity the ability to keep the human body alive far past what was thought possible even fifty years ago. Revolutionary medicines, therapies, and interventions can absolutely cure us physically in many circumstances.

Healing, though, is much broader, and much more precious, than a physical cure. This point is illumined by the biblical witness, Acts 4:8–12 being an example:

> Then Peter, filled with the Holy Spirit, said to them, "Rulers of the people and elders, if we are questioned today because of a good deed done to someone who was sick and are asked how this man has been *healed*, let it be known to all of you, and to all the people of Israel, that this man is standing before you in good health by the name of Jesus Christ of Nazareth, whom you crucified, whom God raised from the dead. This Jesus is 'the stone that was rejected by you, the builders; it has become the cornerstone.' There is *salvation* in no one else, for there is no other name under heaven given among mortals by which we must be saved."

In English, the two words I have italicized are distinct and only loosely related: healed and salvation. One could conjure a relation whereby being physically healed is salvation from illness. For all intents and purposes, however, the words are predominantly unrelated.

This is not the case when they are considered in the original Greek. Both words have the same root, σῴζω. The term serves as the basis for describing a variety of meanings, including: to save from death, bring out safely, save/free from disease, keep, preserve, thrive, prosper, get on well, to save or preserve from transcendent danger or destruction.[7] In verse twelve above, Peter's claim "is about *sōtēria*, 'wholeness,' understood as well-being in its fullest sense: physical and spiritual health."[8]

This holistic understanding of well-being is more powerful than simply physical restoration. True health is centered in our relationship with Jesus: mind, body, and soul. The holistic wellness of the mind, body, and soul is a better thing than solely a physical cure.

Story as Meaning Transmitter

Stories are tremendous transmitters of meaning, in part because of the memorable and powerful nature described thus far. Whether novels, movies, short stories, or cultural folktales, meaning is brilliantly carried within narrative.

This ability to transmit meaning is amplified by the lack of a restriction on a story's length. Consider the *Lord of the Rings* trilogy by J. R. R. Tolkien as an example. One may well begin the first novel with no conception of the world of elves, orcs, dwarfs, and dragons. The length of the story, carried through three novels (four if you count the precursor book, *The Hobbit*), gives ample time to fully understand the depth and contours of this fantasy world. Its length also gives time for the reader to find real-world and real-life meaning in this epic struggle of good versus evil.

Narrative is also a powerful transmitter of meaning because it has the ability to be self-referential. A story can tell you its meaning as it unfolds. Think of a narrator explaining the inner thoughts of a character, or a soliloquy that reveals the meaning a character has gained from an event. Shorter vehicles of meaning transmission, such as metaphor and image, do not have that ability.

Stories are the lingua franca, or bridge language, for transmitting meaning.

METAPHOR

A metaphor is, in simplest terms, "A figure of speech based on the comparison of two things. It describes something in terms of another idea, object,

---

7. BDAG 982.

8. Holladay, *Acts*, 111.

or process."[9] Metaphors are ubiquitous in our thoughts, speech, and culture. Metaphors are so commonplace, in fact, that we often overlook that they are being used. Do you see what I am saying? (That was a metaphor, by the way.)

The Bible, while containing the greatest story ever told, is replete with metaphors as well. Jesus is the bread of life. The Lord is my shepherd. You are the salt of the earth. The wind blows wherever it pleases. Biblical metaphors are an inexhaustible list. (That was a metaphor, too.)

Not only are metaphors the communicative water we swim in, they are actually how we think. As George Lakoff and Mark Johnson put it in their ground-breaking book, *Metaphors We Live By*, "metaphor is pervasive in everyday life, not just in language but in thought and action. Our ordinary conceptual system, in terms of which we both think and act, is fundamentally metaphorical in nature."[10]

It is natural not to believe this. Conventional wisdom would suggest that we think in words. As one reads this page, the sound of words are likely echoing in the reader's mind.

Even so, think about the last dream you remember having. It may have been pretty strange. The brain thinks things in dreams that are impossible in the waking world; things that are incompatible, even, with rational thought. But there is one thing that you are doing right now that is nigh impossible to do in dreams: reading.

It turns out that reading, writing, and most aspects of language are nearly impossible to engage in while dreaming. Harvard University dream expert Deirdre Barrett has noted that this "seems to have to do with our whole language area being much less active."[11] A paper published in 2000 by Ernest Hartmann found that a mere 1 percent of sleepers engaged in those kinds of activities in their dreams.[12]

Yet, brains are active while dreaming. Thus words cannot be the foundation of our thought formation. Instead, metaphors are.

Metaphor as Meaning Transmitter

While not as expansive as story, metaphors are still robust transmitters of meaning—provided there is a shared knowledge base of the terms being

9. Mangum, *Lexham Glossary of Theology*, s.v. "metaphor."

10. Lakoff and Johnson, *Metaphors We Live By*, 3.

11. Tayag, "Can You Read in Your Dreams?," para. 4.

12. Hartmann, "We Do Not Dream of the 3 R's," 103.

used. Take this American metaphor as an example: there may be snow on the rooftop, but there is fire in the furnace![13]

The meaning of this metaphor is that someone who is older remains passionate. The house, which is not specifically mentioned but implied, is the body. Snow is white hair, and the furnace could be likened to the heart, where emotion metaphorically resides. The key to the meaning being transmitted by this metaphor is that "in cold climates, houses are often white on top but toasty on the inside."[14]

Yet, what if the hearer of the metaphor is from a warm climate where snow and furnaces are not part of the cultural understanding? Then this metaphor cannot successfully transmit the intended meaning because it lacks the shared cultural knowledge base.[15]

While many metaphors are intelligible to only a narrow context, others are more extensible for the human family. These are called primary metaphors and they link everyday experience with subjective judgment. These metaphors form as a child grows, and so cut across multiple cultural contexts.

Think about the primary conceptual metaphor *Affection Is Warmth.* We know almost instinctually to identify affection with warmth and aloofness with coolness. The metaphor developed because "our earliest experiences with affection correspond to the physical experience of the warmth of being held closely."[16]

In a similar way, *Knowing Is Seeing* is a primary concept metaphor that is applicable across multiple cultures. At first, a baby's entire world consists literally of what it sees. To see something is to know that it exists. This is particularly true prior to an infant developing object permanence. As the child grows, however, this experience of seeing takes on a metaphorical meaning. The concept of understanding as seeing remains, but it becomes applied to a wider context than just what is literally within the line of sight. Voilà, a primary metaphor is born.

13. Wiktionary, "There May Be Snow on the Rooftop But There Is Fire in the Furnace," https://en.wiktionary.org/wiki/there_may_be_snow_on_the_rooftop_but_there_is_fire_in_the_furnace.

14. Sullivan, *Mixed Metaphors*, 163.

15. Here is an example from a non-Western culture: I have been bitten by a tsetse fly. To most Americans, this is just a flat statement. To the Sukuma people of Tanzania, however, this is a way of saying that someone to whom you owe a debt is pestering you relentlessly.

16. Lakoff and Johnson, *Metaphors We Live By*, 255.

For the human family, metaphorical thought "is unavoidable, ubiquitous, and mostly unconscious."[17] Since they are so intrinsic to how we think and communicate, metaphors are incredibly powerful as meaning-transmitters. Their only limitation is the shared cultural knowledge base of the terms they use.

PROVERB

A proverb is a sentence of cultural wisdom that has gained prominence because its truth has been borne out through lived experience. That truth has withstood the test of time because it has been proven useful when applied to a wide variety of situations down through the years.

One of the proverbs I remember hearing as a youth was "Don't count your chickens before they hatch." The proverb is a warning to not take for granted the occurrence of something that has not yet happened. If one pauses for a moment, then I am sure that any number of proverbs from their past can be brought to mind.

The proverb is one of humanity's most ancient and instructive written art forms. In ancient Sumer, "proverb collections were used as textbooks."[18] The book of Proverbs found in the Bible acted as a similar collection of wisdom for our forerunners in the faith (and for us as well), useful for study and practical application.

While proverbs are wonderful transmitters of meaning, the meaning they transmit is often very old. In one sense this makes proverbs extremely powerful. They speak to certain truths about right living that transcend the passage of time.

In another sense, perhaps because proverbs speak such age-*old* truths, *new* proverbs can lack persuasiveness and gravitas. To illustrate what I mean, what follows is a proverb I created and its explanation: *It's the surprise fly that focuses the chameleon.*

"One real world problem we have is the deeply divided nature of the politics in this country. Despite being drowned in information, each political party seems to be operating within their own data set. They are seeing a picture entirely different from that of the other party. It is like a chameleon, which is the only animal that has monocular vision (both eyes look in different directions) that is movable. Their eyes operate independently, roaming around, and seeing two totally different pictures of the world. But when a fly wanders too close, the two eyes snap forward and the chameleon's vision

17. Lakoff and Johnson, *Metaphors We Live By*, 272.
18. Geary, *I Is An Other*, 185.

immediately becomes binocular, with precise depth perception. Then the tongue shoots out and dinner is had. It takes the surprise fly for both eyes to work together to achieve something that neither eye could do independently. This country needs a surprise fly to bring our two political factions together to do something we can't do independently from each other."

This proverb speaks to a problem in the current cultural context of the United States. It accurately uses the anatomy of a chameleon to describe a solution to the problem posed. In that way, it does what a proverb is supposed to do: it speaks a sentence of wisdom that can be applied to a situation.

Yet, because it is newly created and has only been applied to one situation, it lacks something. It has no prominence or provenance. It carries no patina of the lived experience of past generations. It lacks the *je ne sais quoi* that we have come to recognize in proverbs that have withstood the test of time. Proverbs, while elegant and perhaps even noble, are not the right choice for guiding us in an exploration of liturgical semiotics.

IMAGE

Image is the most terse vehicle for transmitting meaning. Yet this terseness does not detract from an image's ability to convey meaning. A picture is worth a thousand words, as the old saying goes. Those thousand words, however, are sourced from a deep well of shared knowledge.

Think of a family photo album. Each snapshot has the ability to spin a yarn. It speaks to the family's experience of a particular time and place. It is the catalyst for rich reminiscing and spellbinding storytelling. It transmits deep meaning—for that family.

If one is a stranger, though, that photo album holds very little meaning. Perhaps a few things are recognized: "I've been there! . . . We had that same kind of car. . . . Can you believe that those pants were ever in style?" While cultural cues might be picked up on, the rich meaning of the family interaction and experience is lost.

Alternatively, call to mind a stained-glass window from a church. Often the scene portrayed in the glass is a biblical one. To the well-read Christian, the solitary image in the stained-glass brings forth the entire story detailed in Scripture. To the follower of Christ with the shared knowledge base that we call the Bible, the picture in glass is worth a thousand words.

The concept of images of course extends beyond just family pictures and stained-glass windows. An image is the likeness of something or someone. It has representative and symbolic qualities, but it also "is the similitude of something, reflecting or mirroring it."[19] Jesus is described as being the image of God (Col 1:15) and he tells the disciples that whoever has seen him has seen the Father (John 14:9). In fact, humanity as a whole was created in the image and likeness of God (Gen 1:26–27).[20]

This suggests that there is a definite relational quality between an image and the thing that it reflects. It is that relationship that is the conduit of meaning transmission. Whether it is the relationship between the picture of the family and the family, or the relationship between God the creator and we God's creation, it is the fact of the relationship that allows for meaning-making to happen.

The Case of Icons

The Greek word for image is εἰκών, which we render in English as icon. While today the word may most closely associate with something on a computer screen, religious icons are an ancient phenomena.[21]

Traditionally, icons are "flat pictures, usually painted in egg tempera on wood, but also wrought in mosaic, ivory, and other materials."[22] They portray figures and events of importance to the Christian faith: Jesus, scenes from the Gospels, saints, etc. They hold a special place in the life of the Orthodox Church. To a lesser degree icons are also found in the Catholic and Anglican churches.

Icons are robust transmitters of meaning in that the picture often contains many visual cues for the Christian observer. Rublev's *Trinity*,[23] perhaps the most famous icon, provides an excellent example.

At first blush the picture is that of the three angels who visited Abraham at the Oaks of Mamre (Gen 18:1–8). The icon is replete with symbolism, however, that Christian contemplation reveals. A constellation of observations suggest that this is actually a representation of the Holy Trinity (the prominence of the angels, their garments, eyes, hands, body positioning, the lack of Abraham and Sarah in the painting, etc.). Further examination reveals eucharistic overtones in the shape of a chalice that is formed by the

19. Ferguson et al., *New Dictionary of Theology*, 329.

20. Humanity's creation in the image of God is known as the *imago Dei* in systematic theology. Its interpretation, a matter of sometimes zesty debate, lies beyond the scope of this work.

21. The field of semiotics attaches a specific definition to the word icon. That definition is explored in the next chapter.

22. Cross and Livingstone, *Oxford Dictionary of the Christian Church*, 820.

23. See Wikipedia, s.v. "*Trinity* (Andrew Rublev)," https://en.wikipedia.org/wiki/Trinity_(Andrei_Rublev).

outlines of the angels' bodies as they sit around a table. The Oak of Mamre, positioned above the angel representing the Son, suggests both the Tree of Life from the Garden of Eden as well as the wood of the Cross. Similarly, the house being above God the Father, and a mountain being above God the Holy Spirit, invite meaning-making.

The longer one looks upon the Rublev's *Trinity*, the more is revealed to the Christian mind. Ever deepening contemplation of the icon brings more and more meaning to the fore. Icons are often so steeped in symbolism and the potential for meaning-making that their creation is referred to as writing: one writes an icon, one does not paint an icon.

Yet again it must be noted that a deep shared knowledge base is needed. To a non-Christian, Rublev's *Trinity* conveys much less meaning. They might find meaning in it based on their own background and context, but it will not be the meaning that Rublev was trying to transmit when he wrote the icon.

Icon Veneration

Icons are heavily freighted with potential meaning based on the symbolism of their brush strokes. There is a second way that they are transmitters of meaning, however. Icons invite meaning-making with regards to our relationship with Christ through veneration. Consider the icon known as the *Christ Pantocrator*.[24] What follows is a recounting of veneration.[25]

"I gaze at him as he gazes at me. Setting my eyes on his image through my glasses seems to put a barrier between us. There must be nothing between us, nothing to interrupt this relation of being. I take them off and gaze closer. What do I see? I see the differences in the two halves of the image, the details of the clothing, the positioning of the book and the hand. I look beyond it. What do I see? He sees me. He knows. He understands. Impassively and reassuringly this is communicated to me. I feel dwarfed and yet affirmed. In this economy of veneration I lift up gratitude and receive peace. I gaze deeper, letting my eyes lose focus. The image changes, shifting and moving. The eyes remain fixed, but all else churns. It shows the active nature internal to him. We follow a God who is in motion, not static.

My intellect breaks through this experience. Why do I hold this piece of wood so reverently? It's not even an original work, but a mass production

---

24. Meaning "Christ ruler of all," icons of this type depict Christ looking straight at the observer.

25. The author of this account wishes to remain anonymous.

of a piece of artwork. So then why am I careful not to put it face down? There is something more going on here."

At first blush this account might sound as if it is breaking the second commandment. However, what the person engaged in with that image, that icon, was not worship. Instead it was veneration, which is a good thing. This position was affirmed by the Second Ecumenical Synod of Nice, which commented that images "should be given due salutation and honourable reverence . . . , not indeed that true worship of faith . . . which pertains alone to the divine nature."[26] John of Damascus put it this way, "When we venerate an icon, we do not offer veneration to matter, but through the icon we venerate the person depicted on it."[27]

Yet in venerating the icon, what was actually happening? The person was focusing their thoughts on it. Through that action, the object of their focus became not the image itself, but what the image represents: Christ Jesus. It is this type of focus that is key because that which is represented by the image cannot be viewed in any other way. Jesus is not with us in the flesh anymore. It is only through the use of images that something visible can be added to what we think in our minds and feel in our hearts with regards to Jesus. An icon acts as a conduit, or perhaps more accurately a conductor, for divine contemplation.

As noted above, there is a relational quality to an image. St. Basil wrote that "the honour paid to the image passes on to the prototype."[28] Hence, when someone looks at an icon of Jesus, they see Jesus. More than that, He is seeing them see him. It *is* a relationship. In much the same way that two parties are required for a conversation, veneration must exist within a relationship. It is very much a two way street. What happens in icon veneration? We gaze upon grace.

Icon veneration is a transmitter of meaning with regards to our relationship with God in Christ. As Henri Nouwen has put it, icons are written "to lead us into the inner room of prayer and bring us close to the heart of God."[29] There is much meaning,[30] and perhaps the most important kind of meaning, to be made there.

26. "Decree of the Holy, Great, Ecumenical Synod," 1021.

27. John of Damascus, *On the Divine Images*, 89.

28. Basil, *De Spiritu Sancto*, 18.45.

29. Nouwen, *Behold the Beauty of the Lord*, 14.

30. There is even more potential for meaning than what has been discussed to this point. The observer can find meaning simply because the artwork is ancient, or the wood old, or the depiction mysterious. As we will see, the cultural and religious disposition of the observer is at the heart of meaning-making.

NARRAPHOR

Lastly we come to narraphor. A narraphor is, simply stated, a narrative plus a metaphor. To stop there, however, would do injustice to the concept. Leonard Sweet has noted that a narraphor "contains the power of a metaphorical image with the accessibility and approachability of a story"[31] and likens narraphor to parable. This dovetails with James Geary's description of parables as "narrated metaphors"[32] and his comment that parables "are the most compressed and concentrated form of story."[33]

To put it succinctly: narraphor solves the limitation problem of metaphors. By wrapping the metaphor in a narrative, its meaning becomes more easily transmitted. The story that surrounds the metaphor widens the net it casts, thereby catching the minds of more readers and hearers.

It is time to reveal a secret to you. The story that I referenced above, "Welcome to Holland," is really a narraphor. The metaphor is (as paradoxical as it sounds to all parents) "Parenting Is a Vacation." The narrative details that surround that metaphor gives color and life and vibrancy to the message. They also make it more understandable, relatable, and meaning-full.

This was the genius of Jesus' kingdom statements. Jesus gave the metaphor, "the kingdom of heaven is like . . ." Then he would wrap that metaphor in narrative detail that appealed to the shared knowledge base of his listeners. He used stories constructed from the stuff of the world around him. This made the metaphor more comprehensible. This is also why we of the twenty-first century often have to work so hard to grasp the meaning of Jesus' parables. We do not have the shared knowledge base of someone from first-century Judea. Thus more work is required on our part to get at the meaning of the metaphor within one of Jesus' parables.[34]

Choosing a Narraphor

As stated at the outset, the goal of all communication is transmission of meaning. The use of a guiding narraphor harnesses both the deep power of metaphor and the wide accessibility of narrative. By choosing a narraphor

31. Sweet, *Giving Blood*, 37.
32. Geary, *I Is An Other*, 181.
33. Geary, *I Is An Other*, 182.
34. Not that first-century hearers necessarily had an easy time of it. They often found themselves befuddled at Jesus' words. They did, however, at least understand the cultural references.

to be the guiding framework of our exploration of liturgical semiotics, the resulting journey will be more memorable and more meaning-full.

The best narraphors, those which *are* the most memorable and communicate the most meaning, are drawn from the current cultural context they are birthed into. Given our current societal situation, there is one event that presents itself as head-and-shoulders above all else: the COVID-19 pandemic.

Given our utterly toxic political climate, some might identify that as the elephant in the room that is shaping us culturally at the moment. While it is undeniably true that both COVID-19 *and* political polarization have deeply affected our society at present, one of these factors has helped to drive the other. There was political polarization prior to COVID-19. The stress and anxiety of the global pandemic has exacerbated that polarization, or at least put us in a position where we are unable to simply turn away from it and pretend it does not exist or is not that bad. But make no mistake, the real change agent here is the global pandemic. This, then, will be the focus of our semiotic analysis.

When we consider the pandemic, several narraphors present themselves as strong contenders as the main meaning-maker in this time and place. One is the ubiquity of numbers. Whether it is the ticker on your favorite news channel, charts on a pandemic-focused website like covidact-now.org, or chatter on the radio—numbers have been in the offing. How many deaths? How many hospitalizations? What is the number of daily new cases per one hundred thousand residents? We have all become armchair statisticians.

Another possibility is the wearing of masks. Ever since March of 2020, what was once remanded to surgical rooms on television shows has become the universal fashion accessory: should I coordinate my mask with the rest of my outfit? It has also become the focus of our logistics: keep an extra mask in your car and your purse in case you forget to grab one on the way out the door. Lastly, the wearing of masks has been a point of great friction between groups with differing tolerances for personal and corporate risk.

Another narraphor that presents itself is getting vaccinated. Negative COVID-related numbers dropped—because of vaccinations. Masks began to phase out of our wardrobe considerations—because of vaccinations. Cities and states periodically offered better and better incentives in order to get more people vaccinated. Fans of the hit Broadway show *Hamilton* posted pictures of themselves post-vaccination with an apropos quote from the show: "I am not throwing away my shot!" The act of being vaccinated is indeed one of the chief narraphors that has come into being during the pandemic.

There is one, however, that is even more foundational to where we find ourselves; one that is even more fundamental to what has been going on in our culture: breathing.

The act of breathing captures several different cultural streams simultaneously. The act of breathing is what spreads the coronavirus. If you recall, in the early days of 2020 we were not sure *how* the virus spread. There was a run on hand sanitizer and disinfecting wipes as we wiped down our grocery bags and cleaned our hands until they were raw.

What was the real culprit, though? Our breath. If one has the virus, then they carry billions of virions (virus particles) in them. Each breath sends virions spewing into the surrounding air. Wearing a cloth mask will stop virus transmission via respiratory droplets. Cloth masks do little, however, to stop virus transmission via aerosol. Our act of breathing, necessary for human life, has the potential to take human life as well.

The act of breathing is also at the heart of the other pandemic alive and well in this country: racism. The phrase "I can't breathe" has become a slogan synonymous with the Black Lives Matter movement. It rose to prominence in 2014 when Eric Garner, an African American man, was put in a choke hold by a New York City police officer and died as a result. He repeated the phrase eleven times before losing consciousness. The New York Times has reported that this phrase has been used by at least seventy people who have died in police custody.[35]

"I can't breathe" took on new energy when George Floyd, an African American man, was murdered by a police officer in Minneapolis in 2020. The officer knelt on Floyd's neck for nine and a half minutes, killing him by asphyxiation. This brutal act, this death by deprivation of breath, sparked outrage and protests around the country. "I can't breathe" has become the rallying cry and the warning klaxon of those who have had their fill of racial injustice. "I can't breathe" have been the words of far too many black men in this country.

"I can't breathe" have also been the words of far too many patients with COVID-19. The early days of the pandemic in this country saw a shortage of ventilators, as thousands succumbed to an inability to get enough oxygen. The surge of the COVID-19 delta and omicron variants saw this disturbing circumstance come to the fore again as hospitals creaked under the strain of treating the unvaccinated sick.

The most potent narraphor in our time and place is the act of breathing. This is the narraphor we will use as the guide and the exoskeleton for

---

35. Baker et al., "Three Words. 70 Cases."

our exploration of liturgical semiotics. This is why, for instance, each chapter begins with a quote about breathing or breath.

CONCLUSION

In chapter 1 we explored worship as the primary activity that Christians engage in. In this chapter we opened up narraphor as the key to memorable and powerful meaning-making and chose a narraphor to guide our journey moving forward. Equipped with these insights, standing upon this firm foundation, let us now turn in earnest to the subject of liturgical semiotics.

PART TWO

"A Breath of Fresh Air"

THE WHAT

The idiom that titles the second part of this work is not that old. It dates from the mid-nineteenth century. Its antecedents, however, are quite old. Our current *breath of fresh air* took over the idiomatic space occupied by *breath of heaven* and *breath of spring*, which passed out of regular usage at about the same time.

The use of *breath of spring* dates back at least to ancient Rome, where we find it in the letters of Cicero: "Spurinna, indeed, when I told him about it and described your former way of living, pointed out the serious danger to the state if you did not recur to your old habits with the first breath of Spring."[1] The *breath of spring* is a spring chicken compared to the *breath of heaven*, which we can find referenced as far back as the Sumerian *Elid Genesis* creation myth from the twenty-second century BCE: "An and Enlil have sworn by the life's breath of heaven, the life's breath of earth, that he is allied with all of you."[2]

Sourced in the images of Spring and Heaven, over time these phrases took on the more general meaning of newness, freshness, goodness, and life that was associated with those sources. It is this connotation that was transferred over to *breath of fresh air*, which has evolved to include the concept of a new approach or a refreshing change.

---

1. Cicero, *Letters*, 4:178.
2. Barry et al., *Faithlife Study Bible*, s.v. "Ancient Flood Accounts."

THE WHY

That understanding sets the tone for the second part of this book. In one sense, there is a small yet energetic corpus of work that has been done in the area of liturgical semiotics. In another sense, virtually no work has been done in the field of liturgical semiotics. This is because what I mean when I bring together the words semiotics and liturgy is very different from what others have meant when they have joined those terms. Their approach has been systematic and scientific. Mine is artistic and artisanal. In comparison to what has come before with regards to liturgical semiotics, what I am offering is a breath of fresh air.

Part Two consists of chapters 3–5. Chapter 3 explores the base components of liturgical semiotics: semiotics and liturgy. It sketches out different approaches to semiotics and differing understandings of liturgy found in various branches of the Christian family. Chapter 4 lays out my approach to liturgical semiotics as found in the acronyms BREATHE and GASP/RASP. Chapter 5 gives an overview of the work of others in this area (even though previous work in this arena is quite distinct from my own).

3

Semiotics and Liturgy

"Great success in singing is impossible to the vocalist who does not thoroughly understand breathing"

~DAME NELLIE MELBA, AUSTRALIAN OPERA SINGER[1]

THIS BOOK IS ABOUT liturgical semiotics. Similar to how a vocalist cannot be a successful singer if they do not understand breathing, one cannot successfully explore liturgical semiotics if one does not understand the base components: liturgy and semiotics.

First, semiotics is considered. This follows naturally from our phrase "liturgical semiotics." Semiotics is the primary thing. It is the object, the field of study being applied. *Liturgical* is an adjective, acting as a modifier. What kind of semiotics is being examined? Liturgical semiotics.

Next, liturgy is discussed. Thus far, the term liturgy has been used interchangeably with worship. Here we develop more precision and specificity in using that word, and how it is understood by different branches of the Christian family.

With semiotics and liturgy both better understood, the borders of liturgical semiotics are then brought into clearer focus. By the end of this chapter, a description of semiotics and liturgy are fleshed out, and one is prepared to engage with liturgical semiotics directly.

---

1. Murphy, *Melba*, loc. 3804.

WHAT IS SEMIOTICS?

For an answer to this question, let us begin with a conversation that Jesus had with the Pharisees, from Matthew's Gospel: "The Pharisees and Sadducees came, and to test Jesus they asked him to show them a sign from heaven. He answered them, "When it is evening, you say, 'It will be fair weather, for the sky is red.' And in the morning, 'It will be stormy today, for the sky is red and threatening.' You know how to interpret the appearance of the sky, but you cannot interpret the signs of the times" (Matt 16:1–3).

The word that is translated as *sign* in English is the Greek word σημεῖον which means "a sign or distinguishing mark whereby something is known" or "an event that is an indication or confirmation of intervention by transcendent powers."[2] This word is the root of our word semiotics, and is why semiotics is defined at its most basic level as the study of signs.

This begs another question: what is a sign? Traditionally, a sign is considered to be "something that stands for something else" (captured in the medieval Latin phrase *aliquid stat pro aliquo)*. This broad definition implies that virtually everything is a sign. Even the words that one sees on this page are signs, because they stand for something else, namely the things they describe or are associated with.

The ubiquity of signs is made all the more so when considering the subjective nature of interpretation. I may look at a shooting star as just a shooting star. One of the other roughly eight billion inhabitants of the planet may understand the same shooting star to be a sign of something else (e.g., good luck or divine blessing).

If almost everything can be considered a sign, then defining semiotics as the study of signs is to broaden the topic to the point of meaninglessness. Signs are everywhere and we are always engaging and interpreting them. We are all semioticians and life's journey is itself an exercise in semiotics.

This is all true. To try and derive more concrete insights from our endeavor into liturgical semiotics, however, a more focused and intentional understanding of semiotics is necessary. Yes, we are all doing semiotics all the time as a matter of living our lives. Yet multiple approaches to the discipline have arisen over time.

What follows is the briefest of overviews of the history of semiotics. This is as opposed to an exhaustive investigation. One might think of it as walking down the historical hallway of semiotics. We are reading the plaques next to a few of the doors. Behind each one, however, lies a room

2. BDAG 920.

(and often a wing) of semiotic endeavor that we could occupy ourselves in fruitfully for some time.

One for the Stoics

The sophisticated semiotic systems of today can trace their common pedigree back to the rhetoricians of ancient Greece. To be effective at influencing the thought and behavior of an audience, one must be able to not only understand the affect and interest of the listeners, but also the context in which one is speaking. In other words, to be a good rhetorician, one must be a good sign reader. Thus, works on the art of rhetoric like Plato's *Cratylus* (388 BCE) and Aristotle's *On Interpretation* (350 BCE) have been influential on the development of sign theory.

It was the Stoic philosophers (third century BCE to about third century CE), however, who put together the first fully modern semiotic theory.[3] The reader might remember that while the apostle Paul was in Athens, he debated with some Stoic philosophers (Acts 17:18). For the Stoics, words provided a link between forms (signifiers) and concepts (signified). Someone could consider their favorite coffee cup as an example.[4] When they say the word *cup* in reference to their cup, they are linking that word to the concept of what a cup is. The word *cup* is the signifier, and the concept of a cup, its *cup-ness*, is the signified. Someone's particular coffee cup is the referent in this moment, that which is being referenced by the signifier. Furthermore, "Every phenomenon that falls under the concept linked to a certain word form may be a referent of the word constituted by that word form and that concept."[5] So someone's utterance of the word *cup* can also refer to every other instance of *cup-ness*, not just their favorite coffee cup.

It is important to note that the ruminations of the Stoics were focused on signs as related to language. A general semiotic theory was not yet in view in the way one would understand it today.

Dyadic for the Show

Semiotic studies as known today trace their origin to the late nineteenth century. One of the fathers of modern semiotics was Swiss linguist Ferdinand

---

3. Boussac, *Encyclopedia of Semiotics*, 568.

4. If someone does not drink coffee, I suppose they could use their favorite general drink receptacle—if they must.

5. Anward, "Semiotics in Educational Research," 5411.

de Saussure (1857–1913). Saussure never actually wrote a book on semiotics (or semiology as he called it). Instead, his thoughts on the subject came out as he taught a course called General Linguistics. Some of his students posthumously published their notes from his course in 1915.

Saussure was interested in a sign's value (i.e., meaning) within a given system. The system is what creates the *conditions of possibility* for a sign's value. Think of the system as the kitchen and pantry in a house. This includes all of the ingredients, crockery, and materiel that one would need to make a meal. The various meals that can be made are the various signs that can be generated in that system. Note that different houses are going to have different sets of ingredients and artifacts available to make meals with. So there are different, although possibly overlapping, sets of meals that can be made. The width and breadth of sign generation is dependent upon the makeup of the system.

This metaphor works well for considering cultural linguistics. It is common to have experienced situations, or heard of situations, where things were lost in translation. Perhaps a cultural idiom is used in one language that, when translated to another, makes no sense.

An example from the Bible might be when Jesus tells the fishermen brothers Simon and Andrew to follow him and he will make them "fish for people" (Matt 4:19; Mark 1:17). The meaning of Jesus' words can easily become lost in translation because our twenty-first-century American understanding of fishing is very different from that of first-century Judea.

A modern reader who hears these words might envision someone standing on a riverbank by themselves, baiting their hook and casting for fish as part of some lazy Saturday afternoon recreation. If they were to start to really reflect on the metaphor, then they might start wondering about the hook, the bait, and what it might mean to get a "bite" when one tries to fish for people.

Simon Peter and Andrew, and the first-century hearers of the encounter, understood it quite differently. These were commercial fishermen. They worked at night, in teams, by casting nets. There were no hooks. There was no bait. The notion of "fishing" for people carries an entirely different connotation.

More recent examples abound as well. Think of the popular myth that U.S. president John F. Kennedy called himself a jelly doughnut when he famously said *"Ich bin ein Berliner"* in a speech in West Berlin on June 26, 1963. Whether he did say that or not depends on which house he was cooking in, to use the kitchen metaphor. At that time, the word Berliner might well refer to a pastry in Northern, Western, and Southern Germany.

If that was the kitchen that Kennedy was cooking in, he could have made a guffaw-worthy gaffe.

His speech was in Berlin, however. Residents of Berlin and the surrounding region preferred the term Pfannkuchen when referring to pastries like jelly doughnuts. Thus, given the system that JFK was operating in, the sign that is the word Berliner could not have had the value of a jelly doughnut. No resident of Berlin thought that JFK was calling himself a pastry.

To state clearly what may have been inferred, Saussure understood signs to be dyadic. That is to say, a sign consists of two parts: the signifier and the signified. Similarly to the Stoics, Saussure's approach to semiotics focused on linguistics. For Saussure, "The linguistic sign unites, not a thing and a name, but a concept and an acoustic image."[6] Signs are necessarily spoken, and a sign that goes without enunciation is no sign at all.

Triadic to Get Ready

The other founder of modern semiotic study was American scientist, philosopher, mathematician, and logician Charles Sanders Peirce (1839–1914). Peirce was a prolific thinker and hugely productive in terms of generating intellectual output. He also had serious personal challenges.

Peirce's approach to semiotics was a triadic one rather than a dyadic one. For our purposes, we will consider two Peircean triads. The first triad consists of an object, a "representamen," and an "interpretant." The object is the thing itself. The representamen is the object as it is being represented. The interpretant is the sign generated in the mind of the observer that connects a representamen to the object. In other words, "you see any object as a sign (representamen) that makes sense in your mind (the interpretant)."[7] Furthermore, "all three items are triadic in the sense that none is what it is—sign, object, or interpretant—except by virtue of its relation to the other two."[8]

For example, consider a large wooden cross standing at one end of a church. The object is the wooden cross. That the cross is in a church is a sign (a representamen). How that sign makes sense in one's mind (the interpretant) differs depending on the person's context. Some will see the cross as a sign of Christ's atoning sacrifice. Some will see it as the logo of an antiquated institution. A very few may even see it as the glorification of a torture device.

---

6. Saussure, *Course in General Linguistics*, 66.

7. Downing, *Changing Signs of Truth*, 200.

8. Short, *Peirce's Theory of Signs*, 18.

Having introduced Peirce's object-representamen-inteptetant triad, it is now necessary to introduce his index-icon-symbol triad. These three terms lay out the three ways that a sign (representamen) may refer to its object by creating an understanding (interpretant) in the observer's mind.

An index is a sign that points to what caused it. It "involves an actual connection between two things in the real world, for which reason we speak of one of those things as representing the other."[9] Think of smoke indexing a fire. Alternatively, given our times, think of a high fever and cough indexing COVID-19.

An icon, rather than pointing to a cause, "offers a likeness that visualizes what it refers to, like a photograph."[10] Religious icons, for example, are a visual likeness of what they refer to. Or, consider computer icons. Many of them are in a visual likeness to what they refer to (e.g., the trash icon looks like a trash can where someone throws things away).

A symbol, by contrast, does not look like what it refers to. Therefore, words are symbols. Each page of this book is a page full of symbols. A drawing of a heart, which is not shaped like the organ that pumps blood, and is meant to refer to love, would be a symbol. Additionally, a drawing of a shamrock, meant to refer to Ireland, would be a symbol.

Let us again consider the example of a cross. A cross painted on a road sign could be considered a symbol of a church building. A wooden cross in the church could be considered an icon if one recalls that the wooden cross is a likeness of the instrument of Jesus' death. A wooden cross in the church could be considered an index if one intuits that the cross in the church is indexing that which caused it to be there: the resurrection of Jesus.[11]

Given the extensibility of these triads, it becomes clear that Peirce's approach to semiotics was more generally applicable and was not limited to linguistics. Peirce's triads can be applied equally well to linguistics, visual arts, sporting events, and any other number of activities or endeavors.

Narraphor to Go!

A similarity of the semiotic approaches already discussed is that they are all systematic. They strive to codify and categorize our experiences in order to glean meaning. They are examples of understanding semiotics as a science.

9. O'Brien, "Eucharistic Species," 84.

10. Downing, *Changing Signs of Truth*, 206.

11. It is worth noting that the cross in the church could index any number of theological emphases: the saving work of Jesus Christ, the love of God, the indwelling of the Holy Spirit, etc.

Another approach is to consider semiotics as more art than science. This is what happens when narraphor is used as the main hermeneutic for finding meaning. As was discussed last chapter, narraphors (stories wrapped around metaphors) are tremendous conveyors of meaning. It would seem natural for them to find expression as a way to do semiotics.

This approach to semiotics has been pioneered in the modern era by Leonard Sweet. Sweet is a church historian, futurist, and elder in the United Methodist Church. His brand of semiotics has been applied not only to biblical studies, but to cultural analysis and future studies as well. His approach to semiotics, while requiring explanation and exploration, can be summed up as "trusting the story and connecting the dots."

To do this kind of semiotics, one must first be open and receptive to the ubiquity of story and metaphor. As was mentioned in the last chapter, metaphorical thinking and speech is so universal that it often goes unnoticed. As people live their lives, they swim in metaphorical waters (that was another metaphor, by the way).

Stories are equally omnipresent, if one takes the time to look. Every headline, TV show, movie, or person encountered, is a story. Stories are unfolding and intertwining all day, every day. At this very moment, your story and my story are mingling.

Next, while considering a story, first it must be trusted. To trust a story is to trust that the story is how the author intended it to be and that the author is trying to relay meaning through it. The author is not trying to trick or confuse the audience. The author wants the audience to understand the story and is trying to communicate through it.

If someone is watching a movie, then they trust that the movie is how the filmmakers wanted the movie to be and that they are trying to tell them something through it. If someone is reading a book, then they trust that the book is how the author intended it and that it is communicating what the author wants it to communicate. If someone is considering a person's life (or a company's, or a country's, etc.), then they are trusting that the Author of all life is communicating meaning through all that has happened in that life up to and including their point of engagement in it.

To trust the story is not only to believe that the author wants to communicate something through the narrative, but God does as well. God has brought this story into the audience's life in order that they gain something from it. To trust the story is to realize that the "most basic prerequisite for hearing the voice of the Lord speaking . . . is that one must allow of the possibility that one might oneself be the person to whom the word is addressed."[12] God is giving the reader or hearer a word through the story, be it in the form of a newspaper, a neighbor, or a natural wonder.

All this means that one takes the story largely as given. The story is not to be sliced to ribbons trying to analyze the life out of it. Instead, it is to be received as given, and as gift.

This also means that one does their best to understand the cultural context of the story (and that of the author and that of the intended audience). This is because it is a contextual understanding that will transmit the meaning and significance of the story. Signs "are communicated through cultural media and are governed by cultural aesthetics."[13] To grasp the reality of this, consider that "when a person visits another culture, often times that person does not understand the signs; they hold no significance for that individual."[14] In moving from one culture to another, one changes systems . . . and kitchens.

Then, the dots are connected. Once one understands the story, what the author is trying to say, and its context, then one reads the signs and makes meaning. Furthermore, the more beautiful the story, the richer the meaning. In fact, when someone really does trust the story, and they really do read the signs therein, the meaning that is arrived at may be something that most other people have missed. An example of this approach can be found in appendix A.

When using a narraphor-based semiotic, people are practicing the art of making connections, seeing the relationships between things and reading the meaning of those relationships.

IN SUMMARY

Before moving on to a discussion of liturgy, a brief summary is in order. Semiotics has been done for as long as humans have been aware of their surroundings. Beginning with the Greek rhetoricians and philosophers, however, it has been a discrete field of study. It has been conceived in modern times as two-fold (dyadic) or three-fold (triadic) in nature. For our purposes, however, a story-based approach to semiotics, and one that is more artistry than science, is the way forward.

---

12. Barrett, *Wind, the Fountain, and the Fire*, 16–17.
13. Klotz, "Oh, Worship the King," 294.
14. Klotz, "Oh, Worship the King," 294.

WHAT IS LITURGY?

Our English word liturgy "derives from the Greek λειτουργία, a word in turn compounded from two other Greek words—laos (=people, cf. Laity) and ergon (=work, cf. Metallurgy)."[15] Today the word has been popularly translated as "the work of the people" and is synonymous with corporate worship. The original usage of the word, however, was quite different:

> In ancient Greece, particularly at Athens, a form of personal service to the state which citizens possessing property to a certain amount were bound, when called upon, to perform at their own cost. These liturgies were ordinary, including the presentation of dramatic performances, musical and poetic contests, etc., the celebration of some festivals, and other public functions entailing expense upon the incumbent; or extraordinary, as the fitting out of a trireme in case of war.[16]

This connotation of liturgy as services rendered appears in Philippians 2:29–30, "Welcome him then in the Lord with all joy, and honor such people, because he came close to death for the work of Christ, risking his life to make up for those services (λειτουργίας) that you could not give me." The connecting of liturgy with worship stems from the Septuagint's use of λειτουργία to "translate the Hebrew terms shereth and avodah, when these designate worship and its ministers."[17] From there the notion of liturgy being related to worship passed into Christian understanding and eventually became the sole understanding of the word.

In this day and age, different strands of Christianity have different understandings of (and approaches to) liturgy. An overview of some of these differences is helpful because it informs the work that has been done thus far in liturgical semiotics.

For traditions that are steeped in history and hierarchy, such as Roman Catholicism and Eastern Orthodoxy, there is clear documentation for articulating their particular understanding of liturgy. For more de-centralized traditions, like churches birthed from the Reformations, more nuance and finesse is required to determine their understanding of liturgy. As in many things, Anglicanism tries to locate itself somewhere between these two ends of the spectrum.

---

15. Komonchak et al., *New Dictionary of Theology*, s.v. "Liturgy."
16. Whitney and Smith, *Century Dictionary*, s.v. "Liturgy."
17. Di Berardino et al., *Encyclopedia of Ancient Christianity*, 2:584.

What follows is not an exhaustive list of liturgical understandings from every corner of the Christian family. It is, however, a representative swath of the major themes involved.

Roman Catholicism

One of the gifts of the Roman Catholic Church is that it is a tradition that values scholarship, detail, and clarity. Between the *Catechism of the Catholic Church* and the documents coming out of Vatican II, a Roman Catholic understanding of the liturgy is easily discernible.

For Roman Catholics, "the liturgy is the summit toward which the activity of the church is directed; at the same time it is the font from which all her power flows."[18] This potent statement, birthed out of Vatican II, clearly locates corporate worship at the very center of Christian life. For Roman Catholics, there is no more important endeavor.

An equally powerful statement speaks to the agency of corporate worship: "Every liturgical celebration, because it is an action of Christ the priest and of His Body which is the church, is a sacred action surpassing all others; no other action of the church can equal its efficacy by the same title and to the same degree."[19] From a Roman Catholic perspective, worship is not primarily an individual activity, or even a personal one. Worship is something that Christ is doing and we participate in, because we are his body, the church.

In the liturgy, "God is to be honored by the body of the faithful, and the latter is in its turn to derive sanctification from this act of worship."[20] Thus, the purpose of our worship is to do something for God rather than to get something for ourselves (although our act of service toward God does bring benefit to us).

It is also important to keep in mind the timeless aspect of corporate worship. Joseph Ratzinger put it most eloquently in writing that the "historical liturgy of Christendom is and always will be cosmic, without separation and without confusion, and only as such does it stand erect in its full grandeur."[21] The liturgy connects us with worship that has been going on, unceasing, since the days the disciples still walked the Earth and inherently connected to the worship given by all of creation.

---

18. Catholic Church, *Sacrosanctum Concilium*, §10.

19. Catholic Church, *Sacrosanctum Concilium*, §7.

20. Guardini, *Spirit of the Liturgy*, loc. 130.

21. Ratzinger, *Spirit of the Liturgy*, 34.

Lastly, for Roman Catholics the Mass (Holy Eucharist) is the source of all liturgical prayer. The celebration of this sacrament is to be the normative, daily expression of liturgical worship. Thus, any and all liturgical prayer points back to Holy Eucharist. It is this sacrament that lies at the true north of all corporate worship, and each instance of liturgical activity is like a compass needle guiding the worshiper back to Mass.

What we see is that a Roman Catholic understanding of liturgy is on one end of a spectrum. On this end of the spectrum, the emphasis of corporate worship is on the work of Christ, participated in by the gathered clergy and laity. The emphasis is not on the perceived spiritual experiences of individual worshipers. The primary importance of liturgy is not what it does for the worshiper, but what it does for God. Liturgy connects the church across the world and throughout time, from the foot of the Cross to the present day.

Orthodoxy

An Orthodox understanding of liturgy is not as clearly articulated as a Roman Catholic one is. To begin with, Christian Orthodoxy is not a single church in the way that Roman Catholicism is a single church. There are at least fifteen Eastern Orthodox churches and several Oriental Orthodox churches (e.g., Coptic, Armenian, and Ethiopian). The largest Eastern Orthodox churches are Greek and Russian.

Orthodoxy also lacks the clear governmental authority of Roman Catholicism. Instead, it looks toward almost two thousand years of church tradition for articulating its belief system. It is also a branch of Christianity that has a high tolerance for mystery and ambiguity in how it articulates those beliefs.

Despite these considerations, an Orthodox understanding of liturgy can be apprehended. The synopsis of the next two paragraphs is sourced from D. N. Bernardakis's *A Catechism*.[22] While this Greek Orthodox resource lacks authoritative standing throughout all the Orthodox churches, it gives us a satisfactory view into the Orthodox mindset regarding liturgy.

Corporate worship (i.e., Divine Worship) is a manifesting by outward signs of our faith in God. In worship, Divine Grace is acquired through the Holy Spirit by the celebration of the sacraments. The sacraments are celebrated by the priests. The chief rite of the church is the Divine Liturgy, in which the Eucharist is celebrated.

22. Bernardakis, *Catechism*, 20–21.

During Eucharist, the priests and the singers offer prayer aloud, while the rest of those gathered follow along in silent prayer. The Eucharist is a form of service, and a service is understood to be the whole body of prayers and thanksgivings which the priests and singers read and sing before God in the church. Christians should partake of Holy Communion as often as possible, after proper preparation, because partaking of Holy Communion is necessary to salvation.

We are to worship God "on account of his Divine existence, and on account of his Divine perfections," "on account of his creation of the world, and of his Divine Providence over it," and "on account of a retribution; because the righteousness and holiness of God constantly demand the rejection of whoever scorns to pay him worship, or transgresses his holy will."[23]

The Orthodox understanding of liturgy certainly shares space with Roman Catholicism on one end of our spectrum. The liturgy is something primarily done by the up front participants (priests and singers). The rest of those gathered are passive observers and/or silent participants. This is evidenced by what one may see when visiting a large Orthodox church: well-choreographed enactment as the central act taking place, while others mill around on the periphery, only somewhat engaged or focused on icons along the outside of the space.

Protestantism

If Orthodoxy cannot be described as monolithic, then Protestantism can only be described as incomparably variegated. There is such breadth of belief among Protestants on any number of issues that a concentrated exploration of understandings of liturgy would be a book in and of itself. What can be accomplished, however, is to examine a few pieces of evidence that will broadly sketch out where perhaps the balance of Protestantism resides on this issue.

A good place to start with Protestantism is with its birth: the Protestant expressions of the Reformation. The churches of the Reformation Era pushed back fiercely against many aspects of the Roman Catholic Church, including its understanding of worship. The Reformers often expressed their beliefs in the form of various confessions of faith.

One influential confession among the Reformed branch of Protestantism was the Westminster Confession (1646). In it we find the following:

23. Plato II of Moscow, *Great Catechism*, 8–9.

The Liturgy hath been a great means, as on the one hand to make and increase an idle and unedifying ministry, which contented itself with set forms made to their hands by others, without putting forth themselves to exercise the gift of prayer, with which our Lord Jesus Christ pleaseth to furnish all his servants whom he calls to that office: so, on the other side, it hath been (and ever would be, if continued) a matter of endless strife and contention in the Church, and a snare both to many godly and faithful ministers, who have been persecuted and silenced upon that occasion, and to others of hopeful parts, many of which have been, and more still would be, diverted from all thoughts of the ministry to other studies; especially in these latter times, wherein God vouchsafeth to his people more and better means for the discovery of error and superstition, and for attaining of knowledge in the mysteries of godliness, and gifts in preaching and prayer.[24]

This excoriation of "the Liturgy" is illustrative of a crucial difference between the ends of the spectrum of liturgical understanding. The Reformers wanted more flexibility in how their worship manifested. They wanted more extemporaneous prayer and less set forms, for example.[25]

They also wanted more emphasis placed on preaching. The general form of Protestant worship that has developed over time bears this out. In many Protestant denominations, the worship builds toward the act of preaching. In some churches, the majority of time spent in worship consists of the sermon. The Holy Eucharist (or Lord's Supper or Holy Communion) is typically something that may or may not be celebrated, depending on the week, or month.

The decided majority of churches hold some understanding of worship comprising a combination of word, sacrament, and experience. The Protestant end of the liturgical understanding spectrum places more of an emphasis on word and/or experience. The architecture of many Protestant worship spaces puts this on display by locating the pulpit in a higher or more central location than the table.

In identifying the primary act of worship as the sermon, something is implied that may not be readily apparent to the worshiper. Preaching is directed toward the gathered congregation and is done for their edification (albeit to God's glory of course). This suggests that the main point of worship, not the only point but the main point, has to do with the spiritual life of

24. Westminster Assembly, *Westminster Confession of Faith*, 480.

25. This flexibility engendered more participation on the part of the laity, which was an aim of the Reformers.

the worshiper. It is the cultivation and nurturing of their relationship with God that is of first importance.

This stands in distinction to liturgy that places the emphasis on, or builds toward, Holy Eucharist. In the Roman Catholic or Orthodox understanding of liturgy, the primary concern is not the spiritual life of the worshiper but the service rendered to God.

Before moving on from Protestantism, the disclaimer given at the beginning of this section must be touched upon again. There are thousands of denominations that trace their heritage back to the Protestant Reformations. Further, there are thousands of non-denominational churches that also have a Protestant pedigree, even if that pedigree goes generally unacknowledged. Given this wide, deep, and beautiful variety of Protestant expressions, what has been said about Protestantism in this section cannot be applied universally across all of those expressions.

To take one example, think about the Society of Friends (i.e., the Quakers). They do not recognize sacraments. They do not preach sermons (although they do speak out of the silence of their worship). In many ways, they do not fit cleanly into the sketch that has been made of a Protestant understanding of liturgy. This does not negate the value of the insights gained from that sketch, however.

Anglicanism

To prepare for delving into Anglicanism, it is good to pause and consider the lay of the land for a moment. Thus far two ends of a spectrum have been fleshed out when it comes to liturgical understanding. One end places an emphasis on ancient, set forms of worship. That worship is intended primarily to render service to God in the form of the Holy Eucharist. The other end places an emphasis on the preached word for the spiritual nourishment of the worshiper.

Neither end of the spectrum is bad or wrong. Both ends of the spectrum have strengths and weaknesses and are more nuanced than has been described. Yet the two ends are distinctly different, and that must be acknowledged as well as honored.

Anglicanism has been saved for last because it does not inhabit either extreme of our spectrum of liturgical understanding. It sits somewhere in the middle, blurring toward both sides.

Anglicanism lacks both the confessional documents of Protestantism and the clear documentation of Roman Catholicism. Birthed out of the English Reformation, Anglicanism has always held an appreciation for mystery in tension with a certain pragmatism that desires clarity in the face of lived reality.

That pragmatism is what leads Anglicans to look toward their worship to find their identity. Churches in the Anglican Communion typically follow their own Book of Common Prayer (BCP) as their guide for worship.

Considering the Episcopal Church's BCP will help us to locate Anglicanism on the liturgical understanding spectrum. To begin with, the normative worship experience in the Episcopal Church is the Holy Eucharist. Chances are, if someone walks into an Episcopal Church on a Sunday morning, the service of Holy Eucharist is what will be encountered.

This has not always been the case. Prior to the liturgical renewal movement of the twentieth century, the normative expression of Episcopal worship was Morning Prayer. Now, however, the church is one that is Eucharist-focused.

This is also evidenced by looking at other liturgies in the BCP. The liturgy for the Celebration and Blessing of a Marriage, for example, is intended to end with Holy Eucharist. If Holy Eucharist is not included, the wedding service ends with the Passing of the Peace.[26] For a congregation waiting for the bride and groom to walk down the aisle, passing the peace can be an incongruous way to precede that action.

Perhaps even more importantly, Holy Baptism is now specifically to be celebrated with the context of a service of Holy Eucharist.[27] In the prior BCP, there was provision for private baptisms. Now, the linking of Baptism to Eucharist speaks to the importance of the gathered community for the celebration of the sacraments, and to the foundational place of the Holy Eucharist in the life of a faith community.

In one sense, this emphasis on the Holy Eucharist places Anglicanism on the same end of the spectrum as Roman Catholicism and Orthodoxy. This is not, however, the whole story.

In the Episcopal Church, one of the vows that the priest makes upon ordination is to "conform to the doctrine, discipline, and worship of The Episcopal Church."[28] This means that the BCP is to be followed closely and taken seriously in how worship is conducted.

As such, the participation and involvement of all those gathered is crucial to worship. A priest cannot celebrate the Eucharist by themselves, for example, because the liturgy calls for more than one participant. Those

26. Episcopal Church, *Book of Common Prayer*, 431.

27. Episcopal Church, *Book of Common Prayer*, 298, phrases it this way: "Holy Baptism is appropriately administered within the Eucharist as the chief service on a Sunday or other feast."

28. Episcopal Church, *Book of Common Prayer*, 526.

gathered are absolutely necessary in the service that is being rendered to God. This stands in sharp distinction to the Orthodox or Roman Catholic view that it is the priests alone who celebrate the sacraments.

While Anglicanism does inherently carry a high view of the Eucharist, it also carries an understanding of the crucial role of the laity. After all, one of the birthing acts of Anglicanism was to provide worship in the vernacular so that the laity could understand what was going on. The edification of the entire assembly is important in Anglicanism, and this is wed with a high view of the Holy Eucharist. This combination places Anglicanism closer to the middle of our spectrum of liturgical understanding.

CONCLUSION

It is wise to refrain from diving into the subject of liturgical semiotics head-first. Instead, wading into these waters through an examination of semiotics and liturgy as separate subjects is preferable.

Semiotics, while having a long past, has become a focused area of study within the last century. While first finding manifestation in linguistics, the study of semiotics has broadened into an art that can be applied to almost any area. This chapter introduced the semiotic approaches of Ferdinand de Saussure, Charles Sanders Peirce, and Leonard Sweet.

Liturgy was originally understood as acts taken to serve the public good. Over time the term came to be associated with Christian worship in the form of acts taken to serve God. In present times, different parts of the Christian family have different understandings of liturgy. In this chapter Roman Catholicism, Orthodoxy, Protestantism, and Anglicanism were looked at.

The next chapter explores liturgical semiotics proper.

4

BREATHE, and GASP/RASP

"The Church must breathe with her two lungs!"

~POPE JOHN PAUL II[1]

LITURGICAL SEMIOTICS IS THE application of semiotics to the subject of liturgy. This chapter outlines my approach to the concept. The next chapter explores others' work in the field of liturgical semiotics, and the section after that (Part Three) contains practica for applying my approach.

Chapter 2 established the choice of breathing as a guiding narraphor for this work. Breathing is the most robust narraphor of the now, and it presents us with a powerful opportunity for meaning-making and memory seizing.

Like breathing, my approach to liturgical semiotics takes on two separate but complementary parts. First, we must listen to what Jesus is telling us through the liturgy and its implications for our common life together. Second, worship leaders must consider how to engage in the enactment of the liturgy in a more evocative and culturally resonant way. Step one is about receiving; step two is about giving. Step one is about listening; step two is about speaking.

These two steps are intertwined as inhaling and exhaling are intertwined. We must inhale before we can exhale. We must receive the oxygen offered to us by the trees when we inhale before we can offer the gift of carbon dioxide to the trees when we exhale.

In the liturgy the Divine Breath, the Ruach, the Pneuma, offers us meaning through signs. First, we must be receptive to these signs. After we have received those signs and learned from them, we will be able to offer our

---

1. John Paul II, *Ut Unum Sint*, §54.

own breath in return and add to the signs. We will be able to enhance those signs, making them more accessible by worshipers.

We must receive the gift offered to us by Christ, the eternal and heavenly liturgist (Heb 8:2), before we can give the gift of semiotically enhanced worship.

DIFFERENCES BETWEEN BREATHE, GASP, AND RASP

My approach to liturgical semiotics can be staked out, and hemmed in, by the above three acronyms. There are differences among these acronyms that need to be stated to set the stage before delving into their content. One is that BREATHE is a process. It is a step-by-step flow. GASP and RASP are not. Instead, the elements of the GASP toolkit are brought together and applied collectively. RASP is a function that is undertaken for purpose, but not in a linear, step-by-step way.

A second difference is that there is no predetermined result for what the BREATHE process produces. Instead, one faithfully follows and discovers what is (or is not) there to be found. In contrast to this, the semiotician who engages GASP/RASP has an endpoint in mind. GASP is perhaps best thought of as tools that the semiotician uses to help reach the desired endpoint. RASP, while lacking a process flow as such, does have a specific destination in mind.

With this brief orientation of how the acronyms function, it is time to get into the details of what they actually mean.

LEARNING TO BREATHE

The first part of my liturgical semiotics paradigm, the inhalation, involves reading the signs of the liturgy and finding meaning. An acronym to help the intrepid semiotician remember the flow of this process is BREATHE. The acronym breaks down as follows:

> **B**e aware of the context.
> **R**esolve upon a narraphor.
> **E**ngage the metaphor.
> **A**pply Peircean triads.[2]
> **T**rust the story.
> **H**armonize the results.
> **E**xplore what comes next (if anything).

2. Charles Sanders Peirce's triadic approach to semiotics was sketched out in the previous chapter in the section entitled "Triadic to Get Ready."

Leggo my LEGO[3]

When I was a kid, I loved to play with LEGO bricks. I would open a new box and studiously and earnestly build the scene correctly, following the instructions. If I discovered a brick was out of place, then I needed to deconstruct until I corrected the error and then rebuild again. The finished product, once verified against the picture on the box, was a source of pride for me.

There is something in many of us, likely the more structured and left-brain oriented of us, that loves to follow directions. Insert Tab A into Slot B. Do this, *then* that, and then the other. The worship service begins on page 355 and uses these words in this order. If you are not like this, then I suspect that you at least know these types of people.

The BREATHE part of liturgical semiotics is more artistic than scientific. It is to put away the instruction booklet. It is to let go of the expectation for what the finished product is going to look like. The artistry of liturgical semiotics does not come with a picture on the box. Rather, like an artist who stands before a blank canvas or a lump of clay or a block of stone, the semiotician partners with the creative muse (perhaps best described as the Holy Spirit for us Christians) and sees where the process leads.

Be Aware of the Context

Know thyself. To thine own self be true. If you are going to love your neighbor as yourself, then you can't love your neighbor until you love yourself. Put your own mask on before helping others. However you want to phrase it, there is a key point here about knowing or tending to yourself before you can be effective at something else or with other people. Knowing your own context is key before proceeding with liturgical semiotics.

To begin with, what is your background with regards to Christian worship? It could be that you have been born, raised, and continue on in a particular denomination. Or, you might have a rather ecumenical background. Your understanding of Christian worship is going to color the semiotics that you do. Semiotics is a subjective rather than objective task. We think with what we know, and so what you know is going to inform how you read the signs of worship.

Another element of contextual awareness is the liturgy itself. There are many forms of Christian worship, each with its own distinctiveness.

---

3. If one does not know of the iconic "Leggo my Eggo" motto for Eggo brand waffles, this title likely makes no sense.

Semiotics is a practical endeavor in that it is a particular endeavor: we consider a particular liturgy instead of liturgy as an abstract concept.

Resolving Upon a Narraphor

The liturgy is replete with meanings. To try and take in meaning from all of a worship experience at once would be an overwhelming task. Instead, my approach focuses on one piece of the liturgy at a time. A choice is made and then meaning mined.

Narraphor has already been identified as a potent transmitter of meaning. In light of this, a particular narraphor present in the liturgy under consideration is chosen. In delight of this, the same liturgy can be examined many times, each time with a different narraphor as the focus.

Recall that a narraphor is the combination of two things: a metaphor and a story. The process flow addresses each of these parts.

Think about the lighting of candles for worship as an example of a narraphor to resolve upon. Churches today have electric lights, so the lighting of candles is metaphorical, with rich imagery to explore. The story of how that lighting happens could be equally rich. Who is lighting the candles, when, and how? Bringing these two elements together provides even more material with which to weave a tapestry of semiotic meaning. Hopefully this example has proven illuminating.

Engage the Metaphor

Once a narraphor is chosen, the metaphor present within that narraphor is engaged. Leonard Sweet has written that metaphors "involve two different realities that are forced together to form a new reality, with the metaphor itself a frame that connects the conjoined meanings into a revelatory focus."[4]

There is a creative, artistic energy to metaphor engagement. What does the metaphor suggest? How might we turn the metaphor, as one does a precious gem, to reveal different facets? One way this can manifest is to think about one or both of those realities in a more expansive way by themselves and then bring those insights together.

An illustrative example will bring some concrescence to this ethereal epitaph. For engaging metaphors par excellence, we look to the parables of Jesus. Consider Jesus' pronouncement in Matthew 13:3 that the kingdom of

---

4. Sweet, *Giving Blood*, 154.

heaven "is like yeast that a woman took and mixed in with three measures of flour until all of it was leavened."

This metaphor takes the realities of the kingdom of heaven, and of yeast, and forces them together to make a new reality. Engaging this metaphor would involve rumination on the nature of yeast: What does yeast do? How does it function? Then one might ponder the historical context: What is the difference in the use or role of yeast today with how it was understood in the first century? After that, the insights gained about the yeast would seek application as qualities of the kingdom of heaven.

A revelatory word of caution: the art of metaphor engagement is "knowing how far to ride a metaphor—and getting off before it breaks down."[5] In thinking about the kingdom of heaven being like yeast, there is a limit to how applicable yeast properties are to the kingdom. For example, cogitating on how yeast cells reproduce might not shed new insights into how the kingdom of heaven expands.[6]

Applying Peircean Triads

There is some structure to even the most creative art. If there were no guidelines, no rules, no parameters, no borders, then there would be no difference between street art and defacement (and there is a difference).

The Peircean triads discussed in chapter 3 are a useful tool in the semiotician's toolkit. They can be applied situationally, on the small scale. The semiotics rooted in Saussure are often interested in the big picture, the whole system. Peircean based semiotics can do that as well. But the triads that Peirce offers allow for a more granular, episodic approach. This quality lends itself to our endeavor.

The first triad is the object-representamen(sign)-interpretant(how one makes sense of the sign in one's mind) triad. This triad helps to situate or frame the metaphor that is being discussed. Identifying an object helps to draw the borders of the discussion and prevent scope creep as we move forward. Working out the sign is ultimately about taking that object and firmly grounding it in a particular experience. Making sense of the sign in one's mind is a subjective task that makes us acknowledge how we are thinking about what we are engaging in this semiotic process.

Peirce's second triad is that of index-icon-symbol. This triad interrogates the sign to determine just what kind of sign it is. Does it refer back to

5. Geary, *I Is An Other*, 36.

6. Or it might—I haven't done the research. One may perpend on this at their leisure.

that which produced it (index)? Does it resemble what it represents (icon)? Or is it not in the likeness of what it refers to (symbol)?

Once that determination is made, the sign can be contemplated with greater specificity to see if there are new insights to reveal.

Trust the Story

The next letter in our BREATHE acronym is T, as in trust the story. A narraphor is a narrative wrapped around a metaphor. While thus far the metaphor has been dealt with, now the narrative is attended to.

Yet what does it mean to trust the story? It means to suspend one's disbelief and follow through to the tale's conclusion. It means to have a posture of openness and an attitude of curiosity. It means that to really understand something, you must first stand under it.

To give a glimpse of what trusting the story might look like, take John 12:3: "Mary took a pound of costly perfume made of pure nard, anointed Jesus' feet, and wiped them with her hair. The house was filled with the fragrance of the perfume." The next day Jesus and the disciples enter Jerusalem and the events of Holy Week, from John's perspective, unfold.

To trust this story is to consider what narrative facts it gives us, add into consideration historical and scientific facts, and discern what the implications are. One narrative fact to think about is that Mary used an enormous amount of perfume. Only a minute amount of perfume is needed to get the fragrance flowing. Instead Mary used an entire pound. The smell would have been quite powerful, as the text suggests.

The other narrative fact to lift up at this point is that during the foot washing in John 13, Jesus' feet do not get washed. Jesus' washes the disciples feet, but the text does not record that anyone washed *his* feet.

Next we look for historical facts to help contextualize these narrative facts. One that seems pertinent is that bathing customs in first-century Judea were not what they are in twenty-first-century America. The idea of daily full-body bathing was not in view. It thus seems very unlikely that Jesus had a bath between the time of his anointing by Mary and his crucifixion.

The scientific fact to add to this is that scents can remain for quite some time. Given the exorbitant amount of perfume Mary used on Jesus' feet, and the probable lack of a bath in between, the scent of the perfume would still have been present when Jesus was crucified.

To trust this story leads us to the foot of the cross. It is there that we find Jesus, still breathing in the scent of the perfume that Mary anointed him with, as he dies for the sins of the world.

Harmonize the Results

To this point in the process two different avenues have been pursued. A metaphor has been interrogated, and a story has been followed. Each of these investigations has produced some type of result. It could be grandiose or it could be humble, but some artifact has resulted from each of these avenues of inquiry.

Next these two results are brought together. Do they harmonize, or do they contradict? Do they come together like oil and vinegar (making a nice vinaigrette), or like oil and water (making an unmixable mess)? What does the combination of these two results look like?

Then we take a pause. A breath break. Remember that there is no picture on the outside of the box. There is no determined form of our final product. It could be that we have revealed a marvelous piece of art, like the artist who reveals the statue that was already there in the stone. Or, we could find ourselves with a misshapen piece of clay. There is no guarantee that we will find something breathtaking. We may instead find ourselves simply out of breath after our semiotic exertions.

Thus we pause to consider. What have we found so far? Do our results harmonize? Has this parallel pairing of Peirceans triads and story perambulation produced something prêt-à-porter or pernicious?

If there is discord, then the process stops. The liturgical semiotician lives to worship another day, maybe with a slightly lower batting average. The process stops with a single BREATH.

If there is harmony, then the process continues. Our noun (BREATH) becomes a verb (BREATHE).

Explore What Comes Next (If Anything)

In Luke 16:10 we find Jesus saying that "whoever is faithful in a very little is faithful also in much." This process of liturgical semiotics has borne fruit. There is evidence that the semiotician is on the right track. There is something here. It is time to go farther.

Now the artistry of liturgical semiotics can proceed less by rote and more by Rorschach. There can be less guardrails and more gusto. The semiotician continues on, creatively and in conjunction with the Holy Spirit.

Learning to BREATHE is about making some wise choices, and then testing out those choices to see what the Spirit might be saying through that piece of the liturgy. If it seems as though the endeavor has been a worthwhile one, then fertile semiotic ground has been discovered and more action may be taken.

LEARNING TO GASP AND RASP

The second part of my liturgical semiotics paradigm, the exhalation, involves making semiotic adjustments to the liturgy. This happens in two ways.

One way, captured in the acronym GASP, is to make specific changes to parts of the liturgy that are evocative of the day's celebration. This helps to make the worshiper's engagement with the spirit of the day's liturgy (whether a liturgical season, or feast day, or specific event) more robust. The enactment of the liturgy becomes more unified, and hence, the intended meaning of the day's liturgy may be more fully apprehended.

The other way, encapsulated in the acronym RASP, is to change how various artifacts in worship are used in order to make them more resonant with the cultural context of the worshiper. The worshiper thinks with what they know, not only intellectually but culturally. By adjusting how certain elements of worship are presented, sourced, and used, the worshiper's engagement with these symbols will be more resonant with how they understand and live into the world around them.

GASP

This task entails instituting changes that make the liturgy more evocative of the particular meaning one is attempting to transmit to the worshiper. The acronym to help the courageous semiotician remember this undertaking is GASP. The acronym breaks down as follows:

Gestures.
Awareness.
Speech.
Presence.

A Word about Scope and Specificity

The scope of what comprises liturgy, and hence what may comprise semiotic adjustments to the liturgy, may not be readily apparent. Liturgy is not simply the words on the page. It is all that takes place during the worship. It is the depth of words spoken, silences observed, and movements made. It is the breadth of stillness sought, light shone, and music played. The liturgy is everything that happens from the start of worship (including how that is demarcated) to the end of worship. With such a wide and rich understanding of what comprises the liturgy, there is plainly much freedom and possibility as to how semiotic adjustments can be made.

It must also be noted that one does not GASP in a vacuum. If GASP is best described as a set of tools, then there must be something tangible to use those tools on. Similar to the BREATHE process, a particular liturgy, a particular worship experience, needs to be specified as the subject.

Furthermore, within that liturgy, a particular piece should be focused upon. It is fine to have a broader vision, but that vision is best broken down into bite size chunks. For example, one might be interested in evoking the theme of resurrection in worship on Easter morning in a robust way. That can be achieved once the project is considered in more granularity. The question is not "how do I evoke the theme of resurrection in this worship service?." It is more "how do I evoke the theme of resurrection in how we process into the space, or in the music, or in the sermon, or in the lighting, or in the way the bread and wine are acted upon at the altar, or in how we pass the peace, or how we pray for the dead?" Start small and build up.

As just implied above, the theme or message that one is trying to evoke also has to be specified. Whether it is the character of a particular feast day (All Saints Day) or a seasonal theme (Lent) or a celebration (a wedding) or a Scripture passage (Jesus healing Bartimaeus), that which is to be evoked must be identified. It is true that everything we do in worship, "in some manner, directs our attention to God's actions in history, the active presence of God in the present moment, and the anticipation of God's activity in . . . God's future."[7] Within that broad vision, however, certain themes or messages can be chosen for particular emphasis.

With the scope scoped out, and the specificity specified, it is time to examine what GASP comprises.

Gestures

The height of the COVID-19 pandemic forced many churches to stop worship altogether. It also pushed many churches out of their comfort zones and onto their computer screens. Zoom-based worship services limited our use of one of the most incarnational aspects of our worship: gestures.

7. Alexander, *Celebrating Liturgical Time*, v.

We are embodied creatures. As such, our embodiment of worship is of consequence. In reference to this, Patrick Malloy has noted that the "body, mind, and spirit are integrated, and what happens in one, influences the rest."[8]

As an example, consider what you do when you pray. Does your body assume a particular posture? Do your eyes close or do your hands fold? What you do with your body prepares the rest of you to enter into prayer. The body, and what is done with it, can lead the mind and heart.

This is not only true with regards to oneself, but with regards to the assembly as well. There are certain people in worship who become the focus of the assembly's attention at particular times. Let us call these focal participants. The gestures (a.k.a. manual acts or bodily movements) that a focal participant makes can influence the gathered faithful—for good or ill. This influence is to be taken seriously since, as James Turrell has noted, "sometimes both physical gesture and the material objects of the liturgy speak their symbolic meaning more effectively without words at all."[9] Donald Gray has similarly noted that "these ceremonial, visual actions of the priest teach and instruct as surely as do his formal instruction or his liturgical words, in fact perhaps more so."[10]

Awareness

There is an old saying that those who ignore history are doomed to repeat it.[11] This may be a bit melodramatic, but it speaks to an important truth: it is a good thing to be aware of history. This can apply to worship as much as it does to geopolitical concerns.

Christian worship in twenty-first-century America has not simply materialized out of the ether. Our current worship has evolved from earlier forms of worship, which themselves evolved from earlier forms of worship. As Louis Weil has put it, "everything in the liturgy carries a history, an evolution that has been shaped through a wide range of factors, not merely theological, but also historical and cultural, and even through the accidents of history."[12]

8. Malloy, *Celebrating the Eucharist*, 100.

9. Turrell, *Celebrating the Rites of Initiation*, 77.

10. Gray, "Hands and Hocus-Pocus," 312.

11. This is based on a quote from philosopher George Santayan: "Those who cannot remember the past are condemned to repeat it" (Santayan, *Life of Reason*, 284).

12. Weil, *Liturgical Sense*, 7–8.

It is important for a semiotician to have an awareness of the liturgy, or piece of the liturgy, under consideration. What is the history of that aspect of worship? How did it originate, how has it changed over time, and why?

Think of it this way: the worship that happens on a Sunday morning is the visible tip of an invisible iceberg of history and humanity that has led up to it. Each time worship begins, the latest page in a very old story is being written. It is good to know the story thus far. One needs to be aware.

Speech

While it is possible for physical gesture and the material objects to speak their symbolic meaning more effectively without words, the use of words in worship is not to be discounted. Indeed, how one uses words in worship is the eight hundred pound gorilla of meaning-making in worship.

How actively the use of words can be adjusted to be evocative of a theme or message is a function of the rules governing that worship. The more tightly controlled and choreographed the liturgy, the less space there is for semiotic adjustment of any kind, including words. A wonderful exception to this is the sermon time, where in most traditions the only guardrails in place are those placed by the Holy Spirit.

Take the eucharistic prayer as an example. In some traditions, every word said in relation to the bread and the wine is prescribed. In some traditions, the words of institution are required, but otherwise much flexibility exists. Some traditions have even more flexibility in this regard. Hopefully it becomes clear that the less restrictive the tradition is about what can be said in relation to the bread and the wine, the more opportunity there is for the one presiding to craft the words to be evocative of the intended theme.

Presence

Worship is not a sideshow. It is not a theatrical performance. It is not a spectator sport or a town council meeting. Worship is distinct from these things and requires a distinction in how we make ourselves present to it.

Part of that presence is our bearing, or how we carry ourselves. This is important for all those gathered into "the living presence of our Risen Lord through Word and Sacrament."[13] It is of particular importance for focal participants, however. If one carries themselves in a casual or haphazard way, that is being communicated to the faithful as being how worship is

13. Michno, *Priest's Handbook*, 30.

to be enacted. Alternatively, if one carries themselves with an awareness of humility and solemnity before the Author of all life, that will communicate something very different about the nature of worship to those gathered.

Part and parcel of presence is the intentional assumption and exercising of authority. This is as opposed to what Priva Parker describes as a "ubiquitous strain of twenty-first-century culture [that] is infecting our gatherings: being chill."[14] There is a cultural push for being laid back and non-invasive with regards to facilitating gatherings. Yet, when people are intentionally and purposefully gathered, they need to be led intentionally and purposefully. Such mindfulness is important for focal participants.

RASP

The point of RASP is to effect changes to how certain artifacts of the liturgy are used in worship in order to make those artifacts more resonant with the worshiper's cultural context. The RASP acronym breaks down as such: (Re) signing Artifacts to Spark Perception.

Artifacts are understood to mean the things we use in worship. Objects like candles, oil, ashes, incense, hymnals, bread, and wine would all be examples of artifacts. These artifacts carried particular cultural meanings when they first became part of Christian worship. The cultural meanings attached to those objects have changed over time, but their use in Christian ritual may have (and likely has) not. This gap, and reducing it, is what is of interest.

(Re)signing is a process that has been constructed by Crystal Downing in her book *Changing Signs of Truth: A Christian Introduction to the Semiotics of Communication*.[15] This word encompasses two ideas simultaneously. While being *resigned* to the truth of what we are considering, we also recognize the need to *re-sign* that truth, generating fresh signs that make that truth meaningful to contemporary audiences.

It is worth noting that when being *resigned* to a truth, the original meaning of resign is being used: to yield up oneself with confidence to another for care and guidance.[16] In resigning ourselves to a truth we are yielding ourselves up to, and placing ourselves under the care of, that truth.

(Re)signing is something that the church has done for millennia. There just has not been a catchy name attached to it. Consider the case of St. Christopher from the Roman Catholic Church. During the liturgical reforms of

14. Parker, *Art of Gathering*, 73.

15. First referenced in chapter 3.

16. *Oxford Concise English Dictionary*, s.v. "resign."

the latter half of the twentieth century, St. Christopher was dropped from the universal calendar of saints. He was (re)signed. The church was resigned to his importance in the life of the body of Christ: he remains one of the most popular saints still today, and his celebration is permitted locally. Yet there was a re-signing of the qualities of a universally recognized Roman Catholic saint. For a culture which now placed a high value on historicity and verifiable fact, there was no longer room for a saint who was mostly myth and manuscript.[17]

Or, to choose an example from my tradition's history, consider Thomas Cranmer's creation of the original Book of Common Prayer as an act of (re)signing. Resigned to the importance of liturgy in the life of the church, which is the body of Christ, Cranmer re-signed the liturgy in a way that reconnected it to the people by providing it in the vernacular.

In my RASP approach to liturgical semiotics, elements from our worship are (re)signed. While being resigned to the truth of their importance in the worship life of Christians, they are re-signed so that they generate fresh signs which make that truth more meaningful to current worshipers.

CONCLUSION

In this chapter I have sketched out a three part approach to liturgical semiotics, using the narraphor of breathing. On the inhale we read the signs of the liturgy, following the process laid out by the BREATHE process. On the exhale we semiotically adjust the liturgy using our GASP and RASP acronyms as guides.

Early in this chapter I mentioned LEGO blocks, something from my childhood. Here at the end of the chapter I will mention something else from my childhood: interactive fiction. This wonderful genre of books (e.g., the *Choose Your Own Adventure* series by Bantam Books) gave the reader the power to make their own decisions as to how to proceed through the book. I conclude this chapter by offering the reader something similar.

As your adventure continues you find yourself standing before four darkened passageways: one on the left, one in the middle, and two off to the right. From the passage on the left you hear people: engrossed in conversation, but the language does not sound like English. Straining to hear, you think that what you are hearing is Dutch. Also, the terrain in this direction looks a bit more difficult—the going may be slower.

A wind blows out of the two passages on the right. From the near right passage you hear the sound of worship being enacted. From the far right

17. This illustration is taken from Downing, *Changing Signs of Truth*, 26–27.

passage you hear no sound, but you do catch the faint odor of freshly baked bread.

The passage in the middle appears to have the opposite effect of the passages on the right: there is a draft of air flowing into it. You feel air being pulled in, almost as if the passage itself is drawing in breath.

If you want to find out more about others' work in the area of liturgical semiotics, then choose the left passage and turn to chapter 5.

If you want to explore a practical application of GASP, then choose the near right passage and turn to chapter 7.

If you want to explore a practical application of RASP, then choose the far right passage and turn to chapter 8.

If you want to explore a practical application of BREATHE, then choose the middle passage and turn to chapter 6.

5

Previous Work in Liturgical Semiotics

"Overbreathing is undoubtedly one of the most insidious and dangerous behaviours/responses to environmental, task, emotional, cognitive, and relationship challenges in our daily lives."

~PETER LITCHFIELD, GRADUATE SCHOOL OF BREATHING SCIENCES[1]

A DISCLAIMER

IN THE WORDS OF Monty Python, now for something completely different. Or so it may seem at least. This chapter delves into previous work in the area of liturgical semiotics. Much of that work has been scholarly, complex, and quite different from my own. Thus, one may find that the tenor or language of this chapter differs both from what came before it and what comes after it.

I have structured the book such that skimming, or even skipping, this chapter will not prevent someone from getting a firm grasp of what I mean by liturgical semiotics and how to go about doing it. That being said, what is brought forth in this chapter can be quite rich and edifying for those who want to know more about what has already been done in the field, and how (and why) my approach differs.

---

1. Litchfield, "Brief Overview," para. 14. The Graduate School of Breathing Sciences offers, incidentally, a Master of Science Degree in Applied Breathing Sciences.

AN OVERVIEW

This chapter reviews some previous work done in the area of liturgical semiotics. The review is illustrative rather than exhaustive, for three reasons.
One, there is no agreement on what does and does not constitute *semiotics*.
This makes an all-encompassing review a bit of a moving target. Two, the
comprehensive history of semiotics of religion (of which semiotics of liturgy
could be considered a subset), is still needed and has yet to be written.[2] The
field is young and fluid enough to resist a definitive corpus.

The most important reason for doing an instructional review rather than
an extensive one is that my work differs considerably from previous work.
By looking at the work of three previous scholars in this area, it will help to
provide boundary and texture to my approach. Each of these scholars shares a
kind of quality with my approach, while differing wildly in other ways.

In the last chapter, the acronyms of BREATHE, GASP, and RASP were
introduced. The BREATHE process seeks to hear from the liturgy itself what
meaning it conveys. It lets the object under consideration speak. The work
of Gerard Lukken, grounded in the semiotics of A. J. Greimas (hence Saussurean in origin) does something similar.

The GASP and RASP approaches are both motivated by the idea that
there is a limit of receptivity on the part of the worshiper to the meanings
being conveyed in worship. Undertaking GASP and RASP hopes to increase
the opportunity for the worshiper to grasp the meaning being conveyed. The
work of Graham Hughes, in his notion that the sign-receiver has a bounded
ability to receive and complete the sign, is operating under a similar understanding. Hughes's work was also based on a Peircean semiotic, providing a
balance to that of Lukken.

Next it is important to note that my approach to liturgical semiotics is
extremely practical (tactical even). Rather than constructing abstract sign
system theories, I am dealing with specifics. Mark Searle's pastoral liturgical
studies, with its interest in empirical observation, is similarly practical.

In reviewing the work of these three scholars, the shape and definition
of my work is more discernible. Following the review, further comments on
how my work differs from that which has come before will be made.

SEMANET AND GERARD LUKKEN

The work of Ferdinand de Saussure and Charles Sanders Peirce effectively birthed the modern era of semiotic study. During the mid-twentieth

---

2. Boom and Thomas-Andreas. *Sign, Method, and the Sacred*, 1.

century, semiotics became a discipline that was applied to any number of fields. A curious omission in that energetic expansion of semiotic exploration, however, was its application to liturgy. That is, until the mid-seventies.

It was in 1976 that a group of instructors from the theology department of Tilburg University in the Netherlands began to study structural text analysis, a branch of structuralism.[3] After some early shaking out of purpose and identity, the group eventually settled on the name SEMANET, a Dutch acronym of *Semiotic Analysis by Dutch Theologians.* The group also decided early on that it needed to narrow its focus and methods to a single school of semiotic thought. It settled upon the semiotics of A. J. Greimas (1917–92).

Greimas was the founder of the Paris School of semiotics. This branch of linguistic semiotics stood in the tradition of Ferdinand de Saussure and furthered it by developing a metalanguage.[4] This metalanguage allowed a Sassurian approach to semiotics to be applied to non-verbal expressions, freeing semiotics to move beyond text-based study. As such, the SEMANET group believed the metalanguage to be "applicable to liturgy as well, which is at the same time a verbal and a comprehensive non-verbal object."[5]

Based on these decisions about focus and identity, SEMANET began meeting with the French group CADIR, which stood for *Center for Analysis of Religious Discourse.* This group formed in 1971 and had been working to apply the semiotics of Greimas to biblical texts. The work of SEMANET was spearheaded by Gerard Lukken, who has championed and developed this approach to liturgical study until the present day.

Greimassian Semiotics

The semiotics of Greimas terms the object under consideration the *discourse.* It "tries to lay bare the relations of meaning which lie hidden under the discourse as we immediately perceive or read it"[6] by following what it calls the generative trajectory. What is immediately perceptible is the manifestation level, and the generative trajectory explores three levels which lie underneath this level: the level of discursive structures, the surface level,

3. Structuralism is the study of various aspects of human culture that must be understood in their relation to the broader system. This work, in Europe at least, was grounded in the structural linguistics of Ferdinand de Saussure. Recall that Saussure's approach to semiotics concerned itself most with the sign system as a whole.

4. A metalanguage is a language that is used to describe or analyze other languages. A simple example would be the words *verb, adjective,* and *adverb.* They are all words that we use to describe other words. Hence, they are part of a grammatical metalanguage.

5. Lukken, "Semiotics and the Study of Liturgy," 110.

6. Lukken, "Semiotics and the Study of Liturgy," 110.

and the deep level. The levels progress from the most concrete to the most abstract, and each level comprises two components: the syntatic and the semantic.

The level of manifestation is the object encountered as a whole. The entire rite of Ministration at the Time of Death (colloquially known as *last rites*) for instance.

The discoursive level would examine things like the time, places, actors, and themes involved in the liturgy. In our example, this level might identify God, the priest, and the penitent as actors and perhaps themes like guilt and forgiveness.

The surface level examines the more elementary narrative structures that "are the basic relationships and transformations of relations which underlie the more elaborate figures and themes (and their organization) at the discoursive level."[7] The surface level might, for example, explore the words and gestures used in the rite and find semiotic implications therein regarding the concept of transformation and how it plays out in the liturgy.

The deep level deals "with the question of what the final elementary structure governing the signification of a particular discourse might be."[8] This final structure is often stated as two things in opposition with each other and visually depicted via a diagram called a semiotic square. When this analysis was conducted by Lukken on the general confession within the Roman Catholic Holy Eucharist liturgy, the final structure was stated relationally as "/self-oriented/ vs. /goal-oriented/."[9]

Strengths and Weaknesses

Virtually any approach to a subject is going to have strengths and weaknesses. The application of Greimassian semiotics to liturgical study is no exception. Lukken has identified at least three strengths (my terminology) of this approach.

One, this approach offers "a differentiated and new view of various liturgical questions and problems."[10] This makes sense as this was a new endeavor: a semiotic metalanguage had never been applied to liturgy before. That new connections and modes of thinking would be uncovered is natural.

7. Lukken and Searle, *Semiotics and Church Architecture*, 119.

8. Lukken and Searle, *Semiotics and Church Architecture*, 54.

9. Lukken et al., *Per Visibilia Ad Invisibilia*, 358.

10. Lukken, "Semiotics and the Study of Liturgy," 112.

Two, this approach allows for examining what the liturgical discourse itself has to say, rather than what others say about it. With this method, "only the arguments which emanate from the object are of importance. . . . The object itself tells us what it has to say."[11] This prevents presupposition and allows new meanings to come through.

Three, this approach allows for the unlocking of non-verbal as well as verbal sources. Until semiotics came to be applied to liturgy, it could be said "that as a rule liturgical sources [were] analyzed by methods adopted from literary studies."[12] This semiotic approach makes the liturgy more accessible and leads to a more integral theology of the liturgy.

I do not dispute these strengths, per se. I would, however, add a few related weaknesses that I perceive in this approach.

One, this approach is difficult and complex to undertake. Lukken has put it this way, "semiotics is a very difficult matter. It takes a great deal of energy and time to get used to the semiotic set of devices."[13] More than once, Lukken has said that this approach to liturgical semiotics progresses "gropingly."[14] There is a steep learning curve to apprehending and applying the Greimassian metalanguage. This acts as a barrier to its use, particularly by people who are not professionally trained semioticians. Noted semiotician Umberto Eco dismissed it as "an all-too-rigorous narratological grammar."[15]

Two, this approach does not recognize the uniqueness of liturgy as a subject. What is being suggested in applying the Greimassian metalanguage to liturgical study is not any different than what would be suggested in applying it to an operatic performance or a hiring interview. The metalanguage is laudable in its ability to handle non-verbal objects, but it does not account for the presence and activity of the Holy Spirit in the liturgical event.

Lukken appears ready to move in that direction in saying that the liturgical "sources themselves are the primary witnesses of the manner in which Christians come into contact with the ultimate Christian reality."[16] He never, however, appears to move closer to that ultimate Christian reality in his endeavor. He certainly does not consider that ultimate reality to be a partner in the meaning-making process that is undertaken.

11. Lukken, "Semiotics and the Study of Liturgy," 113.

12. Lukken, "Semiotics and the Study of Liturgy," 114.

13. Lukken et al., *Per Visibilia Ad Invisibilia*, 300.

14. Lukken, "Semiotics and the Study of Liturgy," 111; Lukken et al., *Per Visibilia Ad Invisibilia*, 336.

15. Eco, "Semiotics and the Philosophy of Language," 2.

16. Lukken, "Semiotics and the Study of Liturgy," 113.

Semiotician and philosopher Robert Corrington has commented on the uniqueness of religious objects as a subject of semiotic study. According to Corrington, "The problem with any semiotic framework which exists without recognizing the unique features of the religious referent is that it also has a truncated sense of worldhood."[17] One of the things that makes the application of semiotics to liturgy unique is that "these religious signs share more directly in the power of that in which they participate. Religious ritual is an intensification, via repetition and invocation, of the power native to religious signs."[18] There is a unique power at play in liturgy, and our semiotics must take that into account, or even invite it to be a dance partner in the meaning-making process.

Third, there is a lack of attention to humanness in the Greimassian approach. Lukken himself has commented on this: "In the structural approach, the own dynamics and sensuality of human expressions remained out of sight. In all meaning design there are expressions that emanate from the human being as incarnated and sensory subject."[19] An approach to liturgical semiotics that is more artistic than scientific lends itself more easily to taking the humanness of the actors into account.

PASTORAL LITURGICAL STUDIES AND MARK SEARLE

From a look at Greimassian semiotics we turn to the work of Mark Searle (1941–92), who served in multiple capacities at Notre Dame over the course of his career. Our pivot to Searle is natural because he took a sabbatical during the 1988 academic year to study with SEMANET and Gerard Lukken. Searle and Lukken wrote a book together, *Liturgia Condenda 1: Semiotics and Church Architecture*, which was published the year after Searle's death from cancer.

Before Searle turned his attention to the application of semiotics to liturgy, he pioneered what he termed *pastoral liturgical studies*. It was Searle's belief that liturgical studies needed to include the scholarly findings of other fields within the human sciences. This was born out of a growing tension arising from the post-Vatican II liturgical reforms. As Searle put it, "In short, historical awareness and theological depth were enough to persuade church authorities to reform the liturgy, but they were insufficient to ensure any controlled connection between the reform of the liturgical books

17. Corrington, "Regnant Signs," 22.
18. Corrington, "Regnant Signs," 24.
19. Lukken, "Betekenislagen," 118, translation mine.

and the renewal of Christian life."[20] Input from other fields of study could address that.

Pastoral liturgical studies "examines the way in which liturgical celebration relies upon language, symbol, gesture, and human interaction in order to experience God's actual presence, and at the same time, it critiques the way in which the elements of liturgical celebration serve to cloud, or mask, the realization of God's grace."[21] Searle saw this as a third branch of scholarly research into the field of liturgical study, to be held alongside liturgical history and liturgical theology.

This approach to liturgical studies performs three tasks in order to answer three questions: the empirical task seeks to answer "what is going on?"; the hermeneutical task addresses the question "what does it all mean?"; and the critical task considers "who is doing what to whom and how?"

The empirical task is the documentation of what goes on in worship. Not just the words spoken, but all of what occurs. The tools of the social sciences (i.e., field work, surveys, participant observation, and interviews) can be helpful in that task. This documentation of the liturgical event should attend to the surface form (what is actually done) rather than attempting to find meaning in the event. Additionally, the empirical task must include how the entire assembly, not just the focal participants, experience the liturgical event. This means that "people's attitudes, outlooks, lifestyles, and behavior are all open to investigation, as are also their understanding of what liturgy is for, the motives with which they participate, and the account they give of the place it has in their lives."[22] The tools of the social sciences help to examine these elements.

The hermeneutical task is concerned with how the symbolic words and gestures of the liturgy operate when they engage the believing community. This task seeks not to uncover what the liturgy means, but rather how it means. How do worshipers find meaning in engaging symbol and symbolic language? The task examines "(a) the effectiveness of the contemporary presentation of liturgical symbols in communicating the mystery of grace and (b) the capacity of modern people for receiving such communication."[23]

The critical task takes the findings of the first two tasks and compares them with the historical tradition and the theological claims made for the liturgy. In doing so it must pay attention to four areas. One, it must be "attentive to the ways that models drawn from other disciplines are used and

---

20. Mark Searle, "New Tasks, New Methods," in Koester and Seale, *Vision*, 106.

21. Wilbricht, "Mark Searle's Vision," 148.

22. Searle et al., "New Tasks, New Methods," 112.

23. Searle et al., "New Tasks, New Methods," 113.

to the kind of conclusions that might be drawn."[24] Two, it must undertake a critical evaluation of contemporary culture, identifying the dominant features and reflecting on them theologically. Three, the various forms of religious imagination active in the culture must be evaluated, because "it is through the imagination rather than through professed beliefs and conscious attitudes that religious understanding and behavior are filtered."[25] Four, the various ways that the liturgy is alienating must be identified. There is alienation in the liturgy when "the experience and capacities of the many are excluded in favor of the authority of the few."[26] This implies a critical evaluation of official liturgical reforms and their mode of implementation.

Ruminations on Pastoral Liturgical Studies

Searle's life and work were cut regretfully short. Had cancer not ended his life prematurely, I wonder what the trajectory of his work would have been and what its final form might have looked like. While we can never truly know, the possibilities are intriguing.

On the one hand, the amenability of pastoral liturgical studies to input from other disciplines leaves a provocative path open. Searle proposed that the tools of the human sciences be brought to bear in studying liturgy and was interested in how the assembly could be receptive to the communications going on in the liturgy. I wonder what Searle's response would have been to input from neuroscience that metaphor, narrative, and image are more central to humanity's thinking than words are. Would this have led to an openness on his part to narraphor and its role in the liturgy? Were he alive today, would we have found common ground?

On the other hand, Searle's last scholarly turn was toward Greimassian semiotics. He also was primarily interested in the social sciences for their research instruments. He saw pastoral liturgical studies as something to fit alongside and augment the existing structure of liturgical study. Taken together, these points suggest that perhaps he would be less open to the artistic side of liturgical study than I am. Perchance, while we would agree on some points, we might fail to find common ground on others.

---

24. Searle et al., "New Tasks, New Methods," 115.
25. Searle et al., "New Tasks, New Methods," 115.
26. Searle et al., "New Tasks, New Methods," 116.

BRINGING PEIRCE TO THE PARTY

Having explored the application of Greimassian (and hence Saussurean) semiotics to liturgical study, an example of the application of Peircean semiotics is called for. Graham Hughes (1937–2015), in his work *Worship as Meaning: A Liturgical Theology for Late Modernity*, constructs such an application.

What must first be noted is that Hughes refers to his work as liturgical theology rather than liturgical semiotics. As Hughes phrases it, "The only thing on which I would wish to insist in all this is that the entire project of making sense of the signs of worship is to be called liturgical theology."[27] I would argue that the entire project of making sense of signs, regardless of the field of application, is properly referred to as semiotics.

For Hughes, meaning in worship is "'fastened together' in a collaborative work between those who propose meanings and those who appropriate them and . . . bring them to completion."[28] This meaning is transacted in Peirce's three orders of signs: iconic, indexical, and symbolic. Hughes's use of Peirce's icon, index, symbol triad, while not in contravention of how I have described them previously, does bear some explanation with regards to how they each produce liturgical meaning.

Hughes sees the iconicity of worship as having to do with the liturgical event taking place on the frontier of what human beings can fathom as comprehensible. The iconicity, then, "has to do with the degree that we can manage to generate a likeness or similarity between what we do on the known side of this frontier and how we imagine things might be on its far side."[29]

The indexicality of worship has to do with its authenticity with regards to words and actions. Recall that indexes point back to that which they refer to. Because of this, they necessarily participate in, and have a relationship with, the thing they refer to. This is expressed in Hughes's indexicality of worship by the "integrity between 'form' and 'performance.'"[30] It is the internal disposition of the worshiper matching their outward actions. It is to be truly present when one is present. It is to be truly worshiping when one worships.

The symbolic dimension of worship is rooted in the fact that the liturgy draws on a particular depth of tradition in its construction of meaning. It is this tradition that provides the range of meaning inherent in the sign.

---

27. Hughes, *Worship as Meaning*, 254.
28. Hughes, *Worship as Meaning*, 300.
29. Hughes, *Worship as Meaning*, 148.
30. Hughes, *Worship as Meaning*, 148.

One could say that "the meanings of worship . . . are both funded from tradition and are accountable before the tradition."[31]

For Hughes, all of these orders of sign are operative at all times in the liturgy. Rather than the signs acting discretely, "Each of the actions, utterances, artifacts and spatial arrangements carries or combines within it all of these semiotic dimensions."[32]

If meaning is to be successfully transmitted to the assembly, there is work to be done by both focal participants and the gathered worshiping body. Focal participants must be mindful of how all three orders of signs are enacted: it must be clearly signaled that the liturgical event is operating on the boundary of human limit, that there is authenticity in the enactment, and that "here is something . . . forged from millenia-deep sources of wisdom and knowledge."[33]

The work for the members of the assembly is cognitive and grounded in faith. They "have to reach for the meanings being suggested to see where, how, or perhaps whether, these can 'make sense' in terms of a recognizable world."[34] That work is done in faith that there is, in fact, meaning in the signs they are encountering, and that the meaning is something that is worth apprehending.

Lastly, it must be noted that some intended meanings will be unavailable to the worshiper. As Hughes notes, "Human beings construct their meanings (a meaningful world) from the meanings culturally available to them."[35] If the intended meaning of a sign is something that is not within the worshiper's cultural comprehension, then the intended meaning of the sign will not be successfully transmitted.

LITURGICAL SEMIOTICS FROM BELOW: MOVIN' ON UP

Various aspects of the Christian endeavor can be described as being approached from above or from below. By considering an illustrative example of this, Christology, the foundation will be laid for describing how this dynamic plays out in the field of liturgical semiotics.

A powerful expression of Christology from below was developed by the theologian Wolfhart Pannenberg. Pannenberg began his Christological

31. Hughes, *Worship as Meaning*, 176.

32. Hughes, *Worship as Meaning*, 182.

33. Hughes, *Worship as Meaning*, 302.

34. Hughes, *Worship as Meaning*, 302.

35. Hughes, *Worship as Meaning*, 219.

exploration with the resurrection and earthly life of Jesus Christ. From this he then developed dogmatic claims about the divinity of Christ. He started with the practical and moved to the conceptual.

A prime example of Christology from above was championed by Pannenberg's theological sparring partner, Karl Barth. To do Christology from above is to begin with the dogmatic claims about the divinity of Christ and then to work out what it meant that, as John's Gospel puts it, "the Word became flesh and dwelt among us" (1:14). It could be said that Christology from above begins with the conceptual and moves to the practical.

These categories of *from above* and *from below* can be applied to liturgical semiotics as well. The construction of sign systems, which are then applied to liturgy, is to do liturgical semiotics from above. It is to design the conceptual, and then apply it to the practical. Lukken's work with Greimassan semiotics is an example of liturgical semiotics from above. The conceptual, an elaborate metalanguage, is applied to an instantiation of a liturgical event.

The case is similar for the liturgical "theology" developed by Hughes, based on Peirce's work. Hughes takes Peirce's triad of sign orders and casts their definitions in a worship-minded way. This framework could then be applied to specific liturgical events.

In contrast to these, I advocate for a liturgical semiotics from below. As Christians, we may not be of the world but we are certainly in the world. We are mortal creatures who spend our time interacting with the rest of the creation and striving to find meaning in it. We live below, and aspire to "move on up" above our creaturely cares to new life. It seems natural, and makes eminent sense, to start from where we find ourselves and then try to chart a path to where we hope to be. It makes sense to begin with what we know, our lived experience, and ruminate our way to broader insights.

In identifying a starting place for a liturgical semiotics from below, we look, ironically, at Lukken's statement that "the search for signification is most fruitful when it is done in a group. What one person does not see, the other will notice."[36] This notion that semiotics is best done in groups gives us a glimpse of a powerful truth: semiotics is a subjective activity, not an objective one. To create a large sign system or metalanguage is to try and objectivize something that resists such commodification.

I would submit that two semioticians can start with the same set of tools and the same object of study, and arrive at two different results in conducting their semiosis. Think of it this way, if you give two artists the same set of paints and tell them to paint the same bowl of fruit, you are going to

---

36. Lukken, "Semiotics and the Study of Liturgy," 111.

get two quite distinct paintings. Each one will be an expression of the artist's unique identity.

All of these approaches do not pay enough attention to the semiotician themselves, the one actually doing the semiotics. One must be aware of themselves when doing semiotics. What are you bringing to the task (for good or ill)?

Rather than ignoring the self, a liturgical semiotics from below begins with the self. What kind of Christian are you? From whence did you come as a follower of Jesus, and what traditions fed into that?

As part and parcel of this notion, liturgical semiotics from below looks like beginning with the liturgy itself. This book, for example, has been focusing on the Rite II Holy Eucharist as found in the Episcopal Church's 1979 Book of Common Prayer. That is because I, the author, am a follower of Christ in the Anglican tradition. It informs my choices on what liturgy means, and on what kinds or elements of liturgy are more important or less important.

It is through the study of a specific liturgy that more broad principles or concepts can be drawn. This is what the last part of the book gets into. Start with the concrete, the specific. Start with the semiotician. Let that drive the semiosis, and then move on up to broader insights.

NOT SCIENCE VS. ART; SCIENCE AND ART

As human beings we love to codify and compartmentalize. We dissect and categorize whatever we hold in our analytical gaze into smaller and smaller subsets until all the energy and life in the thing is stripped away. It is A but NOT B. It is fruit but NOT vegetable. It is plant but NOT animal. One is a Red Sox fan OR a Yankees fan . . . but not BOTH! There is science, and quite distinctly, there is art!

There is room in liturgical semiotics for it to be pursued as both a science and an art. The entire field of modern semiotic study is quite youthful compared to most disciplines. As such, there is no unified approach that has aligned and regimented its application. In the great battle of how to do semiotics "the right way," there has been no victor. In considering the semiotics of liturgy, the words of Thomas-Andreas Põder regarding semiotics of religion ring true, that it "is very much alive, although there are many blind spots, or even whole fields of blindness, depending on our disciplinary and linguistic backgrounds."[37]

---

37. Boom and Thomas-Andreas, *Sign, Method, and the Sacred*, 9.

Work in the field of liturgical study that has had the word *semiotics* attached to it has trended toward the scientific side. The creation of meta-languages. The application of instruments from other sciences. Even when not employing the word *semiotics*, such as with Hughes, the use of semiotic conceptual constructions has appeared more scientific than artistic.

Yet what we do in the worship of God is not scientific. Searle himself once wrote that "worship is, above all, an act of the imagination."[38] As such, if worship is likened to any human endeavor, it is art rather than science.

To become too focused on liturgical semiotics as science is akin to overbreathing. It is to take something that is useful, but forcing it to over-function to the detriment of the task. Allowing for artistry in liturgical semiotics is to allow for a balance to the breathing.

Worship is filled with story (and metaphor). There is the story of the arc of tradition. There is the Biblical story.[39] Furthermore, we as semioticians, and as worshipers, walk in with our stories unfolding. Worship is an intersection of all of our stories, twisted and woven into a tapestry of meaning for the time that we are together.

My approach takes this tapestry into account. It honors the individuality and context of the semiotician, the worshiper, and the focal participant. Like the artist who partners with the creative muse to produce art, my approach acknowledges the partnership of the semiotician and the Holy Spirit to receive and offer meaning in liturgy.

The field of liturgical semiotics is an extant one. From where I stand, I can see the work of those who have come before me. I am standing, however, in a very sparsely populated part of the field.

38. Mark Searle, "Images and Worship," in Koester and Seale, *Vision*, 126.

39. The importance of story to Christianity is captured in a wing of theology called narrative theology. Traditional theological approaches put doctrinal statements as primary and stories as secondary. Narrative theology, however, puts "stories as conceptually and practically prior to doctrinal formulations or theological systematization, for these could not make sense without a narrative context" (Komonchak et al., *New Dictionary of Theology*, 702).

PART THREE

"Breathe in through the nose, and out through the mouth"

THE WHAT

The epigraph for this part of the book is common cultural advice when it comes to breathing. It even found its way into the 1984 movie *The Karate Kid*. In the movie, an older Japanese man, Mr. Myagi, is training the protagonist of the movie (Daniel) in the ways of karate. The training often takes the form of repetitive menial tasks. Mr. Myagi gives Daniel this common advice about breathing when he is having Daniel wax his car using very specific hand motions. He also notes the importance of breathing to his young ward.

THE WHY

The tasks that Daniel carries out for Mr. Myagi are not only menial jobs, but also careful karate instructions. They are the deliberate application of a particular self-defense philosophy. They are the physical incarnation of karate concepts. And, if you watch to the end of the movie, learning these actions pays big dividends for our protagonist.

This part of the book is doing something similar. In chapter 4, a particular approach to liturgical semiotics was laid out using the acronyms BREATHE and GASP/RASP. The next three chapters turn those concepts into deliberate application.

Chapter 6 is a practical application of the BREATHE approach. The action taken with the bread during the Rite II Holy Eucharist from the Episcopal Book of Common Prayer is focused on. Following the BREATHE process leads to a connection between how the bread and wine are acted upon and the local church's engagement with the wider community.

Chapter 7 is a practical application of the GASP acronym. The tools contained therein are applied to the breaking of the bread from the same service noted above. Semiotic adjustments are made to that action dependent upon the occasion the service is observing (i.e., seven major feast days, a wedding, and a funeral), in an attempt to make the action more evocative of the service's particular emphasis.

Chapter 8 is a practical application of the RASP acronym. Crystal Downing's function of (re)signing is applied to the use of the bread and wine from the same service under consideration. The cultural meaning of bread and wine at the dawn of Christianity is examined. Then how bread and wine are culturally understood today in twenty-first-century America is explored. Then the use of the bread and wine in a way more resonant with the current cultural understanding is imagined.

6

A BREATHE Practicum

"Excellent introduction that is catchy while still mystifying."[1]

THIS CHAPTER IS A practicum. Equipped with a conceptual understanding of liturgical semiotics as an artistic endeavor, we now embark upon the work of semioticians. As semioticians we "analyze how signs make meaning and what gives them value."[2] In an artistic approach to liturgical semiotics, we partner with the Holy Spirit to read those signs of the liturgy, make connections, and follow those connections wherever they may lead. Liturgical semiotics is a place where the mundane and the divine intersect to create art and reveal meaning.

Our practicum will employ the acronym arrived at in chapter 4:

Be aware of the context.
Resolve upon a narraphor.
Engage the metaphor.
Apply Peircean triads.
Trust the story.
Harmonize the results.
Explore what comes next (if anything).

---

1. Freakstyle571, Review of Switchfoot's song, "Learning to Breathe," para. 4.
2. Downing, *Changing Signs of Truth*, 91.

BE AWARE OF THE CONTEXT

Every practical application is operative within a context. The context of this chapter begins with my context. I am Episcopal. Thus, my understanding of liturgy is informed by, and finds expression through, the Book of Common Prayer. Furthermore, as was explored in chapter 3, this means that for me the fullest expression of the liturgy is found in the Holy Eucharist. Within the service of Holy Eucharist, there is a flow. The structure of the liturgy builds toward the actions at the altar.

Even taking the Holy Eucharist as the normative expression of Episcopal worship, there is a choice to make. The BCP offers two rites for the service, "one in traditional language (Rite One) and one in contemporary idiom (Rite Two)."[3] On balance, the Rite Two service of Holy Eucharist is the more celebrated of the two. This, therefore, will be the subject of our semiotic endeavors.

RESOLVE UPON A NARRAPHOR

This particular context has implications for the choice of narraphor as we engage the liturgy. Since the liturgy reaches its crescendo at the altar, it is apt to choose a narraphor from that section of the liturgy. For the purposes of our practicum, we will choose the narraphor of the actions taken with the bread at the altar.

So what happens with the bread during the service of Holy Eucharist? Engaging the bread during the Eucharist involves what is known as the fourfold action. That action was most beautifully described by Dom Gregory Dix, one of the liturgical giants of the twentieth century:

> At the heart of it all is the eucharistic action, a thing of an absolute simplicity—the taking, blessing, breaking and giving of bread and the taking, blessing, and giving of a cup of wine, as these were first done with their new meaning by a young Jew before and after supper with His friends on the night before He died. . . . He had told His friends do to this henceforward with the new meaning 'for the anamnesis' of Him, and they have done it always since.[4]

---

3. Hefling and Shattuck, *Oxford Guide to the Book of Common Prayer*, 362.
4. Dix, *Shape of the Liturgy*, 743.

ENGAGE THE METAPHOR

When considering the narraphor of the fourfold action taken with the bread in the Holy Eucharist, the metaphor that is operative is that the bread is the body of Christ. This is sourced in Jesus' words to the disciples at the Last Supper that "this is my body,"[5] where the *this* was bread. While the church has argued long and hard over the exact way that the bread is Christ's body, our concern at present is simply to accept the metaphor as Jesus' gave it.

There is an additional metaphor that attracts the semiotician's eye, however. The church is also the body of Christ. This is spoken of in several of Paul's letters, including Romans, 1 Corinthians, Ephesians, and Colossians.[6]

That the body of Christ has two metaphors associated with it invites us to apply some mathematical logic.[7] If the bread is the body of Christ, and the church is the body of Christ, then the bread is the church.

On one level, this may sound silly and reductionist. It also, however, opens up an interesting path of inquiry. If we follow this path to its conclusion, then we can find out if that path is straight and narrow—or primrose.

This is an example of an artistic semiotic rather than a scientific one. A scientific approach would trend toward the harsh equating of the bread with the church. The rigidity of this approach does not take us very far or hold up that well to interrogation. The bread of Holy Eucharist is not the church. It would make no sense theologically, sacramentally, or ecclesiologically. Christians would in effect become the cannibals in worship that they were accused of being in the second century CE.[8]

To consider semiotics as art allows us some room to breathe. We can play with these metaphors, trusting that there could be something important in the offing if we take a few more steps forward. Engaging the semiotic imagination, we consider what it might look like for the bread to be the church. Then actions associated with the bread might have something to say about actions associated with the church.

By studying how we engage the body of Christ (the bread) in the liturgy, we might better understand something about the body of Christ (the

5. Mark 14:22 to choose one reference.

6. Colossians 1:18 for example.

7. Depending on how you prefer your math, you could call this the Transitive Property or the Law of Syllogism.

8. The apologist Athenagoras addresses this accusation in a letter to Emperor Marcus Aurelius Antoninus. He says in part, "For we cannot eat human flesh till we have killed some one. . . . But we, deeming that to see a man put to death is much the same as killing him, have abjured such spectacles. How, then, when we do not even look on, lest we should contract guilt and pollution, can we put people to death?" (Athenagoras, "Plea for the Christians," 147).

local church⁹). This comparison of the body of Christ (the bread) to the body of Christ (the local church) is apt for three reasons:

First, they are both the body of Christ. It is reasonable to suggest that one manifestation of Christ's body can teach us something about another manifestation of his body.

Second, the body of Christ (the bread) connects itself to the body of Christ (the local church) through the liturgy itself. As theologian Hans Ur von Balthasar puts it, "Christ's kenotic condition—as bread to be 'eaten' and wine poured out—appears to confer on the table-guests an active and absorbing role. . . . There Christ actively incorporates the participants into his mystical body."[10] Christ's personal gift of himself in the eucharistic liturgy is the "essential bond between the real presence of Christ in the Eucharist and his real presence as Lord living in the Church."[11]

Third, it is rational and stands in good stead to look to a microcosm to learn about a macrocosm. Drawing such an analogy has been a tactic used for millennia. For example, "Various Greek thinkers, perhaps beginning with Anaximenes of Miletus (sixth century B.C.), drew an analogy between man as the microcosm and the universe as the macrocosm."[12] In our present effort, the body of Christ (the bread) will be the microcosm and the body of Christ (the local church) will be the macrocosm.

APPLYING PEIRCEAN TRIADS

Having established Dix's fourfold action of the bread as a base, and engaged the metaphors surrounding them, that fourfold action will be framed using both of the Peircean triads previously described.

First the object-representamen-interpretant triad. The taking, blessing, breaking, and sharing of the bread is the object. In as much as an action can be considered an object, we are doing so. The representamen(sign) is that this action is occurring within the context of the liturgy. We are not acting upon this bread on a street corner, or in a deli, or in your dining room. We are acting upon it in a church, with prayers, and singing, and vestments, and

9. A brief word about scope. The bread is acted upon in a particular setting: the local setting. Whether a tiny country parish or a mighty cathedral, each service of Holy Eucharist is celebrated locally rather than globally. Similarly, it is the local parish that is gathered for each service of Holy Eucharist. Each local church is an instantiation of the universal body of Christ the church. Thus, in our work here we are thinking about both the bread and church in a local context.

10. Balthasar, *Mysterium Paschale*, 99–100.

11. Schillebeeckx, *Eucharist*, 137.

12. Gregory of Nyssa, *On the Soul and the Resurrection*, 34.

all the other jots and tittles that construe worship. The interpretant (how the sign makes sense in one's mind) may be that the body and blood of Christ is being confected and partaken of by the gathered faithful.

Turning our attention to Peirce's index-icon-symbol triad brings up a question: what kind of sign is the fourfold action in the liturgy? It turns out that the action is all three.

The action is an icon. Icons offer a likeness that visualizes what they refer to. The action is in the likeness of the Last Supper, and refers to Jesus' institution of the sacrament. The action is perhaps an even stronger icon of the post-resurrection encounter commonly called the Walk to Emmaus (Luke 24:13–35). This is so because the biblical witness provides an even greater emphasis on the fourfold action in this story than it does in the institution narratives.

The action is an index. An index is a sign that points to what caused it. The action indexes Jesus' command to "do this in remembrance of me." It was his command to his disciples, and hence to us, that caused (and continues to cause) this action to take place.

The action is a symbol. Symbols are not in the likeness of what they refer to. The action is a symbol in that it manifests the thesis of this work. The fourfold action taken with the bread (the body of Christ) is a symbol of (i.e., a sign that refers to) the action that we (the body of Christ) take to participate in God's mission.

Breaking Open the Symbol

As has been said, there is a fourfold action with the bread in the eucharistic liturgy. The bread is taken, blessed, broken, and shared. Let us examine each step involving the bread along with its corresponding step involving the local church.

First, the bread is taken. It is taken as a unitive whole.[13] So too are the people gathered together as one for worship. We are taken and gathered in the hands of the God who loves us.

Second, the bread is blessed. The actions of the gathered community, under the auspices of a God who is faithful to his promises, blesses the bread. In a similar way, the body gathered for worship is blessed by that worship. The "Hebrew word translated 'to bless' means 'to bring a gift to another

---

13. Optically, this may not appear to be the case in churches that do not use a single loaf of bread. Yet liturgically, the gathered wafers are understood to be one loaf just as the gathered people are understood to be one body.

while kneeling in respect."[14] This definition is well-suited to what we find in worship. For example, the people are blessed at the epiclesis, in which the Holy Spirit is called upon to descend and sanctify those gathered.[15] Those gathered are also blessed in their reception of the sacrament, which forgives sins, strengthens their union with Christ and one another, and foretastes the heavenly banquet.[16] Additionally, at the conclusion of the Eucharist, "the Bishop when present, or the Priest, may bless the people."[17]

Third, the bread is broken. The unitive whole is split into several pieces. So too, at the end of our worship, is the gathered body broken by the dismissal. What was a faith community constituted for worship is split into several individuals.

Fourth, the bread is shared. It is distributed to those gathered. It nourishes those who receive it. In a similar way, the individuals of the local church are shared with the wider community. We, after being taken together, blessed, and broken into our individual and family units, are shared with the wider community.

This is the critical point to consider. In the same way that the blessed bread nourishes us as individuals, we as individuals nourish the wider community. Just as the bread is taken, blessed, broken, and shared to feed us, we as the local church are taken, blessed, broken, and shared with the community.

Through a lens of Peircean semiotics, to participate in God's mission takes us out of the church building and into the wider community. We participate in God's mission, not by "initiating something for God but by becoming part of God's initiatives in the world."[18]

TRUST THE STORY

In turning to the narrative part of our narraphor, one might see a problem: the fourfold action taken with the bread does not immediately present itself as a story. Any action, in and of itself, is not a story.

Consider the action of coughing. By itself, coughing is not a story. But as soon as you look at the context of the action, the representamen you

14. Sweet, *Well-Played Life*, 11.

15. This is explicitly stated in Eucharist prayers A (BCP, 363) and B (BCP, 369). It can be inferred in how prayers C (BCP, 371), D (BCP, 375), Form 1 (BCP, 403), and Form 2 (BCP, 405) are enacted.

16. Episcopal Church, *Book of Common Prayer*, 859–60.

17. Episcopal Church, *Book of Common Prayer*, 366.

18. Sweet and Viola, *Jesus*, 275.

could say, then a story presents itself. If I am coughing by myself in my office on an idle Tuesday, that is one story. If I am coughing in a crowded supermarket in the middle of a pandemic, that is a very different story. Context is king. Or, if you prefer, representamen reigns.

To get at the story of the fourfold action, we will interrogate three different representamen: a Biblical representamen, an historical representamen, and our current liturgical representamen. Each one is a story in itself, a narrative. Once examined, the metanarrative will be considered.

The Walk to Emmaus

The story of the Walk to Emmaus is well-known and time-tested. On Easter day two disciples are forlornly leaving Jerusalem. Jesus appears and walks with them, although unrecognized. The fourfold action takes place once the disciples invite their anonymous traveling companion to stay with them that night. Then we read: "When he was at the table with them, he took bread, blessed and broke it, and gave it to them. Then their eyes were opened, and they recognized him; and he vanished from their sight" (Luke 24:30–31).

What are we to make of this representamen? Leonard Sweet suggests the following:

> It's time to use our imaginations. Picture it in your mind: Jesus assumes the role of host. He takes the bread in His hands, gives the blessing, and breaks the bread. At the moment when He reaches out His hands to pass them the bread, and they reach out to take it, they see . . . what? His wounds. Because His hands and wrists were exposed. Then they recognize Him.[19]

We see that in this story, the presence of Jesus is recognized in the fourfold action by his wounds. His hands and wrists are exposed by the action of breaking and sharing the bread, and his presence is perceived. His wounds index his sacrifice upon the cross in the minds of the two disciples, and his identity becomes apparent.

Gatherings of the Primitive Church

Once we pass out of the biblical narrative and into early church history, our representamen changes. The rhizomatic growth of the early church is difficult to track, given the dearth of extant writings concerning it. So too with its customs and practices with regards to the fourfold action.

19. Sweet and Viola, *Jesus Speaks*, 19.

Despite these challenges, it does seem clear that the community came together on Sundays for an evening meal which served a range of purposes.[20] It fed physically in that it was an actual meal. It fed emotionally in that it was a time of fellowship. It also came to feed spiritually in that those gathered actually came to perceive the presence of Jesus among them. At this point, however, the "questions, later so vigorously disputed, of how Christ or his body and the elements of bread and wine are related, are not yet brought up."[21] What is certain is that the satiating of hunger was joined in some way with the celebration of the sacrament.[22]

This story situates the fourfold action within the context of a small group's shared meal. Jesus had commanded them to "do this" in remembrance of him, and so they did. Jesus "had died, but his followers had the visible experience of his continued life and active presence among them, because they, the believers, formed one community by virtue of his death 'for our sins' and his resurrection."[23] Here, the presence of Jesus was recognized in the midst of the gathered community's event. The fourfold action took place as one of several actions executed during the gathering, evidently without being the sole focus.

The Present Liturgical Context

The story of the present liturgy is that the faithful gather for worship. It is not an actual meal. It is not, in a casual sense, fellowship. Rather, the purpose of the gathering is to worship God, and in so doing, make Eucharist.

The flow of the liturgy prepares the worshiper to receive the body and blood of Jesus in the form of the bread and the wine. Jesus is not understood as solely present in the eucharistic elements. Instead, Jesus is present in at least two ways in addition to the elements: in the gathered community, and in the Scriptures. Yet, the primary focus of the liturgical event, the crescendo of its story, is Jesus present in the eucharistic elements.

The Metanarrative

We have looked at three different stories of the fourfold action. Each one has provided a different emphasis with regards to Jesus' perceived presence.

20. Dobschütz, *Christian Life in the Primitive Church*, 60–61.
21. Conzelmann, *History of Primitive Christianity*, 52.
22. Conzelmann, *History of Primitive Christianity*, 52.
23. Schillebeeckx, *Eucharist*, 123.

These emphases coincide with the three different elucidations of Christ's presence in the liturgy: in the elements, in the gathered community, and in Holy Writ.

In the Emmaus narrative, Jesus was recognized by his wounds as he enacted the fourfold action. These wounds indexed his sacrifice upon the cross, and revealed his identity to the two disciples. They recognized Jesus because they recognized his story. In that the Emmaus narrative is part of the Gospels, and the Gospels are the story of Jesus, this is a recursive example of Jesus being present in the Scriptures.

In the primitive church, the early believers gathered for a multivalent meal. The fourfold action was one of several that occurred. The "sharing of the Eucharist after the Ascension became the occasion for recognizing, once again, his continued presence among them."[24] In the midst of the gathered community, Jesus was recognized as present.

In the liturgy as presently enacted, the faithful gather to worship God and, in so doing, make Eucharist. While Jesus is understood to be present in worship in multiple ways, the service builds towards his presence in the bread and wine. The culmination of the work of the people make it so.

The metanarrative of the fourfold action reveals an evolution in the perceived emphases of Jesus' presence over time. There is another evolution to consider, however, as revealed through the metanarrative. That is an evolution surrounding the intention of the event and expectation regarding the presence of Jesus.

The Emmaus story was both unintentional and unexpected. The meeting between Jesus and the two disciples, their journey together, and their shared meal were all unintentional. The two disciples, when their journey began, never intended for any of this to happen.

It was also unexpected regarding a perception of Jesus' presence. The two disciples, neither by inviting the stranger to join them, nor by allowing him to preside at the table, expected to recognize Jesus in the fourfold action.

In contrast, the gathering of the primitive church was intentional and unexpected, at least to begin with. The earliest followers began gathering intentionally. It was not by accident. They did not, however, initially expect to perceive Jesus as present in their midst.

The current liturgical context is both intentional and expected. The faith community gathers on purpose to do many things very intentionally. Additionally, it has very specific expectations around the presence of Jesus.

---

24. Kubicki, "Recognizing the Presence of Christ," 825.

The metanarrative of the fourfold action reveals that what began as an unintended common event (a meal) with an unexpected recognition of Jesus' presence, has become a highly intended specialized event (a carefully choreographed worship service) with very specific expectations about Jesus' presence. This evolution from a casual dinner to a highly ritualized worship service should not be surprising. After all, "once you start looking, ritual is everywhere. Human beings are ritualized animals."[25] Furthermore, this evolution toward a liturgical focus makes sense because, "for the Christian imagination [liturgies] embody the ultimate point of everything, which is the worship of God."[26]

HARMONIZE THE RESULTS

We now reach the penultimate step in our liturgical semiotics practicum (or ultimate, depending on the outcome). It is now time to stand back and consider the finished product. What conclusions may be drawn? How might we harmonize our results?

In considering our context, the Rite Two Holy Eucharist service of the BCP was chosen as our subject liturgy. The fourfold action of the bread at the altar was the narraphor that was resolved upon. By engaging the metaphor, it was determined that the fourfold action of the body of Christ (the bread) might have implications for the actions of the body of Christ (the local church).

Those implication were explored using Peircean triads. Through a lens of Peircean semiotics, the fourfold action of the bread is a symbol of a fourfold action of the people. This leads to the local church being taken, blessed, broken and then shared outside the walls of the church. To this point in our analysis, the meaning gained is that we are called to engage the wider community outside the walls of the church.

This dovetails nicely with the notion that "to be 'blessed' by God means to be in a perpetual state both of joyful thankfulness for God's grace that meets us where we are, and of readiness to give of ourselves to others where they are, as we fall on our knees in humble and joyful service before the Lord."[27] This is a brilliant expression of the local church's experience of worshiping together and then moving out into the wider community to

---

25. Radcliffe, *Alive in God*, 330.

26. Radcliffe, *Alive in God*, 337.

27. Sweet, *Well-Played Life*, 11.

participate in God's mission. Indeed, it would seem that the "church is directed towards the world because God is directed towards the world."[28]

In trusting the story of the fourfold action in the liturgy, the metanarrative has evolved over time from being an unintentional common event with the unexpected recognition of Jesus' presence, to a very intentional specialized event with very specific expectations regarding Jesus' presence.

At this point in the process we pause to consider: are the results in harmony with each other? Do they cohere in some way, or at least co-exist? Or are they situated in opposition to one another?

If they are in opposition, then our semiotic task ends here, as a single BREATH. When one begins a semiotic endeavor, the final form of the art is unknown. Sometimes fresh insights are gained. Other times not. The latter is not a bad thing. Rather, it simply is where that particular artistic effort has ended.

If the results harmonize, however, then our noun (BREATH) becomes a verb (BREATHE). The initial foray of the semiotic process has brought forth artistic insight. Something new and interesting has been revealed, and there is more in the offing. The artistic effort continues.

For our purpose, the insights of the two parts harmonize. Our Peircean perspective concludes that the body of Christ (the local church) needs to move out into the wider community. It does not, however, suggest how to go about doing that.

Trusting the story reveals that the fourfold action in the liturgy has been evolving toward intentional structure and specific expectation. This suggests that the current story of the fourfold action may lend itself well to the creation of a methodology. This methodology may well be the answer to the question of how the local church should go about being shared with the wider community. That is the task we turn toward next.

EXPLORE WHAT COMES NEXT (IF ANYTHING)

The liturgical semiosis of fourfold action of the bread within the Holy Eucharist Rite Two service from the BCP has been fruitful thus far. One of the insights gained is that we are called to engage with the wider community outside the walls of the church.

The step now undertaken is to examine how that sharing happens. How is the local congregation called to engage with the wider community? An exploration of how the bread is distributed during Holy Communion will show us the way.

28. van Rheede van Oudtshoorn, "Symbolising Salvation," 4.

The BCP provides no firm guidance on how the distribution of the bread manifests. It is only mentioned in passing in the following rubric, "The ministers receive the Sacrament in both kinds, and then immediately deliver it to the people."[29] How that delivery happens is left up to the presider.

Liturgical ambiguity is a situation not uncommon to Anglicans. The BCP's terseness in certain aspects leaves presiders without clarity on how to incarnate certain actions. It is at this point that we look to tradition, among other things. How has this action been enfleshed by those who came before us?

Historically, three primary models for the distribution of the bread have presented themselves. Each model can be thought to imply a different way for the body of Christ (the congregation) to engage the wider community.

Model of Regency

I will call the first the model of regency. In this model, the communicants approach the presider. This has been the dominant form of distribution over the arc of church history, and continues to be so today. It can be found in Orthodox liturgies, the Tridentine mass, Luther's *Formula Missae* and *Deutsch Missae*, Calvin's *The Form of Church Prayers* (both Geneva and Strassburg), and early editions of the BCP.

To consider this model semiotically, we would see the wider community coming to the church, and submitting itself to the church's authority or worldview. This is indeed the way that Western civilization operated for hundreds of years. God was considered to be present and active in the world primarily through the rites and activities of the church.

This model might still flourish in a context where the morality and ethics of the church stand in direct opposition to those of the cultural context surrounding it. In a situation where the church truly finds itself "in a foreign land," so to speak, then this approach to missiology might well resonate.

Model of Approach

Next is the model of approach. In this model, the elements are taken to the people in their places. This was done in the early centuries and persisted

29. Episcopal Church, *Book of Common Prayer*, 365.

for a long period in some areas.[30] During the reformation era, this was seen primarily in Zwingli's Zurich liturgy, although the permissiveness of the rubrics in services like the *The Westminster Directory* and the Savoy liturgy would seem to allow it. This model continues to be used in many Protestant circles today.

Semiotically speaking, this model would see the church literally meeting the community where it is. God would be understood to be present and active outside the walls of the church and the congregation is seeking to not carry Christ into the community so much as reveal the Christ already operative within the community. This would find expression in the church joining into extant community activities and undertakings. It would look like the church adding its resources to an already existing task, plan, or action.

This model could succeed in a context where the church has essentially become invisible to the cultural context. In a situation where the church is not diametrically opposed to the wider community, but essentially ignored by it, this approach could bear fruit.

Model of Intentionality

Last is the model of intentionality. In this model, the presider and the communicants meet around the table. This was directed in John Knox's *The Forme of Prayers* and *The Middleburg Liturgy*, and it was permissible in *The Westminster Directory* and the Savoy liturgy. This model often included the people serving the elements to each other. This would have been the distribution model of the earliest Christian gatherings, when the Eucharist was still primarily a shared meal.

Semiotically, this model would see the church intentionally creating situations of engagement with the wider community. God is present and active in the planning and co-creation of the church and the community. The Holy Spirit is manifested in the shared ministry/work of the church and the wider community. This could find expression, for example, in the church arranging a meeting of community organizations to address some important issue arising out of the community's context (where the church also has a voice).

This model might thrive in a context where the morals and ethics of the church are in harmony with the cultural context. In a situation where the church and wider community agree on the need to address an issue, then this collaborative model could do well.

---

30. Hatchett, *Commentary on the American Prayer Book*, 384.

Regency Redux: Peering More Deeply

Often, the divine is in the details. If one peers more deeply into the Regency Model of distribution, the semiotic story changes. If you play the movie in your mind, then a metamorphosis of meaning takes place.

A movie needs a set. For our purposes, the set is a church where the altar is in the front of the worship space, and raised above floor level. There is also an altar rail separating the nave from the sanctuary. This is representative for what is typical in terms of parishioners coming forward to receive the bread.

As parishioners come forward, it is not simply that they walk forward and receive bread in their hands as music plays. Rather, as they come up, the priest comes down. While the music plays, the priest takes the paten and leaves the altar. The people do not receive Eucharist at the altar. They receive it at the altar rail.[31]

A careful observation reveals that not only does the parishioner move forward to receive the bread, but the bread also moves to meet the parishioner. The parishioner and the bread meet at the altar rail. There is movement from each side.

This casts the Regency Model in a new light. This is not about the community coming and submitting itself to the church. This is about there being a nexus point where the church and the wider community intersect. That place, in the liturgy, is the altar rail.

What then would be the altar rail where the church and the wider community connect? What is that nexus point?

Whatever the actual manifestation, it would need to incarnate two principles. The first is teased out by asking what it is that the altar rail does. The altar rail brings people alongside each other; shoulder to shoulder. Regardless of your personage, you are all equals at the altar rail. There is a leveling of the playing field. Whatever the engagement of the church with the wider community, it must be in a form where people are brought together as equals.

The second principle is illuminated when considering the history of the rail. Hatchett puts it this way: "As early as the time of Augustine of Hippo (early fifth century) in Africa and in several other places, a chest-high rail was built around the altar to keep the people from pressing too closely upon the ministers thus impeding their movement in the course of the service. The people then came to such rails to receive."[32] Whatever form

---

31. Also referred to as a communion rail in common parlance.

32. Hatchett, *Commentary on the American Prayer Book*, 384.

the church's engagement with the wider community takes, it must be in a form where the church does not lose its identity. In the same way that the rail around the altar provided space for the ministers to enact their roles, the church's engagement with the wider community must allow space for the church to be the church. There can be no compromise of Christian identity.

What about the Wine?

Our analysis of the bread has revolved around the fourfold action taken with the bread at the altar during Holy Eucharist: it is taken, blessed, broken, and shared. The same can not be said for the wine at the altar. Rather, with the wine there exists a threefold action: it is poured, blessed, and shared.

The difference does not end at the number of steps in the action. The bread is broken and shared. Each communicant gets a piece of bread. It all comes (at least liturgically) from one loaf, but each person gets their own. It is given to them.

The wine, in contrast, all remains in the same chalice. When we receive the wine it is from a common cup. To do the same with the bread would be to bring around a large loaf of bread and each person takes a bite out of it. I hope this mental picture makes clear the distinction.

With this difference in mind, let us apply the Peircean triads to the action of receiving the wine. First the object-representamen-interpretant triad. The pouring, blessing, and sharing of the wine is the object. The representamen is that this action is occurring within the context of the liturgy. We are not acting upon this wine in a back alley, or in a restaurant, or at a vineyard. We are acting upon it in a church, with prayers, and singing, and vestments, and all the other flotsam and jetsam that make up worship. The interpretant may once more be that the body and blood of Christ is being confected and partaken of by the gathered faithful.

Turning our attention to Peirce's index-icon-symbol triad brings up a question: what kind of sign is the threefold action of the wine in the liturgy? As was discovered in our focus on bread, the action ends up being all three (although we will have to do a little more work to get there).

The action is an icon. Icons offer a likeness that visualizes what they refer to. The action is in the likeness of the Last Supper, and refers to Jesus' institution of the sacrament. The presider's action with the cup resembles Jesus's action with the cup at his last meal with his disciples.

The action is an index. Recall that an index is a sign that points to what caused it. The action indexes Jesus' command to "do this in remembrance of me." It was his command to his disciples, and hence to us, that caused (and continues to cause) this action to take place. As was for the bread, so it is for the wine.

The action is a symbol. Symbols are not in the likeness of what they refer to. The action, while not in the likeness of the church, can be considered a symbol for the church. Previous work identified the body of Christ (the bread) as a symbol of the body of Christ (the church).

Next consider the doctrine of concomitance, which states that Christ is present in both species of the Eucharist, the bread and the wine. This doctrine is the reason that receiving just one element is as efficacious as receiving both; it is also the reason that the wine was withheld from the laity for so long in the Roman Catholic Church.

It can be posited that if the bread is symbolic of the church, then through the doctrine of concomitance, the wine can be symbolic of the church as well. The local church is the blood of Christ as much as it is the body of Christ.

Further, it is the church itself which acts as the chalice, in which the faithful are gathered. Additionally, as liquid forms itself to the container it is in, so do the faithful conform themselves to the shape of the church. This is why the building always wins, and why liturgical semiotics dealing with worship space design can be so rich.[33]

With the wine established as a symbol of the church, let us return to the threefold action. The threefold action taken with the wine (the blood of Christ) is a symbol of (i.e., a sign that refers to) the action that we (the blood of Christ) take in following God's call on us to engage the wider community. In the pouring of the wine into the cup, we are gathered in our worship space. In the blessing of the wine, we are blessed by God as we worship. In the sharing of the wine, we work as a church to share the church with the wider community.

This symbology with the wine is a wonderful compliment to that which was explicated with the bread. The bread was broken and shared, meaning that we as the church were broken into our parts (families and individuals) and shared with the wider community. The wine is shared while remaining in the cup. This is the church acting corporately, as a faith community, in the wider community.

A Watery Corollary

There is one more action taken with the wine to consider in our semiotic analysis. That is revealed in the fact that it is not only wine that is in the

33. More on this in chapter 9, "Breathing Space."

chalice. There is water in the chalice as well. The BCP states that it "is customary to add a little water to the wine."[34][35]

In light of the semiotic trajectory we have been taking, what might the cutting of the wine with water suggest? Let us consider the effect of cutting the wine. What does it do? It dilutes the wine, lessening its alcohol level and softening its taste. Cutting the wine with water makes the wine less potent and more palatable.

To translate this into our missiological analysis, cutting the wine would imply crafting the community engagement of the church as a whole as something that is not as strong. If you are not ready for it, or are not used to it, a mouthful of wine can be overpowering. Analogously, the local church can be a bit overwhelming if you are not ready for it or are not used to it.

This is not to say that the way the local church conducts itself is wrong or bad. Even very fine wine can be overpowering to a teetotaler. The point is instead that paying some mind to being more culturally palatable makes it easier to be received. As noted above, however, that does not mean compromising our identity.

Consider how many local churches spend their time. They gather early on the one morning that most people sleep in (Sundays), to "sit on seventeenth-century chairs (which we call pews), sing eighteenth-century songs (which we call hymns), and listen to a nineteenth-century instrument (a pipe organ)."[36] I have painted a picture with a broad brush, and of course all local churches do not fit that scene. Yet the point is a valid one: the local church is often inherently counter-cultural. Being aware of that, and perhaps cutting that wine with a little water when trying to engage the wider community, can only be beneficial.

CONCLUSION

This is a good place to conclude our BREATHE practicum in liturgical semiotics. This does not mean that there is not more that could be done, though.

Thus far it has been determined that the fourfold action with the bread in the liturgy, and the complementary action with the wine, imply that we

34. Episcopal Church, *Book of Common Prayer*, 407.

35. Chapter 8 explores how to go about making the use of bread and wine in the liturgy more culturally resonant. As part of that, the background of adding water to the wine is explored there. At present, the concern is with the semiotic implications of cutting the wine.

36. Warren, *Purpose Driven Church*, 290.

are called as the local church to engage the wider community. The action of the bread points toward us doing this as individuals and families. The action of the wine points toward us doing this as the local church as a whole. The cutting of the wine with water points us toward being aware of our own counter-cultural tendencies as the local church.

A final thought on the process just undertaken. This practicum has shown that the church's worship is tied to its missiology. Christopher Irvine has put it this way, "In the end, perhaps it is a Church shaped by its worship that will be the most effective mission-shaped Church in and for the world."[37] It is more evidence that worship is indeed the primary activity that we engage in as Christians, and that everything else we do flows from that.

37. Irvine, *Use of Symbols in Worship*, ix.

7

A GASP Practicum

"When Jesus had said this, he breathed on them."

~JOHN 20:22

THIS CHAPTER IS A practicum. Similarly to how the last chapter demonstrated the BREATHE process in action, this chapter will be a demonstration of GASP at work. This exercise will involve making semiotic adjustments to the liturgy for the purpose of evoking particular themes or messaging. Our practicum will employ the acronym arrived at in chapter 4:

> Gestures
> Awareness
> Speech
> Presence

As noted in a previous chapter, however, the GASP acronym does not represent a process flow but rather a toolkit. Therefore, some preparatory work needs to be done before the tools can be utilized.

THE CHOICE OF LITURGY AND LITURGICAL FOCUS

To remain consistent with work in other parts of this book, the Holy Eucharist Rite II from the Episcopal Book of Common Prayer will be the liturgy under consideration. It is the breaking of the bread within this rite that will be focused on. The reason for this choice is twofold. First, this focus helps the parts of this work to remain resonant with each other. Two, the breaking of the bread is very important to me, personally.[1] A semiotician who works on something that they are passionate about brings more of themselves to the effort. Given that my approach to semiotics carries an artistic aspect to it, and one that takes into account the context of the semiotician, this passion makes for better art.

DOING VS. MEANING

When considering making semiotic adjustments to the liturgy, it is important to understand the difference between what the liturgy does and what it means. The liturgy does something. It means nothing. This I have written for shock value. Allow me to explain.

The service of Holy Eucharist is efficacious. It does something. Jesus Christ is made truly present through the liturgy in a way that he was not before, as just one example. The liturgy does something, because Jesus said "do this" in remembrance of me.

The service of Holy Eucharist does not inherently mean anything. Its meaning is up to each person to determine, based on their context. That meaning is dependent upon how the person observing interprets the signs apprehended by the senses: the sights, sounds, smells, tastes, and touches. Thus, finding meaning in the service of Holy Eucharist is a semiotic task.

From my context and experience, the sign that speaks the loudest to me is the action of the breaking of the bread (also known as the fraction). Another observer may be more taken by icons, or the distribution of the bread, or the taste of the wine, or the sermon. For me, it is the breaking of the bread. That is where I am most drawn to find meaning in the liturgy, regardless of what the liturgy does or accomplishes in its enactment.

LITURGICAL HISTORY AND THE EVOLUTION OF THE FRACTION

The first GASP tool to employ is awareness. This is employed before the worship even begins. By exploring the history of the fraction, a firmer understanding of its function and place in the liturgy is gained. This situates the earnest semiotician in good stead to make adjustments.

---

1. See appendix B for a personal story about the breaking of the bread.

The history of the breaking of the bread is as old as bread itself. The first time that someone intended to share a loaf of bread with others, bread was broken. The rest, as they say, was history.

The liturgical history of the fraction began as so many of our liturgical actions did: as a practical necessity. Before the advent of wafers, breaking the bread into individual pieces was the only way that those gathered could partake. By the middle ages, however, "when the people rarely received communion and a wafer replaced the loaf,"[2] the practical breaking of the bread gradually gave way to the theologizing force of liturgical evolution.

Over time there is a tendency for practical actions in worship to be theologized. To give a brief example, consider the lavabo bowl and the action of the presider washing their hands (their fingertips really) just before beginning the liturgy of the table. This action began as a practical necessity: in the days when large amounts of unpackaged food was given as an offering, the priest needed to wash his hands before conducting the table liturgy. The washing was a consequence of the nature of the offering.

Once the offering of messy foods ceased, however, the hand washing remained. Freed from its practical application, the action became theologized. The hand washing was "an action, continuing in existence, but no one could see, at a glance, why it was there, and so it began to gather new explanations which, in turn, came to be seen as its rationale and, indeed, its cause."[3] Since the context was a worship service, observers plundered Scripture for an explanation. The presider needed pure hands to conduct the sacrifice, like the purification rites of the Hebrew Bible. It also became a visual reminder of Pontius Pilate washing his hands.

Once theological reasons have been applied to an action liberated from its causal event, it becomes strengthened and buttressed by Scripture verses, collects, and rubrics. It becomes entrenched, solidified, and if done unthinkingly, ossified.

This process has happened to the fraction as well. Originally, a single unit of bread was used and so it was necessary that it be broken in order to be shared. Once the church moved to using wafers, however, the causal event for the breaking of the bread was removed. The action remained, though. Freed from being an action of consequence, it begged for rationalization and explanation.

The medieval Roman Catholic Church engaged in such theologizing with the fraction. From the fifth century:

2. Hatchett, *Commentary on the American Prayer Book*, 379.

3. O'Loughlin, "Liturgical Evolution," 314.

It was the custom for the Pope (or, if not in Rome, the bishop) to break off portions from his Host and send them, by the hands of acolytes or sub-deacons, to every priest celebrating the Eucharist in churches nearby. Each priest put this fermentum, "leaven" as it was called, with reference to Christ's parable of the leaven, into his own chalice. Thus was demonstrated that there was, in reality, only one Mass in place.[4]

There was also a similar tradition whereby a piece of the host would be reserved until the next day. This piece, "known as the santa, the sacred piece, was added to the Chalice of the next day's Mass."[5] This action showed, in a parallel to the previous action, that there was in reality a single Mass in time.

Later, after "these practices disappeared, a portion of the wafer consecrated at that Mass was placed in the cup and given an allegorical interpretation."[6] This might well be considered theologizing of the second order, since it was a replacement for a theologized action that had passed out of usage.

THE TRIDENTINE MASS

The nonpareil theologizing of the fraction, however, comes from the dominant form of Holy Eucharist for about a quarter of Christian history: the Tridentine Mass. This liturgy was the progeny of the Council of Trent (1554–63), and remained as the official liturgy of the Roman Catholic Church until the authorization of liturgies coming out of the Second Vatican Council (1962–65). It standardized not only the actions of every Roman Catholic priest, it also unified the theological meaning assigned to every jot and tittle of the eucharistic service.

Toward the end of the liturgy of the table, we find that the Celebrant "then places the Host on the paten, uncovers the chalice, genuflects, rises, takes the Host, and holding It over the chalice with both hands, breaks It down the middle."[7] From one of the halves, a very small piece (referred to as a particle) is then broken off. The accompanying explanation is that "the Host is broken over the chalice, to indicate that the blood contained in the chalice proceeds from the broken body of Christ. The breaking of the Host into three pieces distinguishes Christ's mystical body according to its various states: the Church Triumphant, the Church Militant, and the

4. Williamson, *Great Prayer*, 190.
5. Williamson, *Great Prayer*, 190.
6. Hatchett, *Commentary on the American Prayer Book*, 379.
7. Juergens, *Roman Catholic Daily Missal*, 904.

Church Suffering."[8] The particle eventually finds its way into the chalice to symbolically express the doctrine of concomitance.

THEOLOGIZING IS NOT SEMIOTICS

What has been described, the theologizing of actions in worship, is decidedly not semiotics. Or, at the very least, it is not very good semiotics. Rather than relying upon the observer to interpret the sign based upon their context, the meaning of the action has already been decided upon. Add to that the reality that the Mass was not conducted in the vernacular, and that people did not have information providing to them the meaning of the actions, and there was a severe disconnect between presider and observer.

The distinction is well illumined when considered in light of a Peircean understanding of semiotics. Semiotically speaking, the breaking of the bread is an object. That the breaking of the bread is happening as part of worship is a representamen, a sign. The interpretant of that sign, how it makes sense in one's mind, is necessarily going to depend upon the context of the observer. Once an interpretation of that sign is assigned by someone who is not an observer, you are no longer engaging in semiotics. Instead, you have crossed into theological pedagogy.

In order for a liturgical enactment to invite semiotic activity on the part of the participants, it must resist giving explicit meaning to actions. Rather, it should provide flexibility such that the person manifesting an action can do so in a way that invites interpretation and evokes certain images or stories in the mind of the observer. Next we turn our attention away from the historic and toward the current.

SUITABILITY OF THE BCP

The current Book of Common Prayer (BCP) is a resource that leaves much room for semiotic promulgation. Rather than theologizing the actions of the liturgy, it merely presents them. This leaves much room to manifest the actions in inviting and evocative ways.

With regards to the fraction, we find simply that "the Celebrant breaks the consecrated Bread"[9] and following that "a period of silence is kept."[10]

8. Juergens, *Roman Catholic Daily Missal*, 905.
9. Episcopal Church, *Book of Common Prayer*, 364.
10. Episcopal Church, *Book of Common Prayer*, 364.

There is no assigning of theological meaning to the act. The meaning of the action is free for the observer to interpret.

There is also no direction about how to go about completing the action. How high up do you hold the bread? Do you break it over the chalice? What do you do with the two halves once you have broken the bread? How long do you remain silent? Do you remain still during the silence?

All of this and more is left up to the presider to determine and enact. To aid the presider in this determination, books like *Celebrating the Eucharist: A Practical Ceremonial Guide for Clergy and Other Liturgical Ministers,* by Patrick Malloy, and *A Priest's Handbook: The Ceremonies of the Church,* by Dennis Michno, have appeared. While neither work concerns itself with semiotics explicitly, Malloy does note that "the breaking of the Bread is not a functional gesture, but a heavily freighted one."[11]

There is ample flexibility in the enactment of this action to craft a particular semiotic message. If a presider wanted to draw attention to the breaking of the bread, for example, then a few things could be done to accomplish that. The presider could use a very large, very dry (and thus good for making an audible snap when breaking) host. This gives the observer a larger visual sign to interpret and a clear auditory sign as well. The host could be lifted high, and once fractured, a lengthy silence undertaken. All these elements could well draw greater attention to the action.

The semiotic action of the fraction can also be enhanced, and crafted to support a particular message, with words. If the presider wants to support a message of the truth of human life's brokenness, they might say, after the period of silence, "this is the way life is . . . broken."[12]

Something that is often missed in Episcopal circles is that the rubric regarding words spoken after the fraction is permissive.[13] The words we find are "Christ our Passover is sacrificed for us;" with a response of "Therefore let us keep the feast." A following rubric states "In place of, or in addition to, the preceding, some other suitable anthem may be used."

This is often used as an opportunity for a choral piece. *The Hymnal 1982*, for example, contains twenty-two options for singing the fraction anthem.[14] The hymnal *Wonder, Love, and Praise: A Supplement to The Hymnal 1982* has another fourteen.[15]

---

11. Malloy, *Celebrating the Eucharist*, 182.

12. Private conversation with Leonard Sweet.

13. Episcopal Church, *Book of Common Prayer*, 364.

14. Episcopal Church, *Hymnal 1982*, S151–S172.

15. Episcopal Church, *Wonder, Love, and Praise*, 865–78.

Rarely, however, does it manifest as a change in the words spoken by the presider. The only approved liturgical resource that acknowledges the possibility is *Enriching Our Worship 1* (EOW). It contains four options[16] for words to speak after the fraction (and one of them is an updated language version of the fraction anthem from Holy Eucharist Rite I).

The brothers of the Society of St. John the Evangelist (SSJE) are a notable exception to this trend. When these Episcopal monks celebrate the Eucharist, the presider says "Behold what you are" after the fraction, with the response being "May we become what we receive."[17] Otherwise, what you hear in the vast majority of Episcopal worship services are either the spoken words from the BCP, a choral anthem, or both.

GESTURES AND SPEECH

Since this ground has not been well-trod, much less turned over, a semiotic exercise is called for. What follows is an envisioning of the fraction in nine different worship service contexts. This consists of the seven Principal Feasts of the Episcopal Church (Easter Day, Ascension Day, The Day of Pentecost, Trinity Sunday, All Saints' Day, Christmas Day, and The Epiphany) as well as a wedding and a funeral. The point of this exercise is to enact the fraction in a way that emphasizes the context of the worship service. It is an attempt to invite the observer to interpret the action, and evoke certain images or stories in their mind.

The Day of Pentecost

Pentecost is the birthday of the church. The image that naturally sticks in the mind's eye is that of the Holy Spirit, like tongues of fire, descending upon the disciples in the upper room. The presider holds the host high for the breaking. During the silence the two halves are rotated and overlapped such that a "V" shape is formed at the top. The pieces are then brought down low and held over the chalice. The shape of the pieces when held together, and the movement of them, is evocative of the Pentecost story from Acts chapter 2, which would have been read earlier in the service. When the silence elapses, the presider says, "The Holy Spirit will teach you everything, and remind you of all that Jesus said" (John 14:26b).

16. Episcopal Church, *Enriching Our Worship 1*, 69.

17. Observed in worship at the Society of St. John the Evangelist in Cambridge, Massachusetts.

Christmas Day

Christmas is the day that we celebrate the incarnation, the nativity, the birth of our Lord and Savior, Jesus Christ. For this context, I envision movement from back to front rather than from top to bottom. The host is held at chest level, closely, by the presider, and broken. During the silence, the pieces are moved forward, toward the congregation, and are separated. When the silence elapses, the presider says "The Word became flesh and dwelt among us, and we have seen his glory" (John 1:14). The movement of the bread toward the congregation is evocative of approach, of coming among.

Ascension Day

On Ascension Day we recall Jesus' ascension to the right hand of the Father. It marks the end of his bodily, earthy (and specifically earthly), ministry and prefigures the coming of the Holy Spirit. On this day, the presider holds the host low over the chalice and breaks it. During the silence, the pieces are raised straight up and separated slightly. When the silence elapses, the presider says "He ascended far above all heavens that he might fill all things."[18] The lifting up of the body of Christ (the bread) is evocative of the lifting up of the body of Christ (himself).

Funeral

At a funeral, the primary message must be about Jesus, not the person who has died. So the fraction must continue to do what it always does: point to Jesus Christ. Here, the presider holds the host high and breaks it. In the silence, the presider's head bows and his arms move out to the sides. When the silence elapses, the presider raises his head and says "I am Resurrection and I am Life, says the Lord."[19] The lowering of the head and the wide movements of the arms evokes death and brokenness. The words, the same words spoken at the very beginning of the service, are a reminder of the hope we have as Christians.

---

18. Episcopal Church, *Book of Common Prayer*, 226, 1st Collect for Ascension Day.

19. Episcopal Church, *Book of Common Prayer*, 491, Burial Office.

Wedding

At a wedding, it can be challenging to keep the focus on God and not on the couple getting married. The bridge is, of course, love. In this context the presider holds the host low over the chalice and breaks it. During the silence, a wide circle is made with the pieces as the presider's arms are raised. At the top of the circle, the presider holds the two pieces together again. After the silence, the presider says "God's love was revealed among us in this way: God sent his only Son into the world so that we might live through him" (1 John 4:9). The movement of the two pieces coming together at the top of the circle is evocative of two becoming one, of wholeness, and the words locate God at the center of love.

The Epiphany

This feast celebrates the revelation of Jesus as God's Son. It is about recognizing Jesus' identity. In this context, the presider initially holds the host behind the chalice and breaks it. During the silence, the pieces come out from behind the chalice and are lifted at an angle, ending with the presider's arms in a "V" shape. At the end of the silence, the presider says "Be known to us Lord, in the breaking of the Bread."[20] Having the host behind the chalice, and then having the pieces come out into view when broken, is evocative of revelation and is a visual representation of the words spoken.

Trinity Sunday

This is the day that we celebrate the holy mystery of God's triune nature: three in one and one in three. The presider begins by holding the host in front of themselves at chest height, and breaks it down the middle. Then the presider breaks one of the pieces again, creating three pieces. These are displayed in silence to the congregation, at the end of which the presider says "We behold the mystery as we worship the unity." The words are my own, inspired by the collect for the day. The breaking of the bread into three pieces is so obvious as to not be evocative so much as it is demonstrative.

20. Episcopal Church, *Hymnal 1982*, S171.

All Saints' Day

This feast is a remembrance of the Christian faithful who have gone before us. The intent is to recall the great cloud of witnesses through the ages. For this feast, the presider holds the host chest high and breaks it. They continue to fold the pieces together and break them along the scored lines until there are many pieces. Then the pieces are displayed in the presider's hands in silence. At the end, the presider says "In the sacred circle of sacrifice and communion, offering and reception, it is the body broken that makes us strong."[21] The breaking of the host into many pieces is meant to evoke a great many gathered together, and all broken. The language of sacrifice and brokenness is indicative of the saints.

Easter Day

Lastly, the Feast of the Resurrection. This is the most grandiose and dramatic day of the liturgical year, or at least it should be. On this day, the presider begins with the host held high and breaks it. Then the pieces are brought down in an arms-length circle. At the bottom of the circle, the pieces are brought up again, finishing chest high. At the end of the silence, the presider says "He has been raised from the dead; and indeed he is going ahead of you" (Matt 28:7). The shape of the manual act evokes a movement of descent followed by ascent. This, combined with the words, brings to mind the dying and rising of Jesus.

PRESENCE

Chapter 4 noted that the focal participants of the liturgy ought not be "chill." The gathered faithful need to be led, and their voluntary attendance is their granting of permission for that leadership. Realizing and acting upon this goes a long way toward having the appropriate comportment for any worship experience.[22]

Another aspect of good presence, regardless of the particular liturgical context, is preparedness. If the focal participants are prepared to enflesh their roles in the liturgy, then those gathered will experience a smoothness and unanimity to the worship. The expectation of this preparedness is a boon to those gathered. If instead "the faithful are uncertain as to the

---

21. Sweet, *Strong in the Broken Places*, 247.
22. As the old G.I. Joe tagline said, knowing is half the battle.

preparedness of the [focal participants], then they will be distracted and therefore not fully present in the liturgy."[23] This would then act as a barrier to effective communication.

While there are some elements to presence which are unchanging, there are ways to adjust one's presence to match the theme or occasion. Much of this has to do with inner disposition, which one might first think has no outward impact.

The truth, however, is that humans have evolved to signal their emotions to others. From the whites of our eyes, to our smooth brow ridge (which accentuates the movement of our eyebrows), to our ability to blush, to the tilt of our head and the angling of our bodies, humans are always signaling how we feel. As Rutger Bregman has colorfully phrased it, "We constantly leak emotions and are hardwired to relate to the people around us."[24]

With this in mind, the various liturgical occasions described previously can be considered. While the presider at the altar need not intentionally signal how they are feeling about the theme or occasion, the fact of their humanity will signal this in some fashion as they execute their liturgical role.

A wedding is a joyous joining of lives, and the focal participants ought to have a joyful presence. This should not lapse into distracting garrulousness. Yet if the presider feels joyful at the altar, that feeling will find appropriate embodiment.

A funeral is an occasion for a pastoral presence. While the joy of the resurrection is kept in mind, it is held in tension with mourning and grief. The presider at the altar need to carry themselves with somberness and gentleness.

The feast days considered do not always easily lend themselves to a particular inner disposition. Christmas and Pentecost are about birth and newness. Easter is about life and victory. Epiphany is about revelation. But how should one feel about the doctrine of the Trinity? What emotion does the Ascension evoke? Theological rumination may lead to more clarity on the vagaries of the church calendar, but the point is made.

CONCLUSION

Semiotics adjustment can be made to the liturgy using the GASP tools in order to be evocative of particular themes or messages. This chapter explored that using the fraction in the BCP's Rite II Holy Eucharist as a focus.

23. Adams, *Shaped by Images*, 19.

24. Bregman, *Humankind*, 69–70.

First an awareness of the fraction's history and function were explored. Then specific gestures and words were suggested for use during the seven major feasts of the Episcopal Church, as well as the occasion of a wedding and a funeral. Then some thoughts on the presence of the presider were fleshed out.

Three concluding points present themselves. One, semiotic adjustments to the liturgy require mindfulness and preparation. An unthinking or unprepared focal participant is only going to detract from the worship experience of the gathered faithful.

Two, semiotic adjustments will be much more successful if they are part of a liturgy that is holistic and unitive in its approach to the theme or message of choice. If Pentecost is being celebrated, for example, then it should not only be the Scripture readings and the fraction that point to the uniqueness of the feast. The preached sermon, the hymn choices, the procession enactment, and whatever else can be done appropriately to point toward the coming of the Holy Spirit should be done.

Three, there is a cultural component to semiotic adjustments that has not yet been addressed. The GASP tools assume that the gathered faithful are all on the same page, culturally. If the presider speaks the words at the fraction in a language that no one present speaks, then the semiotic adjustment has failed. If the presider is attempting to evoke something in the mind of the worshiper that is not there because it is not part of their cultural lexicon, then the semiotic adjustment has failed.

In a society where being a churchgoer is increasingly counter-cultural, this last point carries some energy and urgency to it. The next chapter addresses some issues around how cultural concerns intersect the enactment of the liturgy with regards to the eucharistic elements of bread and wine.

8

A RASP Practicum

"Dead space is the portion of each tidal volume that does not take part in gas exchange."[1]

THIS CHAPTER IS A practicum, in a similar vein to the last two chapters. This chapter is a demonstration of RASP ((Re)signing Artifacts to Spark Perception) in action. This involves making semiotic adjustments to the liturgy for the purpose of using the bread and wine in the service of Holy Eucharist in a way that is in greater harmony with the prevailing culture. This will help to strengthen existing meanings in the liturgy and make new meanings accessible.

This is done through an exercise called (re)signing. As was mentioned in chapter 4, (re)signing is a combination of resigning and re-signing. While being resigned to an important truth, that truth is re-signed so it can be encountered afresh by new generations.

CULTURAL DEAD SPACE

This is not often thought about, but the body does not absorb all the oxygen that it breathes in. This makes sense if one stops to think about it. When a human breathes in, air not only fills the lungs, but the trachea, mouth, and sinuses. Yet it is only the air that makes it to the alveoli in the lungs that exchange that oxygen for carbon dioxide. The air that comes into the body but never makes it to the air sacs in the lungs is inhabiting "dead space."

1. John Hopkins School of Medicine, "Dead Space," para. 1.

Additionally, if the blood flow to some of the alveoli is not that good (i.e., some alveoli are not well perfused), then the gasses do not exchange, increasing the dead space.

This idea of dead space can serve as a useful guiding image for this chapter. Instead of a respiratory system, there is a liturgical event. Instead of oxygen being sent to the alveoli where it can be exchanged for carbon dioxide, there are signs being sent to the worshiper where they can be exchanged for meaning. Successful interpretation of intended meanings could be the parallel of successfully exchanging oxygen for carbon dioxide.

To further the metaphor, consider perfusion. Instead of poor blood flow inhibiting gas exchange, poor blood flow would inhibit the intended meaning being interpreted by the worshiper. The blood flow, the perfusion, is cultural resonance. The better the cultural resonance between the sign and the worshiper, the better chance that the intended meaning is going to be arrived at. The less the cultural resonance, the greater the semiotic dead space where the intended meaning is not within the range of understanding of the worshiper.

Two illustrative examples will prove helpful. The first is a sketch of how a college student found his way into the Episcopal Church:

> "It was the way they worshiped," he said. "I mean, I walked into that place and there was this priest, holding a chalice and saying things like, 'This is my blood.' I was blown away. That's like straight out of *Game of Thrones*."[2]

The second is a question posed by my nine-year-old son during dinner one night: "Dad, in church when you break the bread and hold it in front of you, why does it look like a dead Pac-Man?"

The point here is that interpretation is going to happen by the worshiper. It cannot be stopped, even if one wanted to. Interpretation is as natural to the human condition as breathing.

Was that priest intending to be evocative of *Game of Thrones*? Surely not. When I rotated the two halves of the fractured host and held them in front of me at the altar, was I trying to evoke the image of a dead Pac-Man in the minds of those gathered for worship? Seems unlikely.

Whether in a worship service or walking down the street, as human beings we think with what we know. We use our cultural context to interpret every sign we see, all the time. That unchurched college student drew upon his cultural context to interpret the actions of a priest at the altar and arrived at a popular TV show. Dead space. My son saw a shape that he recognized

---

2. Lee and Davidson, *Gathered for God*, xi.

from a video game, and applied that meaning to what I was doing. No gasses exchanged.

(RE)SIGNING

The intent of this chapter is to (re)sign the use of bread and wine in the liturgy of the Rite II Holy Eucharist in order to make those signs fresh for contemporary worshipers. As was mentioned in chapter 4, (re)signing is a way of referring to the combination of resign and re-sign. While being resigned to a particular truth, that truth is re-signed in a way that allows it to be encountered anew.

For our purposes, while being resigned to the importance of using bread and wine in the celebration of the Holy Eucharist, those elements will be re-signed so that they may be encountered afresh by people of the prevailing culture in twenty-first-century mainstream America. A word about each part of (re)signing follows for clarity.

I am resigned to the crucial nature of the bread and wine to Holy Eucharist. One could argue for its use from a broadly Christian perspective. Not only are bread and wine what Jesus used at the Last Supper, but for the majority of Christians for the majority of Christian history, bread and wine have been the elements used in celebrating Holy Communion.

A more urgent argument, however, comes from the particularity of the task at hand. The BCP specifies the use of bread and wine in the liturgy. There are no rubrics or additional directives that allow for substitutions to happen. While there have been the rare historical instances of different elements being allowed, such as bananas and banana wine used as eucharistic elements by the Anglican Church in Uganda in the late nineteenth century,[3] the testimony and expectation of the Episcopal Church is clear that bread and wine are to be used. I am resigned to this important truth.

The current way that bread and wine are typically used in the service, however, is out of step with how the current culture understands them. Thus, these artifacts will be re-signed by using them in a way more in sync with how the current culture understands them. This will allow contemporary worshipers to encounter these artifacts afresh and find new meaning in them.

First, the cultural meaning of bread and wine at the dawn of Christian worship will be explored. Next their current cultural understanding will be examined. Then, how the bread and wine are typically used in the Holy Eucharist service today will be considered. After that, adjustments will be proposed that bring the use of the bread and the wine more into alignment

3. Tovey, *Inculturation of Christian Worship*, 45.

with the current cultural zeitgeist. Finally, the impact of those adjustments will be considered.

First-Century Bread in the Ancient Near East

As the *Baker Encyclopedia of the Bible* puts it, "A large proportion of the time and energy of mankind since the fall until the industrial revolution has been occupied in the production of bread."[4] While this statement is painting with a very large brush, and lacks a certain refinement, it does point one toward several truths about bread in the Ancient Near East.

To begin with, bread was the foundation of the diet.[5] Whether wealthy or poor, bread formed the basis for one's daily food intake. The difference was in what kind of bread that was eaten. Those of more means ate wheat bread, while those of less means ate barley bread.

Bread was also not mass produced, by and large. Large urban centers did have commercial bakers. Most people did not live in cities, however.[6] The average family, therefore, baked bread daily for their daily needs instead of seeking out a commercial baker. For the John Q Public of the day, the baking and eating of bread was something that happened in close connection, and on a daily basis.

An interesting exception was Rome's Cura Annonae (care of Annona, a goddess). This was a public program whereby the state would supply bread to the poor of the city. It is one of the first examples of a social safety net.

The foundational character of bread had far reaching consequences for the ancient societies. With the exception of a situation like Rome's, where massive amounts of grain were imported to feed the inhabitants, the population of a place was limited by how much bread that place could produce. Bread was a determining factor in settlement size.

Bread's central place in daily life also had economic implications. The price of grain was seen as an index of the economy's health, and "cereal took the place of money in commerce."[7] Along these lines, recall the biblical witness of Hosea paying part of the price of his wife in grain (Hos 3:2).

Bread also helped to connect people more intimately to the land and its natural rhythm. Through annual seasons, as well as those of feast and famine, the people were closely attuned to fortunes of their local geography.

---

4. Elwell, *Baker Encyclopedia of the Bible*, 378.

5. "The necessities of life are water, bread, and clothing" (Sir 29:21).

6. It was not until 2007 that, globally, more people started living in cities than in rural areas (Ritchie and Roser, "Urbanization," para. 4).

7. Martin et al., *New Bible Dictionary*, 145.

They were very aware that they were part of creation, and while they would not have used this term, they were very ecologically minded.

The old saying that bread is "the staff of life" rang true for our forerunners. Bread was brought as food on journeys because it traveled well. Dried hard bread could carry people through from one growing season to the next. It was used as a metaphor for food in general, to the point that "to break bread" meant to eat a meal (e.g., Acts 2:42, 46).

First-Century Wine in the Ancient Near East

To begin the treatment of wine with a statement as bold as that which opened the bread discussion, "Wine has been known in the East as a beverage since the dawn of history."[8] While the invention of bread certainly predated that of wine, humanity's journey with wine is very old: wine-treading installations discovered in Israel have dated to at least the Chalcolithic period (4000–3500 BCE).[9]

Wine's cultural importance to the Ancient Near East is seen in its frequent association with grain and oil. This triad formed the agricultural and economic base for the region, and their bounty meant prosperity. Along these lines we see wine being used as a form of payment, such as when Solomon offered twenty thousand baths of wine as partial payment for assistance in constructing the temple (2 Chr 2:10).

By the New Testament period, wine was in common, everyday use in the region. While there were certainly variations in the types of wine produced, there did appear to be a cultural constant in how wine was consumed. It was mixed with water. In fact, the ancient Greeks considered it barbaric to drink wine that was *not* mixed with water.[10]

Wine also was used for medical purposes. Paul suggested Timothy drink a little to help with his ailments (1 Tim 5:23). Additionally, wine would be applied to open wounds as a disinfectant.[11]

Twenty-First-Century Bread in America

While wheat is the primary grain consumed by Americans, bread does not occupy the same place as the bedrock of civilization as it did in the Ancient

8. Negev, *Archaeological Encyclopedia of the Holy Land*, s.v. "wine."

9. Cole et al., *Eerdmans Dictionary of the Bible*, 1379.

10. Elwell, *Baker Encyclopedia of the Bible*, 2147.

11. Consider the story of the Good Samaritan from Luke 10:25–37, for example.

Near East. Americans still consume massive amounts of grains, but it is not all in the form of bread. Furthermore, bread is now just one of a dizzying array of dietary options to the average American.

One recent cultural trend that is helping to shape the American understanding of bread is a growing awareness of the importance of healthy eating. For many of the health conscious, this finds fruition in a diet that is low in carbohydrates. Hence the importance of bread is diminished.

Another factor is our societal awareness of how interconnected the global economy is. Given this interconnectedness, this interpenetration, every purchase we make comes with a consequence for the human family and the planet we live on. Each time we buy something, that choice finds its location in the intersection of each of four economic-social-ecological relationships:

> (1) between global economic forces and the integrity of creation's biosystems; (2) between human cultivation of the land and ethical responsibility for its protection and preservation; (3) between the dignity of human labor and the exigencies of poverty, migration, and exclusion; and (4) between the drive for profit, accumulation, and growth and the cost to both Earth and her peoples who suffer impoverishment and misery.[12]

The awareness of these relationships lead towards a favoring of smaller, more local food production. It is also leading toward a favoring of artisanal, well-crafted foods over mass-produced fare.

All of this implies a cultural stance regarding bread in twenty-first-century mainstream America: if one is going to eat bread, it ought to be high quality bread that was sustainably and justly made, or that you made yourself using good (in both senses of that word) ingredients.

Twenty-First-Century Wine in America

While one can find wineries in all fifty states, wine does not occupy the same commonplace space that it did in the Ancient Near East. America as a country does produce a massive amount of wine, from large producers to people who grow their own grapes. Wine, however, is seen as a specialty beverage.

In the ancient world wine was the commonplace drink of the day. In that time and place it was almost as common as water. Today that is no longer the case.

---

12. McGann, *Meal That Reconnects*, 190.

Today, drinking wine is a specialized action rather than a general one. It is possible to unthinkingly have a glass of wine with a meal. But even as one hears the phrase *glass of wine*, the mind is likely to picture elegant stemware and a refined atmosphere. This is the cultural understanding of wine today.

We do not simply drink wine today. We pair certain wines with certain foods, or certain events, or certain times of year—or all three at once. Which wine should we serve with the main course? Is it at the right temperature? Is it the correctly shaped glass for that varietal of grape?

We may not even want to sully our wine drinking experience with food. Instead, we may focus all of our attention and energy on tasting the wine. We explore and evaluate the wine using the five S's. See. Swirl. Sniff. Sip. Savor.

There is little disputing it. Our cultural engagement with wine, once so common as to be little noticed, has become refined and specialized. Additionally, the nexus of global relationships mentioned above in reference to bread similarly has its effects on how we understand wine.

How the Bread Is Currently Used

In the service of Holy Eucharist Rite II there are actually only a handful of references to how the bread is to be used.[13] It is specified that representatives of the congregation bring the bread to the deacon or presider at the offering. The presider is instructed to touch the bread when speaking about it in the eucharistic prayer. The presider is instructed to break the bread. Lastly, it is specified that the bread is given to the communicants.

That is all that the liturgy actually describes in terms of the use of the bread. This means that much has been left up to tradition and the discretion of the congregation. What follows is a description of how the bread might typically be used in a normative Rite II Holy Eucharist service.

First, the form of the bread. In most Episcopal churches, wafers are used rather than a regular loaf of bread. Individual wafers are intended for the individual worshipers, and a larger wafer is intended for use by the presider. Also, it is entirely possible that these wafers come from the Cavanaugh company of Rhode Island, who provide a whopping 80 percent of the altar bread consumed in the United States.[14]

---

13. Episcopal Church, *Book of Common Prayer*, 355–82.

14. Gerety, "Buying the Body of Christ," para. 2.

The bread begins the service in the back of the worship space, in a closed metal container called a ciborium. It is brought up, along with the wine and monetary donations, during the offering and placed on the altar.

At the altar the presider unveils the chalice and paten. The larger wafer will be on the paten, and the presider moves it to the side. Then the ciborium is opened and a number of the smaller wafers are removed and put on the paten. Then the larger wafer, the priest host, is placed on top of the other wafers.

If the number of wafers removed from the ciborium is sufficient to communicate those gathered, then the ciborium is removed from the altar and placed on a side table (called a credence table) where it will sit for the remainder of the service. If more wafers are likely needed to communicate those gathered, then the ciborium will remain on the altar.

During the eucharistic prayer, the presider will put a hand on the wafers on the paten (and on the ciborium as well if it is still on the altar). The priest will elevate the priest host so it is viewable by the congregation. The priest may also elevate the chalice and the priest host together, with the wafer held over the chalice. The priest host will be broken during the fraction and held in silence before the congregation. After a call and response, the pieces will be placed back on the paten. The chalice and the paten will together be elevated and the priest will say "the gifts of God for the people of God."

During the distribution, an individual wafer will be placed in the hand of a communicant and words will be spoken. The congregant will reverently consume the wafer. After all have received, any remaining wafers will be either consumed by the presider or reserved in another ciborium.

How the Wine Is Currently Used

The story of the wine's usage in the Holy Eucharist is a similar one. The references to its use in the service are scant. Like the bread, the vessel containing the wine comes forward at the offering. The presider touches the container while speaking about it. It is given to the communicant after the bread. What follows is an enfleshment of what the use of wine typically looks like on a Sunday morning where the Holy Eucharist Rite II is celebrated.

For many parishes, the type of wine used is a port (i.e., fortified) wine. This is for a few reasons. First, port tends to take longer to turn to vinegar than regular wine. Thus an open bottle has less of a chance of going bad before being entirely used, especially for parishes where refrigeration of the open bottle is not convenient. Second, port tends to be sweeter and so is generally more drinkable by the average communicant, even if he or she is not usually a wine drinker. Third, port stains tend to be easier to get out of linens than regular red wine.[15] Fourth, a cheap jug of port is generally more drinkable than a cheap bottle of wine, and many churches strive to keep costs down.

The wine begins in the back of the worship space in a cruet or flagon, of either glass or metal. It is processed forward at the offering and placed on the altar. The presider pours the wine into a metal (or possibly ceramic) chalice. If the amount of wine poured into the chalice is sufficient to commune those present, the cruet will be removed to the credence table. If more wine than what is in the chalice is needed, the cruet will remain on the altar.

During the eucharistic prayer, the presider will lay a hand on the chalice during the words concerning the wine (and also on the cruet if it is still on the altar). The chalice will be elevated after those words, to focus the attention of the gathered on it. As mentioned above, the presider may also elevate the priest host and chalice together. The chalice and paten will be elevated together after the fraction.

During the distribution, the chalice will be offered to the communicant after they are given a wafer. Depending on the local custom, the congregation will either dip their wafer into the wine, or sip from chalice. The person offering the chalice will wipe the lip of the chalice and rotate it so that a different edge of the chalice is offered to the next worshiper. After all have received, the wine remaining in the chalice is consumed by the presider.

An Evolution toward Quality

In the ancient civilizations, most of the population spent most of their time attending to the basics of life. The focus was primarily on providing food, clothing, and shelter for the family. If one wanted to eat, they needed to bake bread, daily, for example.

The world we inhabit today is very different. Yes, there are still many places in the world where the daily tasks of survival take up the majority of people's time. Yet, as a species, we have more time and resources to bring to bear on non-basics than we ever have before. As broken as some parts of this world are, as a whole the global standard of living has never been higher. As an example, consider that more than a billion people have been lifted out of poverty in the last fifty years.[16]

15. At least according to the directrixes of altar guilds that I have known.
16. Sweet and Chironna, *Rings of Fire*, 5.

This means that we, as the human family, are getting better and better at certain things that we are putting our time, energy, resources, and new technologies toward. We are able to produce wines that have never been made before. We are able to do things with bread that have never been done before. One could rightly argue that we are able to make the best bread and wine in human history, right now.

This evolution toward quality lends additional weight to the idea that the use of bread and wine in the Holy Eucharist is ripe for re-signing.

Re-signing Bread and Wine

We have looked at how bread and wine were culturally understood both in the Ancient Near East and how they currently are viewed in mainstream, twenty-first-century America. What follows is an imagining of how the bread and wine might be used in the Rite II Holy Eucharist in a way that is more resonant with the current culture. This re-signing will allow for new meanings to be accessible to contemporary worshipers that were not before.

The Choice of Bread and Wine

First we consider the bread and wine themselves. A quality loaf of bread has been obtained. This is as opposed to the use of wafers. Perhaps it has come from a local bakery, or has been made by a congregant. Its provenance has been ascertained with regards to the sourcing of the ingredients through questions like the following: Were workers paid fairly when they harvested the grain that became the flour? Was the grain processed in an environmentally friendly manner?

Regarding the wine, a decent bottle of wine, ethically sourced, has been secured. This could mean the wine has been made at a vineyard that pays a fair wage to their workers and treats them equitably. Or it could mean that the wine is organic and produced in an ecologically minded way (i.e., free from pesticides and other harmful chemicals). Or it could mean that it was made by a parishioner, or is from a local vineyard.[17] Whatever the ethical tenor of the congregation, the wine chosen should be in harmony with that tone.

This fact should also be advertised to the congregation. It could be through a statement in the bulletin, or information on the church website,

---

17. This could be an interesting twist on the statement in Micah 4:4 that "they shall all sit under their own vines."

or tacked to a bulletin board, or all three. If this information was kept updated (e.g., "This week's wine comes to us from such-and-such vineyard. They do X, Y, and Z, and were chosen for this reason. The bread was made by the Smiths using ethically sourced ingredients"), it would help the congregation to stay connected to the world outside the walls of the church.

At the Liturgy of the Word

Our next step in re-signing the bread and the wine in the liturgy is to bring the people closer to it. Prior to the service, the bread resides on the paten that is to be used at the altar, with a clean white cloth over it. While it would be nice to have the bread viewable by those gathered, we also want to keep the bread as clean as possible prior to its consumption. The bread could be on a pedestal in the midst of the congregation, rather than at the back of the nave.

Prior to the service, the wine is definitely kept in a glass cruet, as opposed to a metal flagon. The cruet would join the bread on the pedestal in the midst of those gathered. This allows the wine to be viewed by many during the service.

This sign might even be heightened by having the wine in a decanter rather than a cruet. Decanters come in a wider variety of shapes than cruets, and so this might be more evocative of wine's specialized place.

At the offertory, the paten and cruet come forward. This movement is an important act of preparation. As Bernard of Clairvaux said, "It is only to places which produce no wine that wine is wont to be brought.[18] The laity play a critically important part in the liturgy by bringing bread and wine to where there is no bread and wine. If they do not, then Eucharist cannot be made. In our envisioned service, as the paten and cruet come forward and are placed on the altar, the congregation comes with it and gathers around the altar.

Alternatively, and to enter a brief excursus, imagine if the bread is brought into the sanctuary at this point, having just been baked in the church's kitchen. The aroma of the fresh baked bread wafts through the assembly as those gathered come around the altar.

If the person carrying the cruet has been gently swirling the wine, then those gathered would also have an opportunity to appreciate the "legs" of the wine once it is placed on the altar. If a decanter with an open, wider mouth has been used instead of a traditional cruet, then the gentle swirling will aerate the wine and help "open up" the flavor.

18. Bernard of Clairvaux, *Sermons on the Canticle of Canticles*, 2:3.

At the Altar

Prior to the consecration, both the bread and the wine are prepared. The chalice is unveiled. The bread would be uncovered.

In the case of the wine it is poured into the chalice (the cruet remaining if it is thought that more than one chalice of wine will be needed to commune those gathered). The liturgy could be slowed and quieted, in order to place more emphasis on this manual action. If the faithful are gathered around the altar, such that they can see and hear this happen, the pouring out can become a multisensory affair. Unfortunately, the Holy Eucharist Rite II liturgy does not provide for words to be spoken during this time.[19]

During the eucharistic prayer, the priest is directed that "At the following words concerning the bread, the celebrant[20] is to hold it, or to lay a hand upon it."[21] It has become traditional to lift the priest host after the words concerning the bread are spoken. In our imagined service, the loaf would be lifted. Depending on the shape of the bread, rotating it so that those gathered are seeing it from the top down, and turning from side to side for the benefit of those gathered on the sides, may strengthen the sign.

Similarly, the priest is directed that "at the words concerning the cup, to hold or place a hand upon the cup and any other vessel containing wine to be consecrated."[22] It has become traditional to elevate the chalice after the words concerning the wine are spoken. This action could be made more robust through a higher elevation and a longer pause, or by moving the chalice from side to side, as to give those gathered a better view of it.

After the consecration, the fraction of the bread receives its own place in the liturgy (as explored in the last chapter) and is accompanied by words. There is no analogous action with the wine after consecration. It simply remains in the chalice, stoic and still. Here we bump up against a limitation: as flexible as the BCP is, its extensibility can be exhausted.

19. There is something called *An Order for Celebrating Holy Eucharist* in the BCP which allows much more flexibility. In that case, an exploration could be made of words spoken during the pouring of the wine.

20. The BCP uses the word *celebrant* rather than *presider*. The terms may be considered interchangeable.

21. Episcopal Church, *Book of Common Prayer*, 362.

22. Episcopal Church, *Book of Common Prayer*, 362.

Receiving the Bread and Wine

Our re-signing of the distribution of the bread and wine first looks at how the bread is received. This is because the bread is, indeed, received first. Then the wine is received.[23]

In our imagined service, the assembly has gathered around the altar. For our purposes, envision an altar rail around three sides of the altar area. In this scenario, the presider would cycle around the altar rail, ripping pieces of bread off of the loaf and placing them in the outstretched hands of the worshipers. As this is done, the presider looks the communicant in the eye and says "The Body of Christ, the bread of heaven."[24] The communicant responds "Amen" before consuming the bread.

The reception of the wine can also be enhanced. When it is time to receive the wine, the communicant could inhale through the nose as the chalice is tipped toward them. As is well known, smell enhances taste. The communicant can also take a moment to savor the flavor of the wine, as well as its body, rather than simply swallowing.

Our imagined service has assumed that the communicants are receiving the wine directly from the chalice rather than by dipping their bread into the chalice (i.e., intinction). While this will be explored more in short order, for the moment let the reason for this be a practical one: most leavened breads do not hold up well to being dipped in liquid. If the congregation intincts, then the chalice will quickly become home to any number of small floating pieces of mushy, consecrated bread.

Not to be lost in this mental exercise is that, as mentioned above, bread and wine of a decent quality should be used. Wafers are inexpensive, yet basically tasteless. Additionally, a church can certainly save some money buying cheap jugs of port or boxed wine. Yet our offerings are to be first fruits, not last. A fine loaf of bread and a good bottle of wine will enhance someone's experience of most things, and Holy Eucharist is no exception.

After the Distribution

Once the distribution of the elements is complete, the leftover bread and wine need to be addressed. The paten with the remaining bread, and the chalice with the remaining wine (and the cruet if it is still on the altar, and

23. This is the normative order of reception in Christian churches. There are some churches, the Byzantine Catholic Church being an example, where the elements are received at the same time. The bread is mixed with the wine and then spooned into the mouth of the communicant.

24. Episcopal Church, *Book of Common Prayer*, 365.

hence contains wine that has been consecrated) are moved to the credence table. They will remain there, covered with a white linen, until the liturgy is over. The service finishes with a postcommunion prayer, blessing, hymn, and dismissal.

Meanings Strengthened and Accessible

Thus we have painted a scene of the Rite II Holy Eucharist that has (re)signed the use of the bread and wine. While being resigned to their foundational importance in the service, they have been re-signed so that they may be encountered afresh. Now the focus turns to determining what effect or impact that re-signing might have had. What existing meanings are strengthened? What new meanings might now become accessible?

The Breath of Christ's Body

First, there is a strengthened sense of the rhythmic creation and nourishment of the body of Christ. In the BCP, the fact that representatives of the congregation bring forward the bread and wine is a sign. One meaning that could be taken from that sign is that what is to become the body (and blood) of Christ comes from the body of Christ (the gathered community). That meaning, however, may be only narrowly accessible depending on the background of the worshiper. It is strongly dependent on a theological understanding of the congregation as the body of Christ.

Our imagined service augments this sign in several ways. The bread and wine begin in the midst of the people. When they are brought forward they are truly coming from *within* the body of Christ.

If the bread has been baked by parishioners, this idea is yet more strongly evoked. It is no longer that the bread is only coming physically from where the gathered community is. It is now also that the bread is coming creatively from that gathered community.

If the wine has been sourced from a local winery, then that wine carries within it the terroir[25] of that community. The wine was produced not only from the geographic and climatic conditions of that community, but by the sociological and spiritual conditions as well. The essence and uniqueness of that community is imprinted on that wine. It too comes from that community, even if not from the churchgoers themselves.

25. *Merriam-Webster*, s.v. "terroir," https://www.merriam-webster.com/dictionary/terroir, defines terroir as "the combination of factors including soil, climate, and sunlight that gives wine grapes their distinctive character."

The body of Christ (the community) offers that which becomes the body of Christ (the bread and wine), which then nourishes the body of Christ (the community). There is a beautiful, rhythmic relationship at play. In our worship, we who are gathered offer that which will be changed and returned to us as nourishment.

It is rather like breathing. We offer our breath, which is then transformed and returned to us in a form that nourishes us. From this perspective, Holy Eucharist becomes the breathing of Christ's body the church.

Actual Meal Characteristic

The Holy Eucharist traces its origins to the Last Supper. It was originally founded as an actual meal. It retained this characteristic in the early years of Christian worship.[26]

Over the centuries, however, the character of the Sacrament evolved. What started as an actual, largely casual meal with symbolic elements, became a highly choreographed and ritualized worship service, heavily-laden with symbolism.

The meal characteristic of Holy Eucharist has been largely lost due to changes in form, quantity, and time. In terms of form, a tin of wafers replaced a loaf of bread in the majority of the Christian world.

With regards to quantity, consider this: how often does one come to a service of Holy Eucharist physically hungry and leave feeling full? What was once a filling meal has been reduced to a nibble of bread and a sip of wine. The Holy Eucharist is rightly referred to as a foretaste of the heavenly banquet, but what is actually consumed barely qualifies as an hors d'oeuvre at said banquet.

In pondering time, think about the last meal you shared with others. How long did it last? How much of that time was taken up with actually eating? If that meal was like most, then the eating was probably drawn out over some time and interspersed with conversation.

This stands in sharp contrast to the eating and drinking that happens in the Holy Eucharist Rite II. The service consists mostly of talking, in the form of prayers, singing, and the sermon. Only at the end of the service does the eating and drinking actually happen, and it does so fairly quickly.

26. First Corinthians 11 and Acts 2 both provide glimpses into the character of ancient Christian worship. Additionally, the Didache suggests a meal has been eaten during worship by giving the following direction after providing instruction for what to say with the bread and the cup: "After you have taken your fill of food, give thanks as follows" (Did 10.1; Quasten, and Plumpe, *Didache*, 20).

The result is that today it is difficult to find the meal meaning in the liturgical event. Again, for the theologically minded, the sign is there in that bread and wine are, in fact, consumed. Yet, to the contemporary observer, what is going on at the altar might more resemble a wine tasting: you eat the cracker as a palate cleanser before sipping the wine and taking notes.

Our imagined service re-signs the bread and wine in a way that makes the meal meaning more accessible. To begin with, a loaf of bread is used rather than wafers. This is an important step toward recapturing a meal characteristic. Even the general instructions for the Roman Missal corroborate this point: "By reason of the sign, it is required that the material for the Eucharistic Celebration truly have the appearance of food."[27]

The bread and wine are also more prominent in the service. They are observable for a longer period of time, and are of a high quality when they are finally engaged. Additionally the worshipers gathering around the altar is evocative of a family gathering around the dinner table. While this does not totally restore the meal characteristic of the Holy Eucharist, it makes forays in that direction.

There is, as has been mentioned, a limit to the flexibility of the BCP. The order of service, for instance, cannot be changed. Thus doing something like interspersing the consumption of the bread and wine throughout the service, instead of building toward it, is beyond our reach in the present endeavor.

The recapturing of the meal characteristic is important for multiple reasons. First, it points the worshiper back to that which caused this service to exist in the first place—the Last Supper.

Second, it illuminates an important character of Christian community: that of intimacy. To share a meal, to break bread together as the expression goes, is an intimate act. When someone sees you eating, there is a vulnerability and a closeness there. Psalm 41:9 speaks obliquely to this in stating that "Even my best friend, whom I trusted, who broke bread with me, * has lifted up his heel and turned against me."[28]

Third, it reminds us that this Sacrament is something that nourishes us. We are fed, spiritually. As the BCP puts it, the benefits we receive in the Holy Eucharist are "the forgiveness of our sins, the strengthening of our union with Christ and one another, and the foretaste of the heavenly banquet which is our nourishment in eternal life."[29] The meal characteristic of the Holy Eucharist is the outward and physical sign of this inward and spiritual grace that is the heavenly banquet.

27. Catholic Church, *Roman Missal*, §320.

28. Episcopal Church, *Book of Common Prayer*, 642.

29. Episcopal Church, *Book of Common Prayer*, 859–60.

Matter Matters

Faith is not just a mental exercise. It does not only exist in our minds. Rather, Christianity is a very fleshy undertaking—it is embodied. God the Son was born as a human, blessing creation and inexorably connecting the divine and the worldly. As the Epistle to the Colossians puts it, "through him God was pleased to reconcile to himself all things, whether on earth or in heaven" (Col 1:20).

The upshot is that matter matters. The physical stuff of this reality has importance. This message can be lost in our worship when we reside primarily in our heads. Multi-sensory inputs and movement help to evoke that messaging.

The re-signing of the bread and the wine make the messaging of this meaning more robust as well. When the worshipers are aware that the elements were made in a sustainable way with ethically sourced ingredients, the connection to the created world is strengthened. The connection with our fellow created beings, who had a hand in the process of bringing the bread and wine into being, is strengthened as well. It helps the worshiper to, as the baptismal creed in the BCP phrases it, "strive for justice and peace among all people, and respect the dignity of every human being."[30]

CONCLUSION

This (re)signing of the bread and the wine makes certain meanings more accessible to contemporary worshipers. But why does that matter?

Consider the cycle of giving and receiving in the Holy Eucharist, what was termed the breathing of Christ's body. The re-signing of the bread has re-connected our modern day worship with worship at the dawn of the church. In the Ancient Near East in the first century, bread was largely a daily activity of families. Having parishioners make the bread for the Holy Eucharist reconnects us with our ancestors in the faith.

It also could have a redemptive quality. One of the activities that many people engaged in during the pandemic quarantine was that they learned how to make sourdough bread. Ostensibly cut off from the outside world, people started baking bread with just the yeast in the air, the flour in their pantry, the water in their faucet, and some salt. This new skill, borne out of a population's pain, can now be used to nourish the body of Christ.

Next ponder the reclamation of the meal characteristic of the Holy Eucharist. As stated, this promotes the closeness of those worshiping. It fosters

30. Episcopal Church, *Book of Common Prayer*, 305.

familial feelings. In a largely secular society that often barely has the church on its fringes, much less at its center, local congregations need stronger and deeper bonds of affection. In this day and age, if a congregation is not close knit, then it is unraveling.

Lastly, the matter of matter and why it matters. The rise of the digital age is drawing us away from the material world. We are in danger of becoming e-beings, who have lost their connection to the planet and to the real neighbors on every side of us. Understanding our incarnationality, not only in connection to the incarnation but also our intersection with the rest of creation (including the rest of humanity), can help to keep us grounded and aware of what is real and really important.

WHAT COMES NEXT

In one sense, there has been a disservice perpetrated in this chapter. Few comments were made about the worship space in our imaginary service. Everything that was envisioned was predicated on the idea that the architecture of the space would support it.

But what if it did not? What if the aisle was not wide enough to have the bread and wine be on a pedestal there in the midst of the congregation? What if the altar space was not configured in such a way that worshipers could gather around it?

To put it frankly, when it comes to making liturgical decisions, the building always wins. This makes a discussion of the semiotics of liturgical space not only prudent, but advisable. The next chapter addresses just that.

PART FOUR

"Breathing Space . . . and Time"

AUTHOR AND SEMIOTICIAN UMBERTO ECO wrote that titles "must muddle the reader's ideas, not regiment them."[1] For instance, of the title of his novel *The Name of the Rose*, he commented that it "rightly disoriented the reader, who was unable to choose just one interpretation."[2]

My hope is that the title of this part of the book, "Breathing Space . . . and Time," comes at you from an unexpected direction, raises for you the specter of several possible (and possibly competing) interpretations, and dis-orients you as to which interpretive path to follow.

To begin with, the term *breathing space* is well known. It dates to at least 1599 in English, and is "some time in which to recover, get organized, or get going."[3] It is, in fact, a time reference. Perhaps I am suggesting that this part of the book is meant as a time of respite?

Yet, the title then mentions time as something distinct from that term. This pushes back against a traditional interpretation of the term. How should the sign of this term "breathing space" be interpreted, then?

Perhaps the surface meaning is what is intended, and space should be understood to be physical rather than temporal. Breathing space could mean just that: a physical space within which to breathe. In choosing this meaning, then the title in its totality could refer to both a location in which to breathe, and the time spent breathing. This is, indeed, the case. Breathing space . . . and time.

The next two chapters deal with the semiotics of liturgical space and the semiotics of liturgical time, respectively. Chapter 9 will explore how the

---

1. Eco, *Name of the Rose*, 543.

2. Eco, *Name of the Rose*, 542.

3. *Merriam-Webster*, s.v. "breathing space," https://www.merriam-webster.com/dictionary/breathing%20space.

configuration of the worship space shapes meaning. Chapter 10 will explore different ways to understand liturgical time and how those understandings might inform our meaning-making.

This makes quite a bit of logical sense if one thinks about a liturgical event, like a worship service. It must happen somewhere (because it cannot happen nowhere). It must happen sometime (because it cannot happen outside of time). Space and time, which are easy to take for granted because of their ubiquity, must now be taken into consideration.

9

Breathing Space

"Close contact is generally defined as being within 6 feet for at least 15 minutes (cumulative over a 24-hour period)."[1]

AT FIRST GLANCE, IT looks like the opening quote of this chapter does not mention breath or breathing. Looks can be deceiving, however. This quote is implicitly about breathing, even though it does not specifically mention breath.

This is because the idea of *close contact* is inherently about breath. When two people are standing close to one another, the air one person exhales has a chance of being inhaled by the other person (and vice versa). The longer that those two people are close to one another, the better the chances that they will exchange air.

Thus, the CDCs definition of *close contact* does not really have anything to do with proximity, but rather probability. The number crunchers have crunched the numbers, and determined that if one has been within six feet of an infected person for fifteen minutes within a twenty-four hour period, the probability of becoming infected has crossed a threshold where certain actions are warranted.

The COVID-19 pandemic is all about breath. How do we protect ourselves from the breath of the infected, which spews millions of virions into the air around them with each exhalation? The answer, it turns out, has to do with air flow.

---

1. Centers for Disease Control and Prevention, "COVID-19."

Remember those two people standing close to each other? There is a much smaller chance that one will breathe the exhalation of the other if they are outside as opposed to inside. This is because air is flowing all around them, even if the day is not windy. If they are standing indoors, that air flow happens much less naturally.

This is why some churches turned to CO_2 meters during the pandemic. There is no way to determine the level of COVID particles in the air. But there is a way to determine how much carbon dioxide is in the air, and that can act as a proxy for the potential presence of COVID particles. The more someone exhales in an enclosed space, the higher the CO_2 level. The higher the CO_2 level, the higher the amount of COVID particles if that person is infected.

Hence this chapter's concept of breathing space. To stay with the pandemic illustration for a moment longer, the space you are in has a large effect on the spread of the virus. If a church, for example, has large windows that are open, then the chances of spreading the virus are lower than if the windows are closed. If a church has air filtration units running, then the chances of spreading the virus are lower than if there are no units. If a church is cavernous, and the service is short, then the chances of spreading the virus are lower than worshiping for a long time in a small space.

The point of all this pandemic postulating is this: in this age of COVID, the space that one is in literally increases or decreases one's chances of survival. This may sound alarmist, but that does not make it incorrect. COVID transmission comes down to air flow, and the space one is breathing in has a profound effect on that.

SEMIOTICS OF THE WORSHIP SPACE

Similarly, space has a profound effect on the semiotics of worship. How is liturgical semiotics impacted by the worship space? A good way to introduce this subject is with a few words from Richard Giles:

> When it comes to the environment of worship, we should never underestimate the influence of our building upon the way we think about God, about each other, and about the relative importance of the activity we have come together to engage in. Our places of assembly need to speak clearly to us of what we are about as the people of God. Such clarity is required, not only in sign and symbol, but also in the very form and shape of the

interior spaces, the texture of the walls and floors, the beauty and excellence of the artifacts we use, look at and handle.[2]

What story is your worship space telling? How is the layout of your liturgical space giving you signs to interpret?

This is an important area to explore because, as a wise liturgics professor once told me (and as was noted at the end of the last chapter), the building always wins.[3] This statement is terribly simple yet remarkably profound. If someone goes to a baseball game and is seated behind a pole, what do they do? They move to see around the pole. The pole does not move so they can see the game from their seat.

This is true for churches as well as baseball stadiums. During the liturgical renewal movement of the twentieth century, in many corners of the Christian world there was a discernible shift toward weekly Eucharist and increased participation on the part of the laity. This movement experienced frustration, however, because "the architecture of existing churches set up barriers—altars against the east wall, choirs placed between clergy and people, and spatial configurations that suggested a passive laity."[4] The building always wins.

This chapter explores different approaches to considering liturgical space. Some of these approaches are complementary and some are not. They all, however, give insight into the importance of the spaces we worship in and what they might mean.

Matching Architecture to Theology

As just mentioned, the disconnect between worship space design and theology of worship can cause frustration. This is true because, as Prya Parker has noted, "Venues come with scripts."[5] The script that comes with Carnegie Hall, for example, is very different from the one that comes with Carnegie Deli.

Much of the work in studying liturgical space has centered on this idea of script matching purpose. Or, to put it another way, of a worship space's architecture and theology being in harmony.

As an illustrative example, take the historical placement of the altar in Episcopal churches. It can speak volumes about how worship is understood.

2. Giles, *Re-pitching the Tent*, 57.

3. Unless, of course, one changes the building. This option is often cost-prohibitive, however.

4. Hefling and Shattuck, *Oxford Guide to the Book of Common Prayer*, 114.

5. Parker, *Art of Gathering*, 53.

Two placements will be considered: the altar against the wall and the altar pulled out from the wall.

In medieval times, the normative placement of the altar in churches was against the far wall (called the east wall in liturgical parlance). This placement is called east facing, because when the priest stands at the altar they are facing liturgical east. This placement was retained in Roman Catholic churches until the reforms coming out of Vatican II. While most Episcopal churches also changed their altar placements during the liturgical reforms of the last century, this arrangement persists in some Episcopal churches today.

The theology of worship implied by an east facing altar placement is that it is primarily the priest who is worshiping. What is done at the altar is some kind of semi-private act between the priest and God, and the rest of the congregation is simply observing. The height of the service for the laity in medieval times was the elevation of the consecrated host, and calls would come "Heave it higher, Sir Priest!" if the bread could not be seen.

Contrast this with an altar that is pulled out from the wall. The priest standing behind the altar, facing the people, creates a wholly different dynamic. On the one hand, the congregation has a clear view of everything happening at the altar. This increases the sense of involvement on the part of the laity.

On the other hand, this arrangement creates what Patrick Malloy calls a complex dichotomy. In other situations where one person faces a group (e.g., a courtroom, classroom, or theater), "the person facing the group holds power, talent, or knowledge to which the rest of the group must listen, attend, and perhaps even submit."[6] The prayers at the altar are addressed to God, and yet the priest is facing the people. This kind of liturgical crosswind can send mixed signals to those gathered.

In this example, the movement of the altar just a few feet has had a dramatic effect on the implied meaning of the liturgical event. Scrutiny of other parts of the liturgical space tells similar stories. The influence of the architecture on the meaning we find in the enactment of the liturgy is not to be underestimated.

Applying Greimassian Semiotics to Church Architecture

In chapter 5, a review of previous work in the area of liturgical semiotics was undertaken. Two of the scholars examined in that chapter were Gerard

6. Malloy, *Celebrating the Eucharist*, 40.

Lukken and Mark Searle. These two partnered on a book, published in 1993, that specifically dealt with the semiotics of church architecture.[7]

In the book, the authors apply the metalanguage of semiotician A. J. Greimas to the analysis of the Roman Catholic church of SS. Peter and Paul in Tilburg in the Netherlands.[8] In the first part of the book, Gerard Lukken gives an overview of Greimassian semiotics and tweaks that approach for architectural application. In the second part of the book, Mark Searle follows through on the practical application of that approach.

In a systematic way, both the exterior and interior of the church are analyzed. For each, form of expression and content are explored, and pains are taken to drill down through the different levels of what Greimas calls the *generative trajectory.*[9]

The exterior examination demonstrates "how the exterior of a building presents itself to be read by those who encounter it, [and] how the form of the expression is articulated with the form of the content to make such a reading possible."[10] The analysis finds that the outside of the building, while blending into the surrounding area, does not do much to proclaim its function. In short, it does not stand out in the neighborhood as a church.

The interior examination reveals that there is a tension in the space between *in the midst* and *beyond,* with traditional symbols of sacredness being both minimized and accentuated. It is in the "incessant negation and assertion of these oppositions that the identity of the church of SS. Peter and Paul is constituted."[11] It is also pointed out, and interestingly so, that this tension corresponds to the namesakes of the church themselves.

The Importance of Names

Our name marks our identity. In one sense they do that by having meanings in themselves. My last name, Olds, was originally Wold at the time of William the Conquerer. It referred to "someone who lived on any of the areas of open upland."[12]

In another sense, however, names mark our identities because they mark the most important parts of our lives. We are named at birth. We

7. First referenced in chapter 5.
8. This chapter does not recount the details of Greimassian metalanguage. The interested reader is encouraged to return to chapter 5 for a quick refresher.
9. The three levels are the Discursive, Surface, and Deep.
10. Lukken and Searle, *Semiotics and Church Architecture,* 95.
11. Lukken and Searle, *Semiotics and Church Architecture,* 128.
12. Ancestry, "Wold Family History."

are often named at baptism, with older liturgies commanding "Name this Child." It is still common for marriage to come with a renaming (for both parties in some cases).

When Jacob wrestled the angel at the Jabbok river (Gen 32:22–31), he was given a new name: Israel. Saul, persecutor of Christians, became Paul, apostle to the Gentiles. Simon becomes Peter, the rock upon which the church was built.

Every cardinal who is elected Pope chooses a new name. In monastic communities it is not uncommon to receive a new name when vows are made. Our name marks our identity.

Thinking semiotically, the same should be true of our churches as well. A church's name should be a sign, in some way, of that community.

One of the churches I have served is called St. Timothy's. Why? Because it began as an offshoot of St. Paul's Episcopal Church a few miles away. As Timothy was sent by the apostle Paul, so this church was sent by its mother church.

Another church I have served is called Church of the Holy Spirit. It was created as a merger of existing churches. The congregations felt the movement of, and guidance of, the Holy Spirit as they lived through the process of becoming one community. To honor that, they named their new church after the Holy Spirit, even though the community was worshiping in one of the existing buildings.

A church's name should have something to do with that community's identity. If that connection is not readily apparent, then work can be done to explore what the sign of that name might mean. I once served a church named St. John's. We endeavored to look at the writings of St. John to see what the hallmarks of a Johannine community might be. That gave us a focus and a path to grow along, as we sought to become more like what our name indicated.

A Different Perspective

An entirely different way to examine liturgical space is to explore where it is someone focuses their attention in the space. Human beings are predisposed to noticing things. It is how the best of our ancestors avoided being eaten by predators on the grassy plains of our species' remote past.

Every time we walk into a space, we take in everything that is around us.[13] We assess what we see, nearly instantly, and our attention is drawn somewhere. The prevailing theory is that whatever is salient, whatever

13. This presupposes that one is not face-down in their smartphone while walking.

stands out, is where our attention goes. We notice bright, shiny objects, so to speak.

A more semiotic-minded theory suggests instead that meaning plays the dominant role in guiding human attention. In a study published in *Nature Human Behavior*,[14] John Henderson and Taylor Hayes tracked the eye movements of people encountering various real world images for the first time. What they found was that "both meaning and salience predicted the distribution of attention, but that when the relationship between meaning and salience was controlled, only meaning accounted for unique variance in attention."[15]

We use our knowledge base to quickly determine what is meaningful in what we see and we look there. Assume, for example, that someone walks into a restaurant that they have never been in before for the first time. Given the multitude of restaurants that they have been in before, they will recognize the *restaurant-ness* of the place. Once that happens, their attention will go to where they find meaning in that room—perhaps the hostess station.

As has been an ongoing theme in our semiotic journey, it is apparent that humans think with what they already know. They see from where they currently stand. Their prior lifetime of experiences informs how they interpret new inputs. We are beings that are continually seeking meaning, and we generate that meaning based on what we have already experienced and found to be meaningful.

In his book *Being in the World*, Swiss psychologist Ludwig Binswanger wrote that "What we perceive are 'first and foremost' not impressions of taste, tone, smell or touch, not even things or objects, but rather, meanings."[16] Meaning is the driver of our perception. This only heightens the importance of the semiotic task.

Grounded in this understanding of how humans interpret the world around them, let us apply this to liturgical space. To begin that process, something needs to be added to the model: expectations.

The above study looked at eye movements based on being shown new images. In real world application, however, we are not being shown images. Rather, we are entering into spaces, and we have certain expectations of what those spaces will be like.

I may have never been in the church I am about to enter into. Yet, I have certain expectations about how that space will be configured since it

---

14. Henderson and Hayes, "Meaning-based Guidance," 743–47.

15. Henderson and Hayes, "Meaning-based Guidance," 743.

16. Binswanger, *Being in the World*, 114.

calls itself a church. I have an idea in my mind of what constitutes *church-ness*. Those expectations help to provide the contours of meaning for me.

There will be variance in those expectations based on the identity of the person observing and what their previous experiences of churches have been like. Yet some expectations will be almost universal. No one is going to expect a liturgical space to look like the inside of their local grocery store, for example.

If a liturgical space meets our expectations, then it is easier for us to locate that which has been meaningful to us in similar spaces in the past. If I see a room filled with pews, then I recognize the *church-ness* of the space. Being focused on the Holy Eucharist, my eye looks toward wherever it is that all the pews are facing, in order to find the altar. In finding a place of meaning for me in the liturgical space, I am better able to enter into an attitude of worship.

If a liturgical space does not meet our expectations, then it is harder for us to locate that which has been meaningful to us in a similar space in the past. If I see a room filled with auditorium seats, all facing a stage, then I may not recognize the *church-ness* of the space even if the space professes to be a church. This presents a barrier to my entering into an attitude of worship.

Yet this issue is not binary. It is also possible for a liturgical space to not meet expectations, but in a positive way. This involves the concept of ostranenie, coined by Russian formalist Viktor Shklovsky.[17] Ostranenie, also called defamiliarization, is to take something that is known and to make it strange. This allows someone to encounter the familiar something in a new way, and find new meaning in it.

Let us return to my walking into a room filled with pews. I recognize the *church-ness* of the space and my eye looks toward wherever it is that all the pews are facing. Instead of that being the far wall, however, I find that the pews all face toward the center of the room. It is there that I locate the altar.

This is disorienting, and strange. How do I make sense of this? Holy Eucharist, as represented by the altar, is still the focal point of the community's worship. It is where everyone faces when they worship. Yet that is not at the end of the room, it is in the center.

A new meaning that I might encounter in an otherwise very familiar liturgy is where I look for God. God at one end of the room is a God who is to be approached reverently and carefully. God at one end of the room is transcendent, reigning from on high. God in the midst of the worshipers is

17. Shklovsky, *Reader*, 80.

already present with us and within us. God in the midst of the worshipers is imminent, and accessible.

While that new meaning may have always been available to me, it was not made manifest in the worship in a way that guided me toward it. My understanding of God was comfortably ensconced in a familiar liturgical space. Once that space was defamiliarized, I was able to encounter it anew and apprehend fresh meaning.

Looking at Results

Another way to consider liturgical space is to explain its use by the results it generates.[18] This is to look at the function or purpose of something in order to better understand it. For example, why is a knife sharp? Because it was designed to cut things. Cutting is the function, or goal, of knives. Hence the sharpness.

Let us apply this kind of thinking to the worship space in three ways. First, what is the purpose of the space in general? Second, what is the purpose of the altar? Third, what is the purpose of the baptismal font?

What is the purpose of liturgical space in general? In answering this, it is useful to recognize that meaning is found in difference. If everything were the same, if reality was wholly homogeneous, then everything would be meaningless. The shadow proves the sunshine, if you will.

Equipped with this perspective, the purpose of liturgical space is to create difference. By identifying a liturgical space, one is also saying something about what is not liturgical space. The function of liturgical space is to mark off and set apart a place that is separate from another place. This place has its own purpose: to worship God.

In ye olden days, say pre-2020, this would have almost exclusively meant physical space, like a church building. It could also mean another physical space that is used as a liturgical space at certain times, like a church plant meeting in a school gymnasium. In current times, this could also mean a digital space, boundaries determined by links or login codes.

Questions that come from this type of rumination on liturgical space might be "What in this space speaks to its being set apart from other spaces?," or "In what ways (if any) does the beginning or end of the liturgical event connect with the boundaries of the liturgical space?"

Next, what is the purpose of an altar? The answer is simple: to sacrifice something. The sacrificial system in ancient Israel was highly detailed and ritualistic, with different kinds of sacrifices undertaken to accomplish

18. This is known as teleology.

different purposes. Yet, at a high level, the purpose of an altar remained the same. Altars are for sacrifice.

This can be hard to reconcile with modern day Christian worship. What are we sacrificing exactly, when a minister offers prayers at the altar? I once heard a Methodist minister exclaim "It's not an altar. Nothing is getting sacrificed!"

It depends on how one looks at it. The answer given in some liturgies is that what happens at the altar is a "sacrifice of praise and thanksgiving."[19] This concept of sacrifice keeps us connected with the activity of our forerunners in the faith.

There is another way to understand what is going on, however. We call the altar an altar, and that drives its purpose. Yet look at its shape. What else does it resemble?

Some would say a table. This makes sense as *communion table* is another name for this piece of liturgical furniture. The imagery of sharing food at the liturgical dinner table is rich.

The problem I see with this approach is where our question of purpose leads us. What is the purpose or goal of a dinner table? To be eaten at. In present day churches, this rarely if ever actually happens. To see the altar as a table means that it is not fulfilling its purpose.

Additionally, altars tend to be about a meter tall. In most churches, they are not the kind of table you could pull chairs up to, unless they were bar stools. In other churches, the communion table may be so small that you could only have an intimate dinner for two at it. Seeing the altar as a table, while theologically rich, does not seem to pass the function test.

What else might an altar resemble? I submit that we might consider this piece of liturgical furniture to be, not an altar, but a kitchen island. This might sound shocking. I hope, at least, that it sounds strange.

The altar, as mentioned, is tall. It is designed to be stood at, rather than sat around. It is free standing (at least in most churches). And what is its purpose? What is the altar used for, in a very practical sense? Food preparation. That thing that the priest stands at, saying prayers and fiddling with bread, wine, and water is a kitchen island.

What is the purpose of a kitchen island? To prepare food. In a formal sense, it is not where the meal is served. Rather, the food is taken to where it will be eaten—perhaps the dining room.

In worship, holy food and drink is prepared at the island. This preparation happens through words and gestures and the activity of the Holy Spirit.

19. Episcopal Church, *Book of Common Prayer*, 369.

Then that food and drink is taken to where it is served (be that at the communion rail, in the transept, or in the pews).

This transformation, not from altar to table, but from altar to island, opens up wonderful areas for theological reflection by the community. For instance, what might this imagery say about the point of Eucharist (to nourish us?) or the role of the clergy (to serve others?)? The jumping off points are many, and the potential new insights plentiful.

Lastly, we turn our attention to the baptismal font. What is the purpose, or goal, of the font? A natural answer might be to say "to baptize someone." This is misleading, however. It is the priest who does the baptizing. The purpose of the font is to collect and hold water.

This is a simple function. In fact, it is so simple that its subtlety belies its importance. This is because places that collect and hold water attract life.

Think of all the life that attaches itself to a pond. Think of the ancient human settlements that grew up around lakes. Think simply of the birds that are attracted to birdbaths.

Watering holes in Africa attract all sorts of life, even at great risk. It is a myth that the animals enter a sort of detente at the water hole and simply drink together. Attacks at water holes happen all the time. Yet, animals that are vulnerable come to the watering hole anyway. It is the only place to get what they need for life.

Similarly, the font attracts spiritual life. This is true in senses both immediate and broad. On a Sunday when there is a baptism, family and friends from all over are attracted to gather at the font for the activity that is to happen there.

More broadly, it is our own activity at the font that is the entry point into the church in many traditions. This is why the font in many churches is near the door, as a symbol of baptism being the entry point of the church. Often water is kept in that font near the door so that those who come in are able to reconnect with that water around which the Christian community has formed.

The Story Your Building Tells

Another approach to the semiotics of liturgical space seeks to observe what story the space is telling. What does this worship space say about the life of the worshiping community?

This approach will consider a few different elements of liturgical space in comparison between two Episcopal worship spaces. This will illuminate the variety of stories that spaces tell. For our purposes we will call these churches Alpha and Beta.

Entrances and Exits

How does one get into and out of the worship space? This journey, which bookends worship, tells a story.

At Church Alpha, there is one primary entrance into the worship space. You enter the narthex[20] from either the parking lot or the driveway. At this point you face a decision: do you turn and go into the worship space, or do you turn and go into the rest of the church (where you find offices, bathrooms, kitchen, parish hall, church school classrooms, etc.)?

At the end of the service you come back out the same door into the narthex. Then you decide whether you leave or continue into the other side of the building for coffee hour. The story being told is that worship is not connected with the rest of the life of the church. There is no flow, or journey, from one part of the church's life to the next. Life in Christ is compartmentalized, siloed, and discrete.

At Church Beta there are at least three different ways into the worship space, depending on where you parked your car or what direction you walked in from. Furthermore, there is an exit that takes you into the rest of the church without going back the way you came.

This story is about worship being the vehicle through which you journey into the rest of your life in Christ. Worship leads to fellowship. Worship leads to education. Worship even leads to administration.[21]

Jesus Has NOT Left the Building

There is a tradition in the Episcopal Church to keep some of the consecrated bread and wine in reserve in an aumbry.[22] This is done so that Communion may be brought to the homebound, those in hospitals, etc. There is typically a candle hung over where the reserve is kept. The candle is always burning. Having this ever-burning light above the reserve sacrament speaks to Christ's constant presence in the reserve sacrament.

At Church Alpha, the aumbry is in a recess in the wall in the sacristy. The sanctuary candle, which would normally be hung over the aumbry, is

---

20. Known in some churches as a vestibule.
21. Worship leads to the bathroom—every metaphor can be taken too far.
22. Known in some churches as a tabernacle.

instead in the back of the worship space hanging over a glass case containing a bible.

The story that this tells has two parts. With regards to the candle, it would seem to be saying that Christ is always present in the word of God. With regards to the aumbry, it says that Jesus is not always present in the worship space. Instead, Jesus is kept off to the side, or needs protecting. Jesus' presence is only important, or needed, when people are gathered for worship.

Church Beta's arrangement is much more traditional. The aumbry is recessed in the wall directly behind the altar, with the sanctuary candle hanging above. On the aumbry are written the Latin words "ego sum via veritas et vita" which translate as "I am the way, the truth, and the life," Jesus' words regarding himself in John 14:6.

The story being told here is that Christ is always present, not only in the worship space, but near the altar. Regardless of the presence of people for worship or not, Christ is in his holy temple.

Baptismal Font

Baptism has historically been the entrance into one's life in Christ. It is the entrance to the church. Thus, it has not been unusual to find a baptismal font in the back of a church rather than the front.

At Church Beta, the font is up front, to the side of the altar rail. This does not emphasize that baptism is the entrance to life in Christ. It does, however, speak to how closely connected the sacraments of Holy Baptism and Holy Eucharist are.

At Church Alpha, the font is in the back of the church. It is also mobile, however. This means that it could be re-positioned as needed—a rare instance of the building not winning. This means that it can be used to tell the story of baptism being the entrance to life in Christ or display the close connection of the sacraments.

When the Living Bury the Dead

Many churches have places where the dead are buried. A church might have a graveyard, or a columbarium in the undercroft. Or, as in the case of churches Alpha and Beta, there is a memorial garden.

At Church Alpha the memorial garden is right next to the worship space. It can be clearly seen from the church through the large clear windows in the sanctuary. There is a door that leads from the sanctuary directly out to the memorial garden.

Part of the story that is told here is that death is always within sight. Even in the midst of our worship, the dead are nearby. A portion of that great cloud of witnesses is only a head-turn away. We are mortal, and there is no escaping that fact. Yet we know that death is not the end of the story.

Another part of the story is that when it is time for the living to bury the dead, the faith family can journey together. For funerals, people have come in the one entrance and into the worship space. After the commendation, people move forward (not back) to process into the memorial garden. It is there, as part of the same gathering and worship service, that the departed is committed to the earth. Then those gathered continue forward (not back) and leave the memorial garden, following a flagstone path.

Church Beta's memorial garden is not visible from the worship space. It is accessible by a small gate and narrow path on the side of the building, providing access to what is essentially a hillside. It is a tight space that is nonetheless visually lovely.

The story told here is that of a fracture between life and death. One can worship without thought of the dead if one chooses because, as the old saying goes, out of sight out of mind. There is also not a natural progression from commendation to committal. The worshipers must come back out and wend their way toward the memorial garden. Most will not be able to join the presider in the garden, needing instead to look on from the above parking lot. There is not a fluid movement of the living journeying with the dead and then continuing onward into the world. The flow is stilted and disjointed and jagged.

When I Survey the Wondrous Cross

A large cross is a feature of many a worship space. The positioning and type of cross can say a lot about the space. A crucifix at the front tells a much different story than a Christus Rex at the back, for instance.

Church Alpha sports a very large wooden cross at the front of the worship space. The cross seems to preside high above and over the proceedings. It is plain and unadorned.

Part of the story told by this cross is that it is central to the entire proceedings. With unobstructed views of it as soon as one enters, the cross is always in the eye of the worshiper. Similar to how cosmic microwave background radiation is the constant universal reminder of the Big Bang, the cross is the constant universal reminder of why we are here (casually, causally, and existentially).

Another part of the story comes from what is not there. This is a large wooden cross—with no nail marks in it. A wooden cross with no nail marks is a cross that has never seen sacrifice. It has never seen the dirty, seamy, and unseemly on full display. It is a cross that has not been both the problem and the solution. It is a cross that has not been a cross.

The cross at Church Beta is not wooden and does not hang at the very front of the worship space. Instead, it hangs over the altar. Provocatively, instead of being made of wood, it is made of nails.

Part of the story told here is that it is at the foot of the cross that we make Eucharist. The one who once was nailed to a cross, has come down from that cross to be nourishment for the world. It was a descent that has lifted us all.

Another part of the story comes from the material. That the cross is made of nails, rather than wooden beams, puts the emphasis on the very real sacrificial nature of the cross. Our savior was on a cross, but it was the nails that kept him up there. They were what ensured that the task would be continued until it was finished.

A FINAL WORD

The arrangement of the worship space itself gives off signs that imply a story of that faith community's shared life. The architecture may speak to worship being the vehicle that leads to other parts of the Christian life, or deep meaning might be found in receiving the Eucharist in the shadow of a cross of nails. The stories told by our liturgical space can help us understand a narrative at play in the midst of a faith community that has gone unspoken.

10

Breathing Time

"Normal respiration rates for an adult person at rest range from 12 to 16 breaths per minute."[1]

IN A 1789 LETTER to French scientist Jean-Baptiste Le Roy, American founding father Benjamin Franklin quipped "in this world, nothing is certain except death and taxes."[2] To this list of certainties I would also add time.

Not that time is immutable. The work of Albert Einstein showed us that time is, in fact, plastic: the closer one travels to the speed of light, the slower time progresses.

Yet time is an inescapable certainty of our reality. Everything that we experience happens within time, and cannot happen outside of time. It takes time to read this sentence. It takes time to worship God. It takes time to breathe.

Hence, an exploration of the semiotics of liturgical time is necessary. Yet what do we mean when we speak of liturgical time? There are many possible answers, some obvious and some less so. This chapter explores seven ways of understanding liturgical time, and what reading the signs of those understandings might look like. This number was chosen because there are seven[3] parts of the respiratory system (i.e., nose, mouth, throat, voice box, windpipe, airways, and lungs).

1. Johns Hopkins Medicine, "Vital Signs," para. 10.

2. Incidentally, the phrase did not originate with Franklin's letter. The phrase dates back to at least 1716, where it was used in the play *The Cobbler of Preston*.

3. This number is a matter of convenience. There could be 8 parts of the respiratory system, for example, if you distinguish between large airways (bronchi) and small

LITURGICAL CALENDAR

The most traditional way to understand liturgical time is to view this as a reference to the liturgical calendar. The liturgical calendar arranges feasts and seasons of the church year by the overlaying of two cycles. The first cycle, called the temporal cycle, is based first and foremost on the date of Easter. Easter occurs on the first Sunday after the first full moon following the spring equinox. Once this date is set, then (in conjunction with knowing that Christmas will always be December 25th) the seasons of the church year can all be planned out: Advent, Christmastide, the Season after the Epiphany, Lent, Easter, and the Season after Pentecost. The second cycle, called the sanctoral cycle, overlays the celebrations of saints or various events on top of the temporal cycle.[4]

On one level, the story told by the liturgical calendar is both obvious and glorious: Jesus Christ. Our yearly journey through the liturgical calendar takes us through the birth, life, death, resurrection, and ascension of Jesus Christ (and the birth of the church at Pentecost and the story of the early church to boot!). It also reminds us of people and events important to the faith after church history extended beyond the biblical witness. It is beautiful, and holy, and to be treasured.

On a different level, however, there are at least two other stories being told. One story is of the primacy of Easter. The rest of the calendar comes together after the date for Easter has been determined. It is our starting place, our beginning point, as followers of Christ.

This implies that there is nothing of more foundational importance to our understanding of Jesus than his resurrection. It is the cornerstone around which the rest of the calendar is built. Perhaps it is the cornerstone around which the rest of our faith is to be built, as well. It is as Paul wrote, "If Christ has not been raised, your faith is futile and you are still in your sins" (1 Cor 15:17).

The other story that the liturgical calendar is telling us is that ours is a living faith of the dead, not the dead faith of the living. This requires a bit of unpacking, and has to do with the evolution of the calendar over time.

The liturgical calendar honors our history, tradition, and roots. The reason that Easter is a movable feast is because Passover is a movable feast in Judaism. Passover always begins on the fifteenth day of the Hebrew month of Nisan. While that is a fixed date, the Hebrew calendar is tied to the lunar

airways (bronchioles).

4. There is no unanimity among the Christian family on any of this. Various churches manifest the sanctoral cycle differently, or do not recognize it at all. Even the date of Easter is a difference between Eastern and Western Christianity.

cycle. So that fixed date actually occurs on a different day on the Gregorian calendar each year. Easter's echoing of the movable feast of Passover is a sign that, while distinct from our Jewish brothers and sisters, we still honor and respect the taproot from which Christianity sprung.

Similarly, over the centuries, the calendar has evolved. It was not written all at once and followed on forever. It has been changing: this season lengthened, that celebration added, etc. This process continues today, for example, with some advocating for a portion of the Season after Pentecost to be made into a season for Creation Care.

This evolution, this story of change, is a sign that our faith is a living tradition. It is the living faith of the dead, not the dead faith of the living. This makes eminent sense, since we serve a living Lord.

TIME WITHIN THE SERVICE

A second way to understand liturgical time is to think about it as the time spent during the liturgical event.

That time can be considered as a whole. In a positive sense, it is that *hour of power* between the prelude and the dismissal when the people of God gather for worship. In a less positive sense, it is *the most segregated hour in America* as Christians of different denominations and ethnicities separate themselves off from those who do not believe, think, speak, or look like them.

That time can also be considered in a more granular sense. How is time being used in the liturgical event? Where is more time being spent? Where is less? How different churches answer this question tells different stories.

Taize

Take as an example the ecumenical community of Taize. This monastic community, founded by Brother Roger in the 1940s, has become a pilgrimage destination for youth. Every year, thousands of young people from around the world come to Taize to live together in a community grounded in multiple prayer services a day.

With youth being a desiccated demographic in so many churches today, that Taize is packed with them is a wonder. What is the secret to their worship? Is it praise bands and laser lights? Is it charismatic preaching? Is it spectacular faith healings? No. It is silence.

At the center of each Taize worship service is a solid block of silence. Gobs of silence. Minutes of silence. It is the center of their worship gravity, around which everything else revolves.

Imagine if you will, five thousand people in a sanctuary. All around you is a sea of humans, and all you hear is your own breathing. As the psalmist wrote, "Be still, and know that I am God!" (Ps 46:10).

The story here is a quiet one, yet it speaks volumes. Without the clang and din of sound entering our ears, we have a better chance of hearing the Spirit that indwells, that personage of God who "intercedes with sighs too deep for words" (Rom 8:26).

Vineyard Vignette

Many churches, rather than spending their time in silence, spend their time on preaching. A narrative which illustrates this is my experience attending a Vineyard church in California for a few months around the turn of the century.

The Vineyard Movement started in the 1970s, originally being a church plant from Calvary Chapel in Costa Mesa, California. Today the denomination has on the order of two thousand four hundred churches scattered across ninety-five countries. It was in late 2002 that I first wandered into the school where a Vineyard church was worshiping, somewhere near Palo Alto in Silicon Valley.

The first part of the service was all praise music (with bagels and coffee). The last half to two-thirds of the service was the sermon. It was clear that the sermon was the main focus of the liturgical event. Not only is it what the service led up to, it was also where most of the time in the service was spent.

It was also clear that the sermon was very focused on the Bible. For instance, the sermon for two weeks was spent reading the Letter of Paul to the Romans. That was it.

The story told by this kind of liturgical time is about words, and the Word. The Word in song. The Word in Scripture. The Word as it is processed in your brain. It recalls the words from Jeremiah, "Hear the word of the Lord, all you people of Judah, you that enter these gates to worship the Lord" (Jer 7:2).

Another Angle

To return to the liturgical event that has been the primary object of interest all along, let us consider the use of time in the Holy Eucharist Rite II. The service is broken into two parts: the liturgy of the word and the liturgy of the table. The liturgy of the word, which comes under the heading of "The Word of God" in the BCP, consists of several parts (i.e., Scripture readings, sermon, Nicene Creed, confession, and prayers of the people). The liturgy of the table (referred to as "The Holy Communion") consists of prayers at the altar and then the distribution of the elements.

On the whole, the distribution of time between the two parts of the service is somewhat balanced. The liturgy of the word typically takes longer, but not disproportionately so. Also, the service leads toward the altar. In a similar way to how silence is the center around which a Taize service revolves, the liturgy of the altar is the destination of the liturgical journey undertaken.

This kind of liturgical time tells a story of the Anglican desire to have their cake and eat it too. We want a lot of Scripture (i.e., a normative Holy Eucharist service will have four readings: a psalm selection, a Hebrew Bible reading not from the Psalms, a Gospel reading, and a New Testament reading not from the Gospels). We want sacrament. We want various kinds of prayer. And we want some hymns thrown in for good measure. The result is a little bit of a lot of different things, rather than a deep dive on any one thing. A generous reading would be that variety is the spice of spiritual life, and it helps us to be well-rounded. A not so generous reading might be that Anglicans become a jack of all spiritual trades, but a master of none.

DAY AND TIME OF THE SERVICE

A third, and somewhat less obvious, way to think about liturgical time is as the day and time at which the liturgy takes place. The normative worship time for most of the Christian family is Sunday morning, and the Episcopal Church is no exception. Let us consider each of the axes which locate our worship in turn.

Sunday

The centrality of Sunday is clearly articulated in *Title II. Canon 1: Of the Due Celebration of Sundays* of the church's canons, which reads as follows:

All persons within this Church shall celebrate and keep the Lord's Day, commonly called Sunday, by regular participation in the public worship of the Church, by hearing the Word of God read and taught, and by other acts of devotion and works of charity, using all godly and sober conversation.[5]

The denominations of today did not invent Sunday worship, however. Sunday has been the normative day of worship for Christians since the church was young. Justin Martyr, writing in about 155 CE, attests to this when he pens that "Sunday, indeed, is the day on which we all hold our common assembly because it is the first day on which God, transforming the darkness and [prime] matter, created the world; and our Savior Jesus Christ arose from the dead on the same day."[6]

While having worship on Sunday can be interpreted theologically, what might we say about it semiotically? While work patterns in mid-twenty-first-century America are in flux, it is still reasonable to suggest that the majority of people do not work at their regular job on Sunday. For many, it may be the only day during the week that they can sleep in.

Sunday, for many, is a free day. It is a day to devote to non-job related activities. Maybe the grocery shopping gets done, or the laundry. Or maybe all the chores were finished up on Saturday, and Sunday really becomes a secular sabbath day—a day to relax and enjoy.

For a generation of people who were not raised on the idea of spending their free time (an increasingly rare and precious currency in twenty-first-century lives) at church, the notion of getting up and going to worship is an entirely foreign concept. The story of Sunday worship in America is that it is an increasingly counter-cultural choice.

Morning

How to interpret the sign of morning as the normative worship time? As a starting point, consider that morning is when the sun rises. Light waxes and darkness wanes. Nocturnal things go to sleep and diurnal things wake up.

Human beings are diurnal animals. We are engineered to be awake when it is light out, and asleep when it is dark. In this sense, Sunday morning worship says that we are worshiping God at our best, biologically speaking. We are refreshed from sleep and offering God the first fruits of our wakefulness.

5. Episcopal Church, *Constitution & Canons*, 93.
6. Justin Martyr, *First Apology*, ch. 67.

On the one hand, we are at our best in the morning. On the other hand, the morning can be the most dangerous time to be human. This kind of paradox is a microcosm of our lived existence in the wider world. We are the dominant species on the planet. Our technological innovations and move toward globalization have raised the global standard of living, with over a billion less people living in poverty today than did in 1990.[7] The future looks bright.

Yet at the same time, we are in extreme danger. A global climate crisis. Mass extinction of species. The loss of "half the planet's topsoil in the last fifty years."[8] The future looks bleak.

In the midst of this jarring juxtaposition we bring ourselves to God. We seek to bring some semblance of sense to this mystery called life. We seek meaning. We seek solace. We offer praise. We offer ourselves.

What story does liturgical time as morning worship tell us? It tells us that this is life.

WHAT YEAR IS IT HERE?

The first memory I have of being in a church is when I was probably not quite five years old. I remember walking from the sanctuary to the Sunday School room. I was young, and my family did not attend that church for very long, so that is also my only childhood memory of that church. My parents stayed in the sanctuary, with its pews resplendent in lime-green upholstery that was incredibly appropriate to the decade. I followed the teacher to the Sunday School room, which I also recall being cold.

About 25 years later I returned to that church. I was in my first year of seminary, and while visiting my hometown I decided to visit the location of my first church memory. I grew up in Central Upstate New York, and so I had a decent chance of finding the church unlocked and open to visitors even outside of worship or office hours.

This was indeed the case, and I passed through the narthex and into the sanctuary. It was there that I beheld, in all their threadbare radiance, the very same lime-green pew cushions. As I looked around, it was very much as if I walked back in time.

Another way to interpret the concept of liturgical time is to consider the question "what year is it here?" This can of course apply to the fashion statements being made by the decor. That is the low-hanging fruit in this endeavor, though.

7. WorldVision, "Global Hunger Facts."
8. Sweet and Chironna, *Rings of Fire*, 7.

After all, some anachronism is baked into most churches. We light candles. We play an organ. We sign old hymns. We read from an ancient book. We are intentionally recalling past events, and so there is a certain "past-ness" that comes part and parcel of being Christian. The Episcopal Church is certainly like that. And the Episcopal Church looks positively cutting edge compared to the "past-ness" displayed by the Eastern Orthodox!

There is a more semiotic way to understand the question of what year it is in a church, however. This would be to read the signs of where authority is residing in the liturgical event. Exploring this requires a quick summation of the journey humanity has been making from premodern to modern to postmodern as a species.

The hallmark of the premodern worldview is an acceptance of authority. Whether it be god or king, the premodern mindset finds its meaning, power, and authority from above. Premodernism is a top down approach to structuring society. Think about the ancient kingdoms.

The rejection of this plea to authority was to place primary importance instead on the self. This is the hallmark of the modern outlook. Whatever our own rational minds can accomplish, deduce, and discern is what should be given the most weight. Modernism looks to reason for meaning-making. Think of the Enlightenment and the move toward rationalism.

This was in turn rejected by the postmodern view. The postmodern worldview sees the oppression and communal brokenness of both premodern and modern societal configurations. To move away from this, the postmodern approach has been to disregard and unravel any system that has failed to protect people from favoritism or oppression. It places its emphasis on the view from the bottom up. Look at the world around us in the twenty-first century.

I see this evolution from premodern to modern to postmodern as representing a shift in where authority is placed. In premodernism, that authority was placed in an outward place (i.e., God, emperor, or king). In modernism, the authority was brought inward and placed on the self. In postmodernism, the authority is distributed to include everyone, because all our voices are supposed to have equal weight. The authority becomes a communal one.

With this view of authority, the arc of history looks less like a series of tussles and tactical responses to specific situations, and instead an overarching metanarrative that has a flow to it. Authority first moved from without to within us as individuals. Then it moved again (or is in the process of doing so since we are still transitioning from modernism to postmodernism) from each of us as individuals to us collectively as a civilization.

With that understanding we can look more specifically at how authority manifests in the liturgical event. In the Holy Eucharist Rite II service, in one sense, the authority resides with the priest.[9] It is the priest that says the most words in the service. Only a priest can enact the portion of the liturgy that takes place at the altar. Only a priest can bless. This suggests that the liturgy has a premodern character.

In another sense, however, authority is more distributed. In the Episcopal tradition, it is not solely a priest that is required to celebrate Holy Eucharist. The liturgy clearly has a place for the People. If there are no people gathered to respond, then the priest cannot proceed through the liturgy. An Episcopal priest, by him or her self, cannot make Eucharist.

In addition to this, authority in the liturgy is reflected in who has the power to make decisions about the liturgy. A quick glance suggests that this authority resides only with the priest, who has canonical authority to make decisions about how worship is enacted. Yet, it is the General Convention of the Episcopal Church that approves liturgies for use.

Without the consent of the General Convention, there would have been no new Book of Common Prayer in 1979. Without consent of the General Convention, no new liturgies would be made available for trial use and eventually authorized for use throughout the church. And the General Convention is made up of both laity and clergy. In this sense, the ultimate authority in the liturgy, the reason in fact that there is liturgy at all, rests collectively in the Episcopal Church.

This perhaps suggests a postmodern expression of authority. The power resides collectively with the church. The priest still exercises authority within the enactment of the liturgy. Yet it is perhaps best to see the priest as being the steward of the power and authority that resides with the General Convention of the church.

PERCEPTION OF LITURGICAL TIME

Another way to understand liturgical time is how we perceive the passage of time in the liturgical event. We have all had the experience of time seeming to pass quickly or slowly. Two hours exploring a museum could feel like a whole day, whereas two hours spent focused on a particular task could feel like almost no time at all.

While science does not know for sure why our perception of time changes, one theory that has gained traction is the Perceptual Theory of

9. Everything that follows for a priest also applies to a bishop. All Episcopal bishops were once priests, and so can perform the functions of priests should they choose.

time. This theory postulates that the perceived "speed of time seems to be largely determined by how much information our minds absorb and process—the more information there is, the slower time goes."[10] The more voluminous and complex the information the brain is trying to process, the more the passage of time seems to slow.

This, incidentally, might be why children often perceive time as moving more slowly than adults—children experience the world in a much more intense, exciting, vibrant, detailed way than adults do. With so much being processed, and vividly so, time seems to pass more slowly. As we grow older, less things are new and exciting, and we notice fewer details. So we perceive time to move more quickly.

What might time seeming to pass more slowly or quickly in worship mean for us? How might we read those signs?

Let us start with the feeling that time is passing more slowly. Going by the Perceptual Theory, this would mean that the brain is taking in and processing more information. A liturgical event that is sensory-rich may well present the worshiper with the opportunity to experience time more slowly.

After all, when enacted in its fullness, an Episcopal service of Holy Eucharist does engage all the senses. The taste of the bread and wine. The smell of the incense. The light of the candles, and the colors of the vestments and paraments. The sound of music, prayers, and preaching. The touch of passing the peace. The movement of standing, sitting, kneeling, and walking up and down the aisle. Even without screens, worship can be a highly sensory endeavor.

Next, let us turn to the feeling that time is passing more quickly. This time the Perceptual Theory would suggest that the brain is taking in and processing less information. The Episcopal tradition might accentuate this as well, oddly enough. From one week to the next, while there is some variation, Episcopal worship services tend to be very consistent. Over time, participation in them can become rote. This leads to less being noticed and less processing of what is going on by the brain. This could lend toward the perception that time is passing more quickly.

Connecting these dots tells a story that happens to fit the experience of some worshipers over time. When someone is new to the Christian faith, they are like children (and I mean this in a positive sense). Everything, including sensory-rich worship, is new to them. They are taking it all in and processing every detail.[11] They can become lost in the experience, and time can be perceived to stretch.

---

10. Taylor, "Why Does Time?," para. 20.

11. This casts Jesus' announcement to receive the kingdom of God as a little child (Mark 10:15) in an intriguing light.

As someone continues to mature in their faith, they can encounter worship less like a child. Less wonder, less noticing, less engagement, less processing. Rather than becoming lost in the experience, they come to know the experience inside and out, and so time can seem to move more quickly. This may help explain why it is not unusual to traverse through a period of spiritual dryness as one's faith matures.

THE TAPESTRY OF STORIES

The concept of a timeline is pretty well known in popular culture. It is the idea that time can be thought of as a straight line. That line stretches back to the beginning of all things, and it stretches forward to the end of all things. Every movie or television show that talks about time travel references this notion.

To ruminate on this image of time as a line, consider that a line resembles a thread. In the same way that time could be visualized as a line, it could be visualized as a thread. This slight sideways shift opens up a new way of envisioning the liturgical event, and how we interpret time as a whole.

Everyone is living out of their own context. We experience everything from our own perspective, as individuals. This goes for our experience of time as well.

While we may be all living in the same time thread (or time line), we experience time as all our own. Imagine that each individual lives out their own time thread. Then, all of our time threads together is what makes up a braided time cord, of a kind.

With this new vision for how we interpret time, let us turn our thoughts to worship. We each enter into the liturgical event, living our time thread. Then, in our joint praise of God, our collective threads weave together into a tapestry of worship.

This tapestry tells a story, like the medieval tapestries of old. The time threads of our individual stories intersect and intertwine in a special way with the Greatest Story Ever Told. That tapestry would be different without our thread. That story would be different. Our time thread matters. Our story matters. God loves us that much.

KAIROS VS. CHRONOS

Yet another way to understand liturgical time depends on what kind of time we are talking about. Is it *chronos* or *kairos*? The interplay of these two Greek words in the liturgical event is insightful. They are both translated in the New Testament as time, yet their definitions are distinct.

Chronos (Χρόνος) is an indefinite period of time during which some activity or event takes place, a point of time consisting of an occasion for some event or activity, or a period during which something is delayed.[12] If you are thinking about minutes, weeks, or a specific day and time, you are thinking in terms of *chronos*. Hence, our English word chronology.

Kairos (χαιρός) is a point of time or period of time with the implication of being especially fit or appropriate for something, and without emphasis on precise chronology. It could also be a period characterized by some aspect of special crisis.[13] When one senses that the time is ripe, or that it is the opportune or decisive moment for something—this is *kairos*.

In the Bible, we see this distinction in action. When Matthew 21:34 mentions that "when the harvest time had come, he sent his slaves to the tenants to collect his produce," it is a reference to *kairos*. The harvest happens when the crop is ready, not on a fixed date. When Matthew 2:7 states that "Herod secretly called for the wise men and learned from them the exact time when the star had appeared," however, the reference is to *chronos*.

Our society has moved over the generations from a *kairos*-oriented way of living to a *chronos*-oriented one. Think about the early days of this nation, during the time of westward expansion. There was less specificity around chronology and more attention paid to opportune times.

When did you get news (and the mail)? When the stagecoach came through. When did you get that toothache taken care of (if the barber could not do it)? When the traveling dentist came through. When did you go to church? When the circuit rider was in town.

Things happened at the appropriate time. Things took place when the time came that everything was prepared for those things to happen. It was a life lived more in touch with *kairos*.

Nowadays, *chronos* rules nearly the entirety of our lives. Whether through the alarm clock, or the calendar, or the appointment reminders that buzz on our phones, we are a regimented and regulated people.

So how does this find expression in the liturgical event? *Chronos* certainly finds expression in the fixed time of worship. The service starts at 9:30 a.m. on Sunday, for example. There may also be an element of *chronos* in some people's expectations on the length of the service (or the length of the sermon!).

---

12. BDAG 1092.

13. BDAG 497.

If *kairos* is all about things happening at the appropriate time, then the Easter Triduum is an example of liturgical *kairos*. In Episcopal circles, this typically refers to Maundy Thursday, Good Friday, and Holy Saturday. While that does carry a certain chronological specificity, the nature of those three days, liturgically speaking, is actually kairological.

This is because these three holy days are actually one liturgical event. In the Episcopal Church, it is traditional to strip the altar at the conclusion of the Maundy Thursday service and reserve consecrated bread and wine so that it may be used at the Good Friday service. The congregation then departs in silence.

The liturgy for Good Friday picks up where Maundy Thursday leaves off, with the ministers entering in silence and without the usual opening words. The liturgy also lacks a dismissal, implying that the liturgical event has again not reached completion.

There is a kairotic flow to these days. The time is not appropriate for celebrating Jesus' resurrection until the other events of Holy Week are recalled. That being said, the triduum's reality is a contemporary experience. The three days of the triduum, leading to Easter Sunday, are a kind of Christian Passover. As our Jewish brothers and sisters "hold their passover festival in the belief that the exodus event is now present, so Christians hold their passover celebrations in the belief that Christ in his redemptive activity lives now in the liturgical assembly.[14]

On a less grandiose scale, the order of service for a regular Sunday speaks to *kairos* as well. In most churches, the flow of the service is purposeful rather than random. To use a simple example, it is intentional that corporate confession takes place before absolution. Otherwise, people would be forgiven before they repent of their sins. That would evidence a very different theology than what we find in 1 John 1:9, "If we confess our sins, he who is faithful and just will forgive us our sins and cleanse us from all unrighteousness."

In Holy Eucharist Rite II worship, the flow of the service leads to the reception of the Sacrament. What takes place leading up to that point prepares the worshiper for that reception. The word of God is proclaimed. God is praised. Sins are confessed. Prayers are given for the church and for the world. The Nicene Creed is stated (and in that stating, assented to).

There is also something critical to the *kairos* of the service, the appearance of which belies its importance. It is the passing of the peace.

---

14. Komonchak et al., *New Dictionary of Theology*, 298.

Passing the Peace

The action of passing the peace in Christian worship is a practice that fulfills the scriptural exhortation that Christians greet one another with "a holy kiss."[15] A more salient biblical reference appears at the end of 1 Peter: "Greet one another with a kiss of love. Peace to all of you who are in Christ" (1 Pet 5:14). The advantage of the 1 Peter passage is that it directly connects the kiss shared between Christians with the concept of peace.

This is helpful, because the kiss of peace has transformed over time. Initially, this peace was given in public, and regardless of different social standing among those kissing. This was seen as scandalous and led to wild rumors about what must have gone on in Christian worship gatherings. Clement of Alexandria put it this way, "We should realize that the unrestrained use of the kiss has brought it under grave suspicion and slander."[16]

The kiss eventually moved to being used only within the context of worship, and in a ritualized way. In the West, the traditional practice "was for the person giving the Peace to place his hands on the shoulders of the recipient, who in turn placed his hands on the elbows of the giver, each bowing their heads towards each other."[17]

In most churches today, the exchange of the peace has typically become a very informal affair. The action usually consists of handshakes or hugs, and a verbal exchange of any kind. In more reserved congregations it may be a nod and a wave.

In many churches, passing the peace has become a foretaste of the heavenly coffee hour. Kibitzing and personal updates push out the ritualized passing of the peace of Christ.

While the form of passing the peace has changed from a kiss on the lips to a hug or a handshake, the point of the action has not. In simplest terms, passing the peace causes people to engage one another prior to receiving Communion. It is an action that satisfies the instruction of Matthew 5:23–24, "So when you are offering your gift at the altar, if you remember that your brother or sister has something against you, leave your gift there before the altar and go; first be reconciled to your brother or sister, and then come and offer your gift." To pass the peace of Christ to another is to reconcile yourself to them prior to you both receiving the body and blood of Christ. It is a preparatory act of Christian unity.

15. Look at the end of Romans, 1 Corinthians, 2 Corinthians, and 1 Thessalonians.

16. Barry, *Lexham Bible Dictionary*, s.v. "Kiss." (quoting *Paedagogus* 3.81.1–82.1).

17. Cross and Livingstone, *Oxford Dictionary of the Christian Church*, 937.

This is *kairos* in action. When is it an appropriate time to receive the Sacrament? When is the time ripe for the body of Christ (the congregation) to receive the body of Christ (the bread and wine)? When that same body is reconciled and at peace with itself.

Worshiping with a *chronos* mindset is to be worried about what you are doing after the service. Are we ahead? Are we behind? How does this specific time, set aside for worship, fit into all the other *chronos* events of the day? It is to feel the burden of responsibility for this segment of time to be executed correctly.

Worshiping with a *kairos* mindset is to be carried along in the flow of the service. It is to know that each thing that is being done, while discrete, is part of the whole. Each prayer, or silence, or movement, or song, is happening at the opportune and appropriate time for God to be worshiped as it is meet and right so to do. It is to know that this worship is in God's hands rather than ours.

To understand liturgical time as a *kairos* event is an invitation to see the rest of our time through a similar lens.

CONCLUSION

Liturgical time is a bit of an enigma. On the one hand, it is ubiquitous in our worship because worship cannot happen without it. On the other hand, it resists a pat definition. In this chapter, seven different ways to understand liturgical time have been explored. There may well be other ways to view it, however. To the liturgical semiotician who takes the time to reflect on time, there are undoubtedly many more insights waiting to be revealed.

PART FIVE

"Deep Breathing Exercises"

THE LIFE EXPECTANCY IN the United States is seventy-nine years old. At about twenty thousand breaths per day, that works out to upwards of six hundred million breaths in the average lifetime. And most of those are done without ever thinking about it.

When we do think about breathing, when we do it intentionally rather than letting it happen autonomically, the benefits are verifiable. It can reduce stress, increase alertness, and boost the immune system. One study found that twenty minutes of intentional breathing significantly reduced levels of a protein linked to stress.[1]

There are a myriad of ways to breathe intentionally. Someone can do Yogic pranayama, military box breathing, belly breathing, or any other number of options. The point, however, is that breathing on purpose is a help. This fifth and final part of the book provides some practices, some deep breathing exercises, that the liturgical semiotician can engage in order to help their efforts.

Chapter 11, "Breathprints," is about the semiotician finding their unique identity. To this point, liturgical semiotics has been practiced from my perspective, which is decidedly Episcopal. This chapter helps someone to develop their own approach and practice of liturgical semiotics.

Chapter 12, "Breath Marks," is about providing jumping off points for further semiotic engagement. Various worship services are presented, and a point of semiosis is introduced for each. These points are then associated with a story from the Gospels, and some connections are made. The reader is left with insights to consider and questions to ponder.

---

1. Twal et al., "Yogic breathing when compared to attention control reduces the levels of pro-inflammatory biomarkers in saliva: a pilot randomized controlled trial," Results.

I I

Breathprints

*"Researchers have shown that exhaled human breath contains a charac-
teristic molecular 'fingerprint.' Stable, specific 'breathprints' unique to an
individual exist and may have applications as diagnostic tools in personal-
ized medicine."*[1]

DNA IS THE GOLD standard in terms of being a unique identifier for a human
being. Fingerprints are the classic example of how to determine one person's
unique identity, being used as evidence in criminal cases since 1910. As it
turns out, one's breath is also a unique identifier. Someone's specific body
chemistry finds expression in their exhalation. Top to bottom, stem to stern,
there are no two people who are quite alike. While we are all created in the
image of God, each of us is a distinct and unique child of God.

This uniqueness does not mean that learning how someone else does
something is a bad thing. Indeed, imitation is the sincerest form of flattery.
In fact, this was how the education of rabbis happened in first-century Judea.

The age of adulthood for Jewish males was fourteen. It was at that time,
if they were passionate about studying Torah, that they would find a rabbi
to study under. In the rabbinical tradition, a "learner" or "student" (תלמיד,
tlmyd) attached himself to a rabbi (literally "my great one," with the additional meaning of "teacher" or "master") or to a movement.[2]

First, the prospective student would need to convince the rabbi to
take them on as a student. If they were successful in that attempt, then they

1. ETH Zurich, "Exhaled Breath," summary.
2. Barry, *Lexham Bible Dictionary*, s.v. "Disciple."

would move in with the rabbi. At that point the student would begin learning by watching the rabbi's every move. How the rabbi spoke, taught, and argued—the student attempted to absorb every nuance of their *great one*. If the rabbi had a distinctive gait, or any identifying tick or mannerism, the student emulated it. It was said that the identity of a student's teacher could be deduced by observing the habits and mannerisms of the student.

This continued until the age of thirty. It was at this point that the learner became a teacher and was able to take on students in their own right. And thereby the cycle perpetuated itself.

To borrow this image, thus far I have been the rabbi and the reader has been the student. The student has been learning liturgical semiotics by watching how I do it. How I go about manifesting BREATHE, GASP, and RASP. How I make decisions about which aspects of the liturgy to focus on, and which to pass by. How I choose which cultural context to read and what to do with the results.

For the student to do liturgical semiotics by imitating me can provide only limited benefit though. This chapter provides some broader strokes so that the enterprising semiotician can begin to do liturgical semiotics in their own way. Whether one thinks about it in terms of DNA, fingerprints, or breathprints, semiotics is an endeavor unique to the individual. This chapter will help the student to claim their unique identity as a living, breathing semiotician.

A METAPHOR TO FOLLOW

Before being able to exhale, we must inhale. A baby cannot scream its lungs open until it draws in air. Before I respire, I must inspire. Likewise, before someone can exhale their unique breathprint, they must first let the process of inhalation run its course.

Our lungs are the organ that gets all the credit for our breathing. This is warranted in that they exchange gasses and oxygenate the blood. Yet they are not the active agents of the aspiration apparatus. That designation belongs to the diaphragm.

Inhalation happens when the diaphragm muscle contracts and flattens, which draws it down toward the abdomen. This increases the size of the chest cavity. This increase in size creates an area of negative pressure, a vacuum if you will. When the pressure on the lungs decreases, they expand to fill the increased space. This expansion draws in air through the airway.

This anatomy lesson provides the outline for what follows. The diaphragm of our effort, the active muscle that provokes inhalation, is the process of choosing a liturgy. That action is what precedes, and provides for, the gas exchange that is the essence of breathing.

THE DIAPHRAGM: CHOOSING A LITURGY

One cannot engage in liturgical semiotics without choosing a liturgy. Liturgical semiotics as I pursue it is an applied endeavor rather than an abstract one. This means that an actual liturgy needs to be selected before the work of semiotics can begin. In the same way that the diaphragm drives the process of breathing, choosing a liturgy is what drives the process of liturgical semiotics.

This process begins with the semiotician. Liturgical semiotics, as this book has developed it, is not simply an academic exercise. It is an artistic endeavor. An artist makes their best art when they are invested in, and passionate about, what they are doing.

Thus, the question to begin with is this: what kind of worship, or what regarding worship in general, is someone passionate about? For me, the Holy Eucharist is the center of gravity around which my worship life and spiritual life orbit. It is not only what is important to me, but it is what I am passionate about. It was the core of my call to the priesthood.

The answer to the question of passion in worship is going to differ wildly depending on who is answering it. Perhaps someone is passionate about preaching. Or maybe it is being a prayer warrior on Sunday mornings that stokes their spirit. Someone might find their love for Christ awash in the waters of baptism more so than anything else. Another might find that their worship life is most passionately expressed while they are engaged in liturgical dance. There are a wide variety of answers to embrace.

Once someone has identified what they are passionate about with regards to worship, they can choose a liturgy to focus on which incorporates that passion. It is important to consider the liturgical event in its entirety rather than just a segment of it. As a fish needs water to swim in if it is to breathe, so does a liturgical element or action need the context of the entire worship event. A spirit-filled sermon given from a pulpit on Sunday morning to the gathered faithful is a liturgical action set within the context of the entire worship event. A sermon given on a street corner of a busy city as indifferent commuters walk by is decidedly not.

After a type of liturgical event is identified, it is time to consider a particular manifestation of that liturgical event. For me, choosing the Episcopal service of Holy Eucharist was important. Yet I also needed to be aware of the community that service was being celebrated in the midst of. Holy Eucharist being celebrated in a small, local church in the countryside is going to be different than it being celebrated in a cavernous cathedral in a major city.

With a specific liturgical event in a specific place in hand and in mind, the possibility of semiotic engagement is opened up. Now that the diaphragm muscle has opened the chest cavity, there is room to BREATHE (and GASP and RASP). What follows are some recommendations on how to go about engaging these acronyms.

BREATHE[3]

The BREATHE process is about receptivity. It involves reading signs in the liturgy and drawing connections between those signs to find meaning. Then that meaning can find expression in the life of the faith community. In chapter 6, for example, how the bread is acted upon in the Holy Eucharist informed how the local congregation might engage the wider community. What follows are a few points to keep in mind when desiring to start to BREATHE.

Point 1: Remind Me

This is the title of a song by Norwegian electronic duo Röyksopp. The song points out that regardless of where one goes, they are always reminded of other times and places they have been. That sentiment is not only an efficient synopsis of semiotics in general, but of the content of the first point in particular: pattern recognition.

As an illustration, think about how really good chess players win games. Part of winning chess is calculation, of course. Seeing one move farther ahead than your opponent goes a long way toward winning.

Another part of chess success, however, is pattern recognition. Over the course of hundreds of games, chess players begin to recognize certain hallmarks of generally successful chess positions. Ah, when the pawns are arranged like this, my knights are typically more effective than my bishops. My opponent has both of their rooks lined up in this part of the board—I could be in big trouble here.

In a similar fashion, over the course of hundreds of worship services of a particular type, the liturgical semiotician will begin to recognize certain hallmarks of various liturgies. Ah, it does not say this in the bulletin, but I

3. Chapter 4 lays out the definition of BREATHE, and chapter 6 walks through a BREATHE practicum.

know this priest is going to silently pray in her seat after the sermon. The thurifer has not brought out the thurible yet, they might be trying to re-light the charcoal and are having trouble.

I draw this comparison to suggest that, if someone wants to read the signs of a particular liturgy, it is helpful to have a lot of worship experience with that liturgy. Even with the most detailed bulletin or customary,[4] there is much that happens in a liturgical event that evades documentation. Only experience will reveal some elements, actions, and motifs.

This also implies maintaining an awareness of what is going on during the enactment of the liturgy. If one is not being intentional about observing the goings on of the worship service, then there is much that could go unnoticed.

This is not to say that one cannot be genuinely worshiping and observing at the same time. I am of the belief that both can be done at once. In fact, from a particular perspective, our attention to the details of how we worship God can be a form of worshiping God in itself.

This awareness can be enhanced by engaging in a form of ostranenie (a.k.a., defamiliarization). Try to walk into and experience the worship service as if for the first time. In taking something familiar and making it strange by encountering it as a stranger, many things can be encountered afresh and noticed anew.

Point 2: I Know What I Know

This is the title of a song by Paul Simon. A question that the protagonist of the song keeps asking has to do with their worthiness to interact with the wind. The second point to keep in mind when deciding to BREATHE is all Greek to me.

The ancient Greek word for *know* is γινώσκω. The fullness of its meaning is broader than simply having knowledge of something. It also encompasses the idea of perceiving or realizing something.[5] Thinking in these terms, I know what I know could just as well be I realize what I realize, or I perceive what I perceive.

In one sense, this message could be the title for this book. After all, semiotics is all about perception and recognition. We are perceiving signs and recognizing their meaning all the time.

---

4. A customary is a "book containing (1) the rites and ceremonies for the services, and/or (2) the rules and customs of discipline, of a particular monastery, cathedral, or religious order." Cross and Livingstone, *Oxford Dictionary of the Christian Church*, 443.

5. BDAG 199.

Yet in our attempts to BREATHE, what we are trying to perceive is the presence of the Pneuma. What we are trying to recognize is the restlessness of the Ruah (רוּחַ). The Holy Spirit is active and present in the liturgical event, providing signs for us to read, and working with us to read those signs and make meaning from their connections.

It is important to know that one is not alone in doing liturgical semiotics. Instead, we are partnering with God's Spirit. In our striving to read signs and make meanings, we are collaborating with the divine. That collaboration is a conjunction of the Spirit's prompting and our prowess.

Carrying ourselves in a posture of awareness and openness to that pneumatic partnership will help us work with the Holy Spirit. Working with God's Spirit is our aim and intent. We are indeed worthy to interact with the wind.[6]

GASP AND RASP[7]

While the BREATHE process is about receptivity, GASP and RASP are about proactivity. Instead of observing a liturgical event to read its signs, these two acronyms involve making semiotic adjustments to the liturgy.

GASP is about making those adjustments such that the liturgy is more evocative of a particular theme or message. RASP is about making adjustments to how certain artifacts of the liturgy are used in worship in order to make those artifacts more resonant with the worshiper's cultural context. While there is a notable difference in those two intents, they both concern making changes to the liturgy. This similarity means that there are a couple of points that are applicable to both.

Point 1: Determine How Flexible the Liturgy Is

Before making any changes to the liturgy it is important to determine how much flexibility one has in making semiotic adjustments to that liturgy. The answer to this question will be driven by a combination of someone's denomination and vocation.

Some denominations have a set liturgy that has very little flexibility. The Roman Catholic Church is an example of this. Even the gestures that are made by the priest during the liturgy are often predetermined.

6. If you found this reference to wind to be vexing rather than vivifying, know that the Greek and Hebrew words for spirit can also be translated as wind.

7. Chapter 4 introduces the acronyms. Chapters 7 and 8 offer practica of GASP and RASP, respectively.

Some denominations that do not have set rules around liturgical changes have strong traditions that must be taken into consideration. In some churches, for example, there may be nothing specifically stating that bread and wine (or grape juice) are the only elements to be used for Holy Communion. At the same time, the notion of changing from bread and juice to some other elements might be scandalous to the point of being clearly unjustifiable.

Other churches, including many independent and non-denominational churches, may have very few impediments to liturgical flexibility. The sky might be the limit, as it were.

For me, as an Episcopal priest, this principle has been manifested in the Book of Common Prayer. The BCP is the embodiment of how the Episcopal Church has agreed to conduct itself in worship. In order to uphold my ordination vows as I understand them, I must conduct worship as laid out therein.

In some ways, the BCP is inflexible. On Sundays and major feast days, for example, the Nicene Creed must be part of the service of Holy Eucharist.[8] This is whether or not I want to include it or even feel like saying it that day.

In other ways, the BCP is quite flexible. While the presider is encouraged to give a blessing at the end of the service of Holy Eucharist, there is nothing to indicate the content or phrasing of that blessing. It is a blank slate, allowing the presider the flexibility to craft the blessing as they see fit.

Another factor in determining liturgical flexibility is one's vocation. In most denominations, there is a limit to who is allowed to make liturgical changes, and what kinds of changes. In the Episcopal Church, the priest has ultimate authority at the local level over liturgical choices. The bishop of the diocese, however, can approve some liturgical changes for use at the local level that would otherwise be beyond the reach of priests. In some churches, this authority may rest with a committee rather than the pastor, or perhaps even reside corporately. The point is that it is important to know who can (and cannot) make liturgical changes.

In sum, the liturgical semiotician must know the borders or limits to what is possible (or at least advisable) with regards to making semiotic adjustments to the liturgy.[9]

8. There are a handful of times during the year when the Baptismal Covenant may be substituted for the creed, but the point is made.

9. It must be noted that there are times when "holy rule breaking" is appropriate. These times are few and far between, however, and should involve group discernment and a measure of gravitas. The 1974 ordination to the Episcopal priesthood of eleven women, even though women's ordination was not yet allowed in the Episcopal Church, could be considered an example of the Holy Spirit moving those involved to prophetic

Point 2: How to Introduce Change

Once the borders and boundaries of liturgical adjustments are determined, one needs to consider how to go about making those changes. There are two elements to keep in mind when pondering liturgical changes.

The first element to keep in mind is the difference between experience and education. Many of the folks who gather on Sunday for worship may have a great deal of experience around liturgy (meaning that they have participated in liturgical events quite often), but not a great deal of education around liturgy (meaning that they do not know the history of what we do in worship or why we do things the way we do).

I am put in mind of someone who trained acolytes in a church I knew. This person had been worshiping in this particular church for decades and knew every jot and tittle of what the acolytes were to do in that space. Stand here. Move there. Hold this. Do that. They knew what the acolytes needed to do in that church even better than the minister, who had not been there very long.

Yet, if that person found themselves in a different church they would have mostly been at a loss on how to advise the acolytes. Their experience, while vast, was tied to one reference point—their home church. Without an education in the *whys* of acolytes, the reasons underpinning all that one sees acolytes do, the foundational understanding of what the ministry of the acolyte is, they would be fairly limited in their ability to recreate the acolyte role in a new space.

The point of this story is that education is key for the congregation. Faith is perhaps the most intimate and important aspect of our identity as human beings. Thus, we can hold the expressions of that faith (i.e., how we worship) in quite high regard. If a congregation experiences a change in the liturgy, but they do not have an understanding of why that change has taken place, then it can be a disturbing event for them.

So liturgical changes, especially very noticeable ones or ones that involve parts of the liturgy that people hold quite dear, need an introduction. What that means depends on the parish. That could mean something announced prior to the change. It could mean a coffee hour forum. It could mean a Christian formation offering that delves into the whys of the liturgical change. It could mean the creation of a worship committee so that the faith community has some ownership of the change.

---

and holy rule breaking. A lone priest deciding to baptize without water as a statement about the worsening climate crisis, for example, would not be.

The second (and related) element has to do with trust. Even if people do not understand the reason for a liturgical change, they may be okay with that change if they trust the person making the change.

If a minister is new to a church, for example, then immediately making several impactful changes to worship could come with risk. If the clergy person has taken the time to cultivate strong relationships with parishioners, however, then some of that relational capital can likely be exchanged for making changes to a worship service that is held dearly by the faithful.

Cultivating those relationships is also important because it helps the semiotician to learn about the people that make up the congregation. Changes are made to the liturgy in order to present a sign to those worshiping. The better someone knows the worshiping community, the better equipped that person will be to present those signs in a way that the worshiping community will grasp.[10]

UNIVERSAL POINTS

Some points raised above are specific to reading the signs of the liturgy. Other points have been tailored toward making liturgical changes. There are a couple of points, though, that are applicable to both efforts to BREATHE and to GASP/RASP. Rather than duplicate them under each section above, I offer them here.

Point 1: Know the History

It has already been commented that worship does not happen in a vacuum. Rather, it can only happen in a context. When a worship service happens, it is a specific liturgy in a specific place.

A worship service also does not happen in a vacuum with regards to time. It is the latest worship service of years (or centuries) of worship in that space. It is also connected to Christian worship down through the ages, inheriting its form and content from a particular strand of the Christian family.

With regards to the BREATHE process, knowing the history of the liturgy under observation is a boon. Suppose that someone wants to apply the BREATHE process to a wedding liturgy and the narraphor resolved upon has a visual emphasis. In other words, the use of color and the interplay of

10. One way to avoid much of the risk around making liturgical changes is to start a new service at a different time or on a different day. That service will not carry the same weight of expectation that the existing service bears.

dark and light are consequential. In that case, it would behoove the semiotician to know that the tradition of a bride wearing white is a somewhat recent phenomena, becoming popular only after Queen Victoria chose white for her wedding dress in 1840.

In considering making adjustments to the liturgy (GASP and RASP), knowledge of a liturgy's history in a place can be very important. If the semiotician wishes to use blue rather than purple for the color of the candles in the Advent wreath, for instance, then they should know whether or not a current parishioner's family member left a candle endowment to the church (and if their favorite color was purple).

A less tongue-in-cheek example could have to do with the organ. A semiotician may have a persuasive argument for making changes to what kind of music is played in worship and what instruments are used. If they are not aware of that church's long history of truly talented and well-trained organists, however, then they could be in danger of doing more harm than good with the proposed changes.

Point 2: Embrace Failure

No one bats a thousand. Not every drive finds the fairway. Whatever the sports metaphor, the message is clear: we all fail. The same is true for practitioners of liturgical semiotics.

The BREATHE process takes this into account. Sometimes the process stops at BREATH because the results do not harmonize. And that is okay. The process has moved forward, in a hopeful yet realistic way. Some new insight may be there to be gained. Or it may not. Failure is an option.

A similar story may be told when looking to make semiotic adjustments to the liturgy. It could be that a change made is not evocative in the way that the semiotician intends. This makes sense, because not everyone is going to pick up on the same signs or read the signs they do perceive in the same way.

One way to mitigate against that, as mentioned above, is to have a greater knowledge of the worshiping community. Another way is to be very clear about the goal that one has in mind while making semiotic adjustments. Having a goal of "being more reverent" is much less clear than having goals of "bowing more deeply," "standing up straighter when processing," and "not fidgeting while sitting."

Even so, failure will happen. God, however, will still be praised and glorified through our worship. The liturgy is efficacious; it is effective. It does something irrespective of what meanings are either signaled or received. God is worshiped, even when we do not semiotically succeed. That is a source of great comfort.

LITURGICAL HICCUPS

Earlier in this chapter, I likened choosing a liturgy to the diaphragm of the breathing process. If this is the case, if choosing a liturgy is the diaphragm of liturgical semiotics, then we must figure out what to do about hiccups.

Hiccups are involuntary contractions of the diaphragm. Now it is true that the diaphragm contracts involuntarily anyway. If it did not, then we would need to consciously make each breath happen. What defines a hiccup is that the contraction is spasmodic—it happens suddenly.

This section title, liturgical hiccups, presents us with semiotic uncertainty. How are we to interpret it? Do we understand it within the context of the metaphor? Or, do we interpret it colloquially, understanding a hiccup as a mistake? Both. One way corresponds to reading liturgical signs, while the other involves making liturgical changes.

Within the Metaphor

If choosing a liturgy is the diaphragm of liturgical semiotics, then a hiccup might be considered a situation where the liturgy is chosen by someone other than the semiotician. This could be an ecumenical gathering, for instance. Or, it could be a regional worship service within one's denomination. For our purposes, however, let us consider the situation of being a visitor to another church.

There is an implication in this situation. Previously, the semiotician was encouraged to discern what they are passionate about in worship and then choose a liturgy which incorporates that. With this type of liturgical hiccup, there is every chance that the semiotician is faced with a liturgical event that they are not passionate about (or at least much less passionate about).

How should someone go about reading the signs of worship if they are not passionate about the proceedings? To borrow from Psalm 137:3–4, "Our captors asked us for the words of a song; Our tormentors, for joy: 'Sing for us a song of Zion!' But how could we sing a song of the Lord in a foreign land?" (NASB)· Hopefully visiting another church is not as bad as all that, but it can be a place that feels like a foreign land.

When faced with a liturgy that one did not choose, where personal passion may not play a part, I encourage the liturgical semiotician to look for passion. Where is the passion of those gathered on display? Is it in the joy on the face of a choir member? Is it in the furrowed brows, and perhaps even tears, of someone deep in prayer? Is it in the rapt attention of someone listening to the sermon? Is it in the thick stillness of a time of silence?

Where there is passion, meaning is being transmitted and received. Look to those places, begin reading those signs, and making those connections.

Colloquial Meaning

A hiccup can also be taken as a minor mistake or setback. There was "a hiccup in the process," for example. How does one go about responding to making a mistake in executing semiotic adjustments?

The first step is to comprehend that a mistake has been made. The interested and studious liturgical semiotician ought to engage people in conversation in order to see how their adjustments were perceived and received. Maybe that happens in ad hoc coffee hour conversations. Maybe it happens at intentional forums. The hope is that it happens proactively.

Here is a hypothetical example of this kind of liturgical hiccup: Envision a mixed-culture congregation made up primarily of local Americans and British expatriates. In an effort to make the theme of self-love more evocative, the priest decides to make a semiotic adjustment to the passing of the peace. In addition to giving a peace sign to those in the congregation, he also turns his hand and gives himself a peace sign.

The intent is that the priest is modeling a reconciling with oneself. Being at peace with who you are, before you receive Holy Communion. The problem is that the gesture of the peace sign becomes something very different to a certain swath of people when the palm faces inward rather than outward. To people in places like the UK, Australia, India, and Ireland, this gesture is the equivalent in mainstream American culture of showing someone your middle finger.

Once the liturgical semiotician knows that there has been a hiccup, they can correct the situation. In these situations, it is good to remember that Christianity is supposed to be a religion that is grounded in grace.

ARE YOU A NOSE BREATHER?

Some people breathe through their nose, and others breathe through their mouth. Nose breathing is the more beneficial of the two for the body. Nasal hairs filter out dust and allergens, preventing them from getting to the lungs. The air drawn through the nasal cavity is also warmed and moistened. This natural humidification process helps the air reach body temperature prior to entering the lungs. Lastly, the nose releases nitric oxide when someone breathes nasally. This widens the blood vessels and can therefore help improve circulation.

While that is all well and good, where do we locate nose or mouth breathing in our constructed metaphor? Choosing a liturgy is the diaphragm. The actual breathing in and out is the doing of liturgical semiotics. What then would it mean to be a nose breather?

We can look at nose breathing as a way to add something beneficial to the doing of liturgical semiotics. It is something that can be done, but does not have to be done. After all, someone could breathe through their mouth. It is just that they are going to miss out on the benefits mentioned above.

So what is the optional yet beneficial thing that can be added to the doing of liturgical semiotics? Prayer. This can at once seem obvious and surprising. Of course we should be bathing the entire process of liturgical semiotics in prayer. We are Christians. Praying is what we do!

Yet, at the same time, there are plenty of times when we do not intentionally pray about something we are about to do, in the midst of doing, or have just done. This can be particularly true if the *something* has an academic or a systematic bent to it.

Nevertheless, one's efforts to do liturgical semiotics will benefit from prayer. For one, this will help the semiotician develop their unique breathprint. They will likely pray in a way commensurate with their tradition, which is somewhat identifying. Furthermore, everyone has their own individualized prayer life with the Almighty (even if they are unaware of it). Praying is a unique endeavor, and when someone bathes their semiotic efforts in prayer, those efforts become unique as well.

In addition to driving individuality, praying can help to keep our hearts open and antenna up for the movement of the Holy Spirit. I have mentioned that liturgical semiotics is an artistic undertaking. We are not solo artists, creating our own masterpieces. Instead, we are co-creators with God's Spirit. Prayer can help to keep us attuned and ready for that collaboration.

Many worship leaders pray before worship begins. Why not pray before a semiosis of worship begins? Worship itself is replete with prayer. Why not pray while conducting liturgical semiotics? In fact, why not pray after the fact as well as a way to aid in the holy debrief of discerning what worked, what did not, and what insights may be gained from the semiosis? As we say in my tradition before praying: let us pray.

CONCLUSION

With almost any new skill, we first learn by being taught. Maybe it is learning how to play a sport. Or it could be encountering a new subject in school. Or it might be taking on a new life skill. Most often, we first learn under the watchful eye and instructive words of another.

If we continue to pursue something, then eventually it becomes time to branch out on our own. The teenager eventually drives away without the parent. The student studies a subject of interest on their own without the teacher's input. The athlete takes ownership of their own advancement and improvement.

At this point, we are able to add our own personal touch, or imprint, to what we are pursuing. We engage our area of interest in a way all our own, finding the intersection of our identity and our passion. To end where we began, we develop our breathprint.

A semiotician's breathprint is their unique way of going about the artistic endeavor that is liturgical semiotics. It is a product of their identity. Their passions, faith background, prayer life, and vocation all mix to create a one-of-a-kind approach to finding meaning in liturgy and making semiotic adjustments to those liturgies. When done in conscious conjunction with the Holy Spirit, this breathprint becomes a holy halitosis.[11] At this point, their efforts lapse in doxology, for the betterment of themselves and the church.

11. While I am using this phrase in my own way, it was first coined in print by Leonard Sweet.

12

Breath Marks

"There are unique places to take a breath in a piece. Follow your private instructor and band director's recommendation. They know the tricks of the trade that you will learn in time."[1]

HAVE YOU EVER SEEN a musical notation that looks like an apostrophe hanging out between notes on sheet music?[2] That notation is called a luftpause, also known as a breath mark. It indicates where the singer should breathe as they are singing.

Someone is going to breathe while they sing. It cannot be avoided. Whether they are singing in the shower, in church, around the campfire, or on stage, singers breathe while engaged in their task.

In most cases, that breathing is going to happen naturally and without conscious thought. After all, we breathe all the time and rarely think about it. Yet for those who are singing in a more specialized setting, breath marks can help their breathing be more intentional and fruitful.

In a similar fashion, everyone does semiotics all the time. As human beings, we are constantly taking in the world around us and trying to make sense of it. Whether in church, in the office, around the campfire, or watching a stage play, we are always reading signs and making meaning. We are all semioticians, born and bred.

1. Grey, "Breath Mark Guide," para. 5.
2. An example can be found at Wikipedia, s.v. "Breath Mark," https://en.wikipedia.org/wiki/Breath_mark.

For those who are pursuing semiotics in a more specialized setting, however, having some breath marks can help to make the task more intentional and fruitful. This chapter does just that.

If one thinks of different liturgies like different musical scores, then the luftpauses could be considered to be specific places within the liturgy where some intentional semiotic work ought to take place. What follows is an observation of four liturgies that each identify a different type of breath mark. The four types of luftpauses demonstrated are object, words spoken, posture, and action.

In each event, five steps will take place. First, the liturgical event is introduced from an Episcopal perspective. There are no liturgical events that are neutral and without context. Rather than try and create something that does not exist, I choose to look through the lens with which I view the world (my own hermeneutic, if you will) and give of that perspective.

Second, some ecumenical contouring of the event takes place. Not all corners of the Christian family have auricular (i.e., one-on-one) confession as a liturgical event, for instance. Yet many Christians of those persuasions may find themselves in a semiotically similar situation: one-on-one counseling with someone where there is a clear power differential. The semiosis of private confession may well yield insights that would be more widely applicable.

Third, the luftpause within the event is identified. This could be an object (such as wine in the Holy Eucharist), or an action (such as laying on of hands at ordination), or a posture (such as being prone during ministry with the dying), or words spoken (such as the marriage pronouncement). Whatever it is, the breath mark identifies where some intentional semiotic rumination could be a boon.

Fourth, a related Jesus story is considered. As Christians, the answer to most of our questions should have Christ somehow involved. A story from the Gospels that bears a similar breath mark as the liturgical event under discussion will guide further insight.

Lastly, a few insights are offered and questions asked to help frame the liturgical semiotician's further reflection.

LUFTPAUSE #1: HOLY EUCHARIST

The service of Holy Eucharist has been the focus of this entire book. Much semiotic territory surrounding it has already been trod. That being said, there is still more to say.

Episcopal

The importance of the Holy Eucharist within the worship life of the Episcopal Church is well established. It is described in the catechism found in the Book of Common Prayer as "the sacrament commanded by Christ for the continual remembrance of his life, death, and resurrection, until his coming again."[3] The same section also states that the benefits we receive in the sacrament are "the forgiveness of our sins, the strengthening of our union with Christ and one another, and the foretaste of the heavenly banquet which is our nourishment in eternal life."

As a vehicle of continual remembrance, and because of the benefits it brings, it is celebrated regularly. Additionally, other services (e.g., baptisms, weddings, and funerals) are designed to be celebrated within the context of the Holy Eucharist.

Ecumenical

Whether it is called Holy Eucharist, Holy Communion, or the Lord's Supper, this is a service that is celebrated by virtually every part of the Christian family, in some form or another.[4] To some it is a sacrament, while to others it is an ordinance. To some it is a vehicle of the real presence of Jesus, while to others it is solely a memorial. To some it is the weekly (or daily) heartbeat of the faith, while to others it is a much more occasional endeavor. Some churches use recognizably baked bread while others use wafers. Some churches use wine while others use grape juice. Yet however it manifests, this service occupies a foundational space in the greater Christian landscape.

Breath Mark

Plato is often falsely attributed with the quote "nothing more excellent or valuable than wine was ever granted by the gods to man."[5] Even though Plato did not write these exact words, he did write quite a bit about wine in *The Laws*.

It has been at least since Plato's day that wine has captured not only the imagination of the common person, but of the most learned as well. Humanity's long love affair with wine is undeniable, with it being a rich

3. Episcopal Church, *Book of Common Prayer*, 859.

4. To my knowledge, the only denominations that do not practice Holy Communion in some form are the Salvation Army and the Quakers.

5. The actual origin of the quote appears to be lost to history.

element of several cultures across the world and throughout history. This could be because, as Roger Scruton has put it, "Throughout recorded history human beings have made life bearable by taking intoxicants."[6]

While an historical overview of humanity's history of intoxication is beyond the reach of this chapter, Scruton's bracing sentence does remind us that wine is indeed an intoxicant. It is, in fact, the only intoxicant sanctioned for use in Christian worship.

The breath mark I would identify, with regards to the service of Holy Eucharist, is the wine. For some, this will mean grape juice.

Jesus Story

The story explored is that of Jesus' first miracle: turning water into wine at a wedding in Cana of Galilee, found in John 2:1–11.

This was Jesus's public ministerial debut. What is it that kicked off his world-changing ministry? It was not a miraculous healing that brought both physical and societal restoration to one who was broken. It was not a sermon that enflamed hearts and engaged minds. Rather, it was changing water into wine.

That Jesus would choose this as the way to inaugurate this earthly ministry speaks to the importance of the act. There are at least four facets of this viniferous activity that stand out.

One, it is a story about transformation. Jesus turns water into wine. More specifically, Jesus turns regular water into very good wine.

Two, that transformation has a positive effect on the situation. It prevents the host from accumulating shame as it would be a major faux pas to run out of wine. It also keeps the party going, with all the good relational implications of that.

Three, it breaks convention. The normative practice, according to the chief steward, was to bring out the inferior wine after the guests were already intoxicated. Jesus' miracle turns that expectation on its head, and saves the best for last.

Lastly, it provides an enduring effect. This point requires some explanation. While there is not certainty on the historical location of Cana, the likeliest candidate for the town is Kirbet Kana, which is located on a hill above the Netufa Valley about fourteen kilometers north of Nazareth.

Let us hold together a series of observations. One, in performing this miracle, Jesus created a huge volume of wine. Given that the jars each held twenty to thirty gallons of water, and Jesus instructed the servants to fill the

---

6. Scruton, *I Drink Therefore I Am*, 1.

jars to the brim, we are talking about one hundred twenty to one hundred eighty gallons of wine.

Two, the wedding celebration had already been going on for some time. Not only had the wine run out, but the chief steward had expected inferior wine to be brought out by this point in the affair.

Three, given the archeological evidence and the historical witness, Cana was not a large town.

Four, there is a complex of caves in the hill under the town.

Now let us connect these dots. There would have been much wine left over from Jesus' miracle at this wedding reception that most (if not all) of the population of the town would have attended. While there is no certainty on what happened to all that excess wine, two possibilities stand out: the wine was auctioned off, or it was stored.

Let us take the former possibility first. It was not unusual for the left-over wine to be auctioned off after the celebration. This helped to defray the cost of the wedding. Yet, this was not a usual wedding celebration. This man Jesus, who was not known at that time as a miracle worker, had worked a miracle. If anything was going to disrupt usual practices, something like that would do it.

Add to this the probability that the residents of the small town of Cana were basically an extended family. This was typically the case in small towns in Galilee.

Now consider the latter possibility. The excess wine could have been stored in the underground cave system, an ordinary practice for the time. This would have helped it stay good longer. Jesus, in effect, would have left the town a cache of wine.

Every time a household in town drank that wine, that very good wine instead of their normal wine, they would remember Jesus and that wedding reception. As they sat around the table, engaged in food and conversation, Jesus would have been interwoven into their time together.

Jesus was just beginning his ministry. He was just starting to reveal his glory. In fact, he needed his mother's prompting to get started. This gift of wine would have ingrained him into the minds and hearts of the entire town, and not just because of the momentary miracle. In an ongoing, daily way, thoughts of Jesus would have stayed with the townsfolk as long as that gifted store of wine remained.

Jesus was always accomplishing more than one thing with his miracles. His signs and wonders were multivalent. Did his changing water into wine solve an immediate problem? Yes. He saved the honor of the bridegroom and allowed for this community (and family) celebration to continue. He also delivered a theological message about the new covenant which he would enact (the new wine being superior to the old, which had run its course). Yet he also initiated a table ministry of sorts with the townsfolk of Cana, something that he would continue to do throughout his ministry.

This transformation of water into wine had an ongoing effect.

Ruminations

These themes can be carried through from Jesus' miracle in Cana back to the service of Holy Eucharist. If we attempt to draw some parallels, then we are left with interesting questions to ponder.

Jesus' miracle was about the transformation of water into wine. What might this tell us about the transformation of wine into the blood of Christ (either literally, symbolically, or something in-between depending on one's doctrine)? What might it also say to us about the process that led to the transformation of grapes into the wine that is used (this may take us into the arenas of sustainable ecology and social justice for laborers)?

The transformation had an immediate positive effect. Hopefully Christians can all agree that Holy Eucharist, regardless of one's particular doctrine regarding it, is a good thing. It has an immediate beneficial effect on those gathered. How might that effect be highlighted or pointed toward during the liturgical event?

The transformation broke convention and overturned expectation. The connection to Holy Eucharist here is right in front of us, but may be difficult to see given how deeply ingrained this service has become in the Christian consciousness. Allow me to state it plainly: We believe that a nibble of bread and a sip of wine are true food and true drink that allow us to abide in Jesus, and he in us (John 6:55–56). How might we go about recapturing the unconventional and expectation-overturning nature of the Lord's Supper in our worship?

The transformation had an enduring effect. Our celebration of Holy Communion ought to have an enduring effect on we who follow Christ. Yet the enacting of our liturgy is a discrete event. One way to think forward with this is to look to the practice of reserving bread and wine after the service. Some traditions believe that Jesus' presence in the bread and wine is an enduring one, and so some of the elements are kept after the service so they may be taken to the homebound or the sick.

Even in traditions that do not subscribe to an enduring real presence in the eucharistic elements, the notion of bringing bread and wine (or juice) from Communion to share with others can be a semiotically rich offering. It connects the sick or homebound person with their worshiping community.

It acts as a physical reminder of a spiritual relationship, both with the rest of the congregation and with Jesus. The possibility of adjusting the liturgical event to heighten the setting apart of bread and wine for later sharing is worth exploring.

LUFTPAUSE #2: ORDINATION

"Then the priests in all their vestments prostrated themselves and entreated the supreme God to aid in the present situation" (3 Macc 1:16).
The next worship service to consider is that of ordination.

Episcopal

In the Episcopal Church, there are three types of ordinations. Someone can be ordained as a deacon, as a priest, or as a bishop. There is also a sequential flow to this. If someone ends up being ordained a bishop, they have first been ordained a deacon and then a priest.

While three different ordination rites can be found in the BCP, and there are differences to be found within parts of those liturgies, they all follow the same basic flow. The service takes place within the context of Holy Eucharist. The candidate(s) is presented at the beginning of the service. Later, after the sermon and the Nicene Creed, in place of the Prayers of the People, the ordinand is examined and then consecrated to their new vocation.

Ecumenical

The different parts of the Christian family certainly have different doctrines around ordination. Disparate answers will be given by various denominations to questions like: Does ordination entail an ontological change? Is ordination permanent? Does it have a geographic boundary? Does this ordination stand in the apostolic succession?

Even though there is a broad spectrum of answers to these and similar questions, there are a few points that most denominations can agree upon. There are those who are set apart whose call it is to administer sacraments and oversee the faithful in some way. Sometimes that setting apart is called ordination, other times it is a kind of licensing. The marking of those who are set apart involves some type of ritual, and often that ritual is a worship service.

Breath Mark

Ordination services across denominations can vary quite a bit. Great difference is likely to be found in the music played, the prayers prayed, the sermons
preached, and the Holy Communion administered (if that is even a part of
the service). Yet there is one element that has been present in every ordination I have witnessed, regardless of denomination: the laying on of hands.

The laying on of hands as a religious act stretches back at least to the
time of the Hebrew Scriptures. In that context, it had a sacrificial connotation as the priests laid hands upon the animals that were to be sacrificed.

By the time of the New Testament, the action had lost its sacrificial
meaning and was related "to healing, blessings, baptism and the Spirit, and
assignment to a given task."[7] The tying of the action to ordination may be
what is in view in Acts 6:6, "They had these men stand before the apostles,
who prayed and laid their hands on them."

Jesus Story

Jesus did not ordain the disciples by laying hands on them. Indeed, any time
that Jesus lays hands on someone in the Gospels, it is almost always overtly
associated with healing. Take Jesus healing the bent over woman (Luke
13:10–17) as an example.

The one time that Jesus' laying on of hands is not specifically attached
to healing is when people were bringing children to him. Yet even then, the
purpose was for healing: "Those who brought children to Jesus that he might
touch them recognized his healing power (transmitted through the hands)
and no doubt hoped that his touch might protect the children from the "evil
eye" of others who had lost children in childbirth or at an early age."[8]

When Jesus healed it was not simply a physical cure, however. There
was also a relocation of that person into a place of harmony within their
community. To return to our example of the straightened woman, think
about her situation before her healing. She could not look anyone in the eye.

This is significant because the eye was a source of great power in the
understanding of the ancients. The eyes were seen as proactive organs rather
than receptive ones, as modern science now understands them. What was
in one's heart, evil or good, could be projected at someone through the eyes.

---

7. Robert F. O'Toole, "Hands, Laying on of (New Testament)," in Freedman, *Anchor
Yale Bible Dictionary*, 6:48.

8. Pilch, *Cultural Handbook to the Bible*, 176.

With this understanding of eye function, known as the extramission theory of vision, some biblical passages can be conceived of in a new way. When Jesus says that the eyes are the lamp of the body (Matt 6:22), it is supportive of the idea that what is in you shines out through the eyes. When Peter and John heal the man outside the Beautiful Gate (Acts 3:1–10), that process begins with them looking intently at the man. With an extramission understanding of eyesight, the disciples may be understood to be projecting healing power through this action.

When the woman stood up straight, she was visually integrated into the community. Beyond mere physical healing, this engendered a wholeness that was lacking before.

Excursus: Disability

It is necessary to pause here and engage a non-trivial excursus regarding disability. Physical disabilities are only such when measured against a society's structure. Someone in a wheelchair, for example, is not disabled until presented with a building that can only be entered via stairs. If a person is considered disabled, then it is best understood as a sign of society's brokenness rather than the person's.

Jesus' healing miracles were an indictment of the brokenness of society's structure in the first century. Through those miracles, people were brought into a place of wholeness and integration with a flawed structure. That the acts of healing were necessary to effect that integration is what indicted that society's structure.

Ruminations

The touch of Jesus was related to healing. What guidance might this give for reading the signs of the breath mark of laying on of hands during ordination?

The church is known as the body of Christ. Could we consider that when someone has hands laid on them at ordination that it is, through the church's identification with Christ's body, Jesus' hands that are touching them?

If so, then ordination is a form of healing. It is not a physical healing, but it does effect an integration or wholeness. Our journey is one of always becoming more and more who God is calling us to be.

There is a certain segment of Christians who are called to be clergy. When that happens, they are growing more into who God is calling them to be. They are becoming more integrated with that unique child of God that is them in fullness and wholeness.

How might the theme of wholeness be more strongly evoked in the ordination liturgy?

LUFTPAUSE #3: THE WEDDING CEREMONY[9]

Marriage occupies a singular place in the liturgical landscape. It is located at the intersection of the secular and the religious. Lots of people without a religious affiliation, even atheists, get married.

Most liturgies are entirely within the purview of the religious. Things like baptism, Holy Eucharist, and confirmation sprung out of the religious milieu. Even funerals have a distinctively religious character as humans face their own mortality. Marriages may be grounded and founded in religion, but they do not have to be.

Marriage also predates the church. Not only did any number of ancient civilizations have marriages, there is archeological evidence which suggests that even prehistoric cultures had some kind of rituals around life partnership.

Episcopal

The BCP states that the purpose of a wedding is to come together in the presence of God to witness and bless the joining together of two people in Holy Matrimony. It also signifies to those gathered the mystery of the union between Christ and his church.[10]

The flow of the service bears hallmarks of other Episcopal services. After an opening section, which includes a declaration of consent from all gathered, there are Scripture readings and a homily. The marriage itself follows, and the blessing thereof, followed by prayers. Then the service moves into the liturgy of the table.[11]

9. See Appendix C for an alternative semiosis of this service which focuses on the vows and provides a way to consider the difficult future the institutional church is facing.

10. See "The Celebration and Blessing of a Marriage" in Episcopal Church, *Book of Common Prayer*, 423.

11. The service is at least designed to move into the liturgy of the table. Anecdotally, fewer couples are choosing to include Holy Communion as part of their marriage ceremony.

Ecumenical

The idea of a wedding ceremony is universal across the Christian landscape. Regardless of denomination, there is some way that the joining together of two people in a lifelong covenant will be recognized before God.

Breath Mark

Christian weddings can manifest in a wide variety of ways. This is not only true regarding how different denominations go about creating these liturgical events, but also how much the service is secularized. Will it be in a church or at a "destination"? Will readings be from the bible or from non-Christian sources?

Questions like these can make a breath mark difficult to identify. An appeal to our cultural consciousness, however, guides us toward an answer. In most movies or television shows, the most poignant scene of the wedding is the dramatic words "I now pronounce you husband and wife!" This is followed by "the kiss."

While the kiss is a picturesque moment, it is the pronouncement that signals that the deed is done. The one doing the marrying of the couple has accomplished that task. In the Episcopal liturgy it goes like this: "Now that N. and N. have given themselves to each other by solemn vows, with the joining of hands and the giving and receiving of *a ring*, I pronounce that they are husband and wife, in the Name of the Father, and of the Son, and of the Holy Spirit. Those whom God has joined together let no one put asunder."[12]

There are two reasons that I am suggesting this pronouncement as the breath mark. One, it marks the fulfillment of the goal of the gathering—that the couple be married. Yet the second reason is the more salient one: this pronouncement is creating a new family.

Jesus Story

Even during his crucifixion Jesus was continuing his world-changing ministry. It is while Jesus is on the cross that we find this: "When Jesus saw his mother and the disciple whom he loved standing beside her, he said to his mother, "Woman, here is your son." Then he said to the disciple, "Here is your mother." And from that hour the disciple took her into his own home" (John 9:26–27).

---

12. Episcopal Church, *Book of Common Prayer*, 428.

While hanging upon a cross, and nearing his mortal death, Jesus makes this pronouncement. In so doing, he creates a new family.

Ruminations

Marriage is about creating a new family where there was no family. In Jesus' words to his mother and the disciple whom he loved (presumably John), Jesus does just that. He acts as the hinge point, bringing these two separate souls together as a new family. This happens in the wedding ceremony as well. Jesus's words speak into being a new relationship, that of a mother and son. In the wedding liturgy the minister speaks into being a new relationship, that of a husband and wife.

The pronouncement in the wedding ceremony is an act of creation. Because it is done within a religious context, it is an act of creation in Christ. How might the motif of creation be made more evocative in the wedding ceremony?

LUFTPAUSE #4: MINISTRY WITH THE DYING

We next turn to the liturgical event at the end of life. This is known in our cultural consciousness as "the last rites." This is a different kind of service in several respects. First, it does not happen at a predictable, set time. Rather, it happens when it needs to happen. Second, it is a service predicated on intimacy. Rather than a large crowd, there are only family and the closest of friends in attendance.

Episcopal

In the Episcopal Church, liturgy at the end of life is called Ministration at the Time of Death. It is a short service that includes a prayer for a person near death, a Litany at the Time of Death (that the gathered are encouraged to join in), a commendation at the time of death, and a commendatory prayer. There are also resources for a prayer vigil prior to a funeral, and the reception of the body at the church.

Ecumenical

The Roman Catholic Church calls this rite Viaticum (Latin for *provision*, meaning sustenance for a journey). The Orthodox churches call it Holy

Unction. Several parts of the Christian family, however, have no set liturgy to address this time of transition from mortal life to life eternal.

That does not mean that pastors of those denominations do not engage in a ministration at the time of death. Anyone that has prayed at a death bed has done it. Anyone who has sat silently with family, as they sat silently with their dying loved one, has done it. It is an experience that cuts across the breadth of the Christian family, and also something that can cut us to the core.

Breath Mark

There are certain elements that are no doubt universal to ministration at the time of death. Some kind of prayers are prayed. There is some kind of ministry of presence, as a pastor bears witness to great weakness blurring into great strength. There is either a transition or a palpable sense that transition is imminent.

The breath mark that I am suggesting is not found in the words prayed or the silences observed. It is not found in anointing with oil, or the offering of Holy Eucharist. It actually has not to do with the minister, but with the dying person.

It is their position as prone. Someone who is actively dying is lying down, typically in bed.

Jesus Story

There is a story in the Gospels where Jesus is at his house in Capernaum when he is mobbed by people seeking healing.[13] Four friends try to bring their friend, a paralytic, to Jesus. They are unable to do so because of the crowd. Then they find an innovative solution: they cut a hole in the roof of Jesus' house and lower the man through it on a mat.

The term in Greek that is rendered as *mat* in English "refers specifically to the type of sleeping mat used by nonelites."[14] The parallel renditions of the story in Matthew and Luke use a different term that more directly translates to *bed*. Regardless of which Gospel version you choose, this man is lying prone on a bed when he encounters Jesus.

Jesus was the source of the man's healing. But what was the cause of the man's healing? What made his healing possible?

13. The story is recounted in Matt 9:2–8; Mark 2:1–12; Luke 5:17–26.
14. Malina and Rohrbaugh, *Social-Science Commentary on the Synoptic Gospels*, 153.

It was the love and faith of the man's friends. It was their love for their friend. It was their faith in Jesus' ability to help him. These two, love and faith, are what motivated the men to bring their friend to Jesus.

Ruminations

It is because of love and faith that the men bring their friend to Jesus. It is because of love and faith that family and friends call a pastor to the bedside of a dying loved one. It is their love for the dying person. It is their faith that the rites of the church are needed, and beneficial.

Ministry with the dying is often focused solely on the dying person, and understandably so. Yet this time of ministration would not be taking place were it not for the love and faith of the person's family. In the Gospel story, it is only after Jesus acknowledges the faith of the friends (Mark 2:5 for example) that the man is healed.

It is also worth noting that in all three versions of the story, Jesus tells the healed man to go home. To return home to God is one way to understand our mortal death.

Finally, how does the story end? With God being praised. There was a restoration of wholeness to the man: physically and communally. So too in mortal death. Restoration to one's loving God and a fullness of self, health, and integration with community that eclipses ever what was had previously in mortal life.

In our ministry with the dying, how might we cast signs of restoration? How might we point toward or evoke signs of the love and faith of those gathered?

CONCLUSION

Breath marks tell singers where to breathe while following sheet music. Breath marks can also tell the semiotician where to focus their efforts within a particular liturgy. Some such luftpauses have been identified in this chapter.

These are not intended to be the only places to do semiotics in these liturgies, though. To do liturgical semiotics in earnest is to explore new places and ways to ply the craft. A different object, an alternative gesture, other actions or words: the possibilities are many. Not every point in the liturgy will yield deep insights, but one never knows until they try.

Conclusion

"To the last, I wonder with thee; From Heaven's heart, I sign at thee; For love's sake, I bless my last breath at thee."

THE QUOTE THAT BEGINS these last words is an uplifting twist on the last words of Captain Ahab in *Moby Dick*.[1] While Ahab and I may both be accused of being monomaniacal (mine being focused on liturgical semiotics rather than a white whale) hopefully my mania has manifested in a way that leads to creation and light rather than destruction and darkness.

This conclusion has four pieces. The first piece will revisit the kindness described in the book's introduction. The second piece is an overview of the territory covered over the course of the book. The third piece is a look at how one might prepare to go on from here. The fourth and final piece is a blessing.

A KINDNESS REVISITED

The introduction of this book stated that the work's thesis is that the doing of liturgical semiotics will lead to the discovery of new meanings in existing liturgies, improvements in the enacting of those liturgies by making them more evocative of the intended emphasis of the event, and bring the use of worship artifacts more in line with current cultural understandings.

The BREATHE process[2] uncovered missiological meaning in the actions taken with the bread and the wine during the Holy Eucharist. The actions with the bread informed our engagement with the wider community

---

1. "To the last, I grapple with thee; From Hell's heart, I stab at thee; For hate's sake, I spit my last breath at thee." Melville, *Moby Dick*, loc. 8507.

2. Introduced in chapter 4 and practically applied in chapter 6.

as individuals and families. The actions with the wine informed our engagement with the wider community as the local church.

Use of the GASP toolkit[3] presented ways in which the breaking of the bread could be more evocative of the day's particular emphasis (e.g., Pentecost, Easter, wedding, or funeral). The results were adjustments to the liturgy that brought the whole of the liturgy more in line with the theme or message of the day.

Work with RASP[4] (re)signed the use of bread and wine to make certain meanings more accessible to contemporary worshipers. This (re) signing has the potential to reconnect us with the ancient roots of our faith, redeem part of the pain undergone during the pandemic, bring a local congregation closer together, and revitalize our relationship with the earth and the world around us.

With all these observations in hand (another metaphor), it is clear that a successful proof-of-concept has been achieved. Liturgical semiotics as I have cast it has not only produced some fruit, but there is the potential for many bountiful harvests. The laborers, however, are few: help is needed. After a recap of the journey thus far taken, we will turn to how one can join the fray.

LOOKING BACK OVER THE JOURNEY TAKEN

Years ago, before we had kids, my wife Jill and I visited Hawaii. One of the things we did there was to go for a hike in Volcanoes National Park. The trail that we hiked took us down into a crater and across the floor of it. The floor of the crater seemed very much like walking on the moon, except for the couple of spots where we could see steam escaping from the ground. When we got to the other side and started the ascent out of the crater, we looked back, and it was breathtaking. We could see the trail winding its way all the way back across the floor of the crater and disappearing into the treeline on the other side. We both had the same reaction: astonishment. We couldn't believe that we had come all that way and we had been through all that terrain. At the end of that part of the hike, by looking back at the journey we had taken, we were able to see it in a new light and from a new perspective.

Our shared hike through the field of liturgical semiotics, winding through the pages of this book, has reached a similar point. Here is a good place to catch our breath and look back over the terrain. In doing this, we

---

3. Introduced in chapter 4 and practically applied in chapter 7.
4. Introduced in chapter 4 and practically applied in chapter 8.

will both remind ourselves of how far we have come, and begin to see liturgical semiotics from a new perspective.

Part One, "With Bated Breath," encompassed chapters 1 and 2. Chapter 1 posited that worship is the most important activity that Christians engage in. Chapter 2 explored various vehicles for meaning transmission, ultimately choosing the narraphor of breathing as the guide for the rest of the text.

These two chapters combined to form a firm foundation upon which to build an approach to liturgical semiotics. Before addressing liturgy specifically, it was necessary to make the case for the indispensable place of worship in Christianity. Before addressing semiotics as a discipline concerned with meaning-making, it was necessary to identify the best vehicle for meaning-making and choose one as a framework for our further efforts.

Part Two, "A Breath of Fresh Air," consisted of chapters 3 through 5. Chapter 3 explored the base components of liturgical semiotics (i.e., semiotics and liturgy) by sketching out different approaches to semiotics and differing understandings of liturgy found in various branches of the Christian family.

Chapter 4 laid out my approach to liturgical semiotics as distilled into the acronyms BREATHE and GASP/RASP. The BREATHE process is about reading the signs of the liturgy. GASP and RASP are both about making semiotic adjustments to the liturgy. The adjustments of the GASP acronym aim to make the liturgy more evocative of the day's celebration. The adjustments of the RASP acronym have the goal of using various artifacts of worship in a more culturally-resonant way.

Chapter 5 gave an overview of the work of others in the area of liturgical semiotics. Three scholars were picked, the work of each corresponding in some way with one of the acronyms described above. The work of Gerard Lukken was matched to the BREATHE process. The work of Graham Hughes was partnered with GASP/RASP. The practical nature of my approach was offered alongside that of Mark Searle.

Part Three, "Breathe in through nose, out the mouth," comprised chapters 6 through 8. Each of these chapters was a practical application of an approach to liturgical semiotics conceptually outlined in chapter 4. Chapters 6, 7, and 8 corresponded with BREATHE, GASP, and RASP respectively.

These chapters provided real world examples of this trinity of liturgical semiotic engagements. This was necessary because liturgical semiotics, as I have laid it out, does not happen in a vacuum. Rather, it is inherently practical. It is a "where the rubber meets the road" kind of endeavor. Additionally, providing case studies is a tried and true pedagogical method.

Part Four, "Breathing Space . . . and Time," was made up of chapters 9 and 10. Chapter 9 explored different ways to draw meaning from liturgical space. Chapter 10 examined different ways to understand liturgical time, and how that might lead to meaning-making.

These chapters were necessary because space and time can become invisible in their ubiquity. Everything we do takes place at a particular time and in a particular place. To ignore their impact on liturgical semiotics would be like being a marine biologist who completely ignores water. Maintaining an awareness of these larger stages upon which the liturgy plays out helps to broaden our perspectives and keep our minds and hearts open to a greater range of insights.

Part Five, "Deep Breathing Exercises," covered chapters 11 and 12. Chapter 11 provided insights and resources to help someone develop their own unique way of pursuing liturgical semiotics.[5] Chapter 12 provided semiotic insights about different liturgies and suggested some jumping off points for further semiosis.

PREPARING FOR THE UPCOMING JOURNEY

The Boy Scouts of America motto is "Be Prepared." So too with the liturgical semiotician. The question is begged, though, how does one prepare to undertake the semiotic journey? As with most things, a look at Scripture will shine some light on the issue.

In the Gospels we find Jesus sending out the disciples on their own for the first time (Matt 10:5–15; Mark 6:7–9; Luke 9:1–6). They have spent some time learning from Jesus, and are now ready to do a bit of ministry without him looking over their shoulders. While I do not claim to be Jesus, how he sends out the disciples may well inform how someone preparing to do liturgical semiotics on their own might proceed.

In Mark's Gospel, we find Jesus sending out the disciples in a specific way: "He called the twelve and began to send them out two by two, and gave them authority over the unclean spirits. He ordered them to take nothing for their journey except a staff; no bread, no bag, no money in their belts; but to wear sandals and not to put on two tunics" (Mark 6:7–9). One takeaway from Mark's text is that Jesus sends the disciples out in pairs rather than solo.

Travel in that place and time was not nearly as easy and carefree as it is in twenty-first-century America, even in the midst of a pandemic. Most travel, especially for the lower classes, was by foot and therefore slow. Many

5. As opposed to doing liturgical semiotics like an Episcopal priest, which is the only way I know how to do it. My desire is not that everyone does liturgical semiotics like I do, but that they develop their own way of doing it that is true to who they are.

roads were also not safe to travel alone, and so there was more safety in traveling with others.

It is not dangerous to do liturgical semiotics on one's own, per se. Yet it can be done so much more readily in pairs or even in groups than when it is done by oneself. Because semiotics is an individualized endeavor, different people will see different things in the liturgy and make different connections. It is when we hold our perspectives together that even greater insights can be made. This is especially true if the people come from different racial, gender, or generational locations.

Matthew's version of the disciple-sending story does have an important difference from what we find in either of the other two versions: "Go nowhere among the Gentiles, and enter no town of the Samaritans, but go rather to the lost sheep of the house of Israel" (Matt 10:5–6). Jesus is telling the disciples that they are not to simply go about haphazardly. There is an order to these things: go to your own people first.

When it comes to Christians looking to do liturgical semiotics, go to your own people first. There is no doubt much to be learned from studying the liturgies of other denominations or other religions. First, however, one should attend to what they know best. This is why I started with Episcopal liturgies, and it is why someone else should start with the liturgies of their own people.

Luke's version of the story differs from Mark's in what the disciples are to take with them. For Mark, the disciples are to take a staff and wear sandals but not various other things. In Luke's text we find this instead: "Take nothing for your journey, no staff, nor bag, nor bread, nor money—not even an extra tunic" (Luke 9:3). We can spend time and energy trying to reconcile these two contrasting statements and what they might mean. Time and energy is better spent, however, by synthesizing the overarching message: be reliant upon God for what you need on your journey.

The situation is similar when undertaking the journey of liturgical semiotics. You may have paired up with someone, but there are more than two of you there. You may be sticking with *your People*, but there are more than just Episcopalians (or Presbyterians, or Pentecostals, etc.) in the room.[6] God is present and active as well: in the liturgical event and in your semiosis.

---

6. This eye toward the beauty of variety also opens up conversation about variety in any number of ways: racially, ethnically, etc.

A FINAL BLESSING

We come at last to the end of our shared journey together. The final blessing I offer is tripartite, as many excellent blessings are.

The first part is a poem. It comes from Ciel Sainte-Marie and, though brief, provides a rich commentary on breath. It also, I believe, touches on semiotics.

The second part is a liturgy. Part of the Episcopal ethos is the daily office. This is a series of liturgies to be prayed throughout the day at various times. It is a way that some Christians, particularly monastic Christians, have marked the passage of various times and occasions down through history. What I offer is a little office of liturgical semiotics, patterned after An Order for Noonday.[7] One might find it useful to pray (either on one's own or with a partner or group) before engaging in the work of liturgical semiotics.

The third part is a prayer and words to send you out with (also known as a blessing and dismissal).

A Poem

Semiotics, the art of the sign,
embraces liturgy, bows toward the divine.
Inspirations at worship, gift from above,
meaning discovered, proof of God's love.
Oxygenate. Respire. Breathe.[8]

A Liturgy: An Order for Liturgical Semiotics

Officiant: O God, make speed to save us.

People: O Lord, make haste to help us.

Officiant and People:
Glory to the Father, and to the Son, and to the Holy Spirit: as it was in the beginning, is now, and will be for ever. Amen.
Except in Lent, add Alleluia.
A suitable hymn may be sung. One or more of the following Psalms[9] *is sung or said.*

7. Episcopal Church, *Book of Common Prayer*, 103–7.
8. My own work, written for this book.
9. Psalms are taken from the Book of Common Prayer rather than the NRSV.

Psalm 33 Exultate, justi

1. Rejoice in the LORD, you righteous; * it is good for the just to sing praises.

2. Praise the LORD with the harp; * play to him upon the psaltery and lyre.

3. Sing for him a new song; * sound a fanfare with all your skill upon the trumpet.

4. For the word of the LORD is right, * and all his works are sure.

5. He loves righteousness and justice; * the loving-kindness of the LORD fills the whole earth.

6. By the word of the LORD were the heavens made, * by the breath of his mouth all the heavenly hosts.

7. He gathers up the waters of the ocean as in a water-skin * and stores up the depths of the sea.

8. Let all the earth fear the LORD; * let all who dwell in the world stand in awe of him.

9. For he spoke, and it came to pass; * he commanded, and it stood fast.

10. The LORD brings the will of the nations to naught; * he thwarts the designs of the peoples.

11. But the LORD'S will stands fast for ever, * and the designs of his heart from age to age.

12. Happy is the nation whose God is the LORD! * happy the people he has chosen to be his own!

13. The LORD looks down from heaven, * and beholds all the people in the world.

14. From where he sits enthroned he turns his gaze * on all who dwell on the earth.

15. He fashions all the hearts of them * and understands all their works.

16. There is no king that can be saved by a mighty army; * a strong man is not delivered by his great strength.

17. The horse is a vain hope for deliverance; * for all its strength it cannot save.

18. Behold, the eye of the LORD is upon those who fear him, * on those who wait upon his love,

19. To pluck their lives from death, * and to feed them in time of famine.

20. Our soul waits for the LORD; * he is our help and our shield.

21. Indeed, our heart rejoices in him, * for in his holy Name we put our trust.

22. Let your loving-kindness, O LORD, be upon us, * as we have put our trust in you.

Psalm 130 De profundis

1. Out of the depths have I called to you, O LORD; LORD, hear my voice; * let your ears consider well the voice of my supplication.

2. If you, LORD, were to note what is done amiss, * O LORD, who could stand?

3. For there is forgiveness with you; * therefore you shall be feared.

4. I wait for the LORD; my soul waits for him; * in his word is my hope.

5. My soul waits for the LORD, more than watchmen for the morning, * more than watchmen for the morning.

6. O Israel, wait for the LORD, * for with the LORD there is mercy;

7. With him there is plenteous redemption, * and he shall redeem Israel from all their sins.

Psalm 150 Laudate Dominum

1. Hallelujah! Praise God in his holy temple; * praise him in the firmament of his power.

2. Praise him for his mighty acts; * praise him for his excellent greatness.

3. Praise him with the blast of the ram's-horn; * praise him with lyre and harp.

4. Praise him with timbrel and dance; * praise him with strings and pipe.

5. Praise him with resounding cymbals; * praise him with loud-clanging cymbals.

6. Let everything that has breath * praise the Lord. Hallelujah!

At the end of the Psalms is sung or said
     Glory to the Father, and to the Son, and to the Holy Spirit: *
     as it was in the beginning, is now, and will be for ever. Amen.
     One of the following, or some other suitable passage of Scripture, is read

Jesus said to them again, "Peace be with you. As the Father has sent me, so I send you." When he had said this, he breathed on them and said to them, "Receive the Holy Spirit." John 20:21–22.

People: Thanks be to God.
or the following
For wisdom is more mobile than any motion;
because of her pureness she pervades and penetrates all things.
For she is a breath of the power of God,
and a pure emanation of the glory of the Almighty;
therefore nothing defiled gains entrance into her.
Wisdom of Solomon 7:24–25.

People: Thanks be to God.
or this
Then the Lord God formed man from the dust of the ground, and breathed into his nostrils the breath of life; and the man became a living being. Genesis 2:7.

People: Thanks be to God.
A meditation, silent or spoken, may follow.
The Officiant: then begins the Prayers
Lord, have mercy.
Christ, have mercy.
Lord, have mercy.
Officiant: and People:

Our Father, who art in heaven,	Our Father in heaven,
hallowed be thy Name,	hallowed be your Name,
thy kingdom come,	your kingdom come,
thy will be done,	your will be done,
on earth as it is in heaven.	on earth as in heaven.
Give us this day our daily bread.	Give us today our daily bread.
And forgive us our trespasses,	Forgive us our sins
as we forgive those	as we forgive those
who trespass against us.	who sin against us.
And lead us not into temptation,	Save us from the time of trial,
but deliver us from evil.	and deliver us from evil.

Officiant: Lord, hear our prayer;
People: And let our cry come to you.
Officiant: Let us pray.
The Officiant then says one of the following Collect. If desired, the Collect of the Day may be used.

O God, whose blessed Son made himself known to his disciples in the breaking of bread: Open the eyes of our faith, that we may behold him in all his redeeming work; who lives and reigns with you, in the unity of the Holy Spirit, one God, now and for ever. *Amen.*[10]

Eternal Father, you gave to your incarnate Son the holy name of Jesus to be the sign of our salvation: Plant in every heart, we pray, the love of him who is the Savior of the world, our Lord Jesus Christ; who lives and reigns with you and the Holy Spirit, one God, in glory everlasting. *Amen.*[11]

Heavenly Father, in you we live and move and have our being: We humbly pray you so to guide and govern us by your Holy Spirit, that in all the cares and occupations of our life we may not forget you, but may remember that we are ever walking in your sight; through Jesus Christ our Lord. *Amen.*

Almighty and most merciful God, grant that by the indwelling of your Holy Spirit we may be enlightened and strengthened for your service; through Jesus Christ our Lord, who lives and reigns with you, in the unity of the Holy Spirit, one God, now and for ever. *Amen.*[12]

Free intercessions may be offered. The service concludes as follows
Officiant: Let us bless the Lord.
People: Thanks be to God.

Prayer and Parting Words

May God the Father wake you from the sleep of the everyday as you seek him in worship and seek to worship him. May you encounter the liturgy anew, empowered by the Holy Spirit to read signs and make connections. May you be the hands and feet of Christ as you enact the liturgy, an apt instrument of the heavenly liturgist. And may the blessing of God Almighty: Father, Son, and Holy Spirit, be with you this day, and always. Amen.

Go in peace: a kingdom of meaning, and the meaning of the kingdom, awaits.

10. Episcopal Church, *Book of Common Prayer*, 224–25.
11. Episcopal Church, *Book of Common Prayer*, 213.
12. Episcopal Church, *Book of Common Prayer*, 100.

Appendix A

What follows is an exercise in trusting the story, focusing on Paul's calling of Timothy.

THE ACTS OF THE APOSTLES 16:1–5

Timothy Joins Paul and Silas

Paul went on also to Derbe and to Lystra, where there was a disciple named Timothy, the son of a Jewish woman who was a believer; but his father was a Greek. He was well spoken of by the believers in Lystra and Iconium. Paul wanted Timothy to accompany him; and he took him and had him circumcised because of the Jews who were in those places, for they all knew that his father was a Greek. As they went from town to town, they delivered to them for observance the decisions that had been reached by the apostles and elders who were in Jerusalem. So the churches were strengthened in the faith and increased in numbers daily.

Timothy's Circumcision

The typical interpretation of this story is that Paul recruits Timothy because Timothy was of a mixed marriage, his mother being a Jew and his father being a Greek. Given this background, Timothy would be a good person to use for evangelizing the Gentiles.

Yet that reading of the story misses something crucial that the author of Acts was trying to tell us. Consider that after calling Timothy, Paul "took him and had him circumcised because of the Jews who were in those places, for they all knew that his father was a Greek" (Acts 16:3). If the primary reason that Paul wanted Timothy was to appeal to the Gentiles, then he would not need to do something to assuage the Jews in the area. Furthermore, if Timothy were a Gentile, there is no reason at all that he should be circumcised, given the Council of Jerusalem's decision in 48 CE that Gentile Christians need not be circumcised. If we are to trust the story, however, Timothy's circumcision has to make sense.

An interpretive key lies in Luke's intended audience. The reader will recall that the Gospel of Luke and the Acts of the Apostles were written as a two-volume set. They were written to Theophilus, "so that you may know the truth concerning the things about which you have been instructed" (Luke 1:4).

It is possible that Theophilus could have simply been a literary device and that he was not a living, breathing person. It would not have been an extraordinary choice for the author to make. The story as written, however, is that he is a real person—the intended audience of Luke and Acts. Furthermore, "dedications of the time customarily referred to real persons."[1]

If the reader suspends their disbelief long enough to trust the story as given to us, that Theophilus was a real person, then there are some interesting dots to connect. The wording of the dedication seems to imply that Theophilus is a convert to the faith since he has received instruction and the books are to further that instruction.

The question becomes, a convert from what? Theophilus is a Greek name. But was Theophilus a gentile or a Hellenized Jew? Consider that Christianity at the time of Luke-Acts was still intertwined with its Jewish roots. In light of this, let us follow the path of Theophilus being a Hellenized Jew and see where that may lead.

If Theophilus was a Hellenized Jew who had converted to Christianity, then the intended audience of Luke-Acts was a Jewish one. This then changes the nature of Timothy's call and his circumcision makes sense. If Luke is "talking" to a Jewish audience, then in mentioning that Timothy's father was a Greek, he would actually mean a Hellenized Jew. This is because, "in Israelite in-groups, 'Judean' meant 'barbarian,' that is, following the customs and language of Judea, while 'Greek' meant 'civilized,' following Hellenistic customs and language."[2] Such Hellenized Jews would not have their children circumcised, even though "Jewish law required that all Jewish males—and male converts to Judaism—be circumcised."[3] They would have seen themselves as too sophisticated, too civilized, for such barbarous acts.

---

1. Robert O. Toole, "Theophilus (Person)," in Freedman, *Anchor Yale Bible Dictionary*, 6:511.

2. Malina, *Timothy*, 101.

3. Patterson, *Forgotten Creed*, 11.

It makes sense for Paul to circumcise Timothy if he is a Jew and if he is intending to be ministering among Jews. Once circumcised, Timothy could appeal to both Judean Jews and Hellenistic Jews. He was "a perfect homophilous candidate to assist Paul in his diffusion of innovation activity among Israelites in majority non-Israelite locations."[4]

By trusting the story, and reading the sign of Timothy's circumcision, we have made sense of Paul's circumcision of Timothy and gained new insights into Paul's ministry.

4. Malina, *Timothy*, 107–8.

Appendix B

A PERSONAL STORY

I find the breaking of the bread, also known as the fraction, to be the most poignant and meaningful action in the Holy Eucharist. Allow me to share a personal story.

I was halfway through my first semester at my first seminary and I was suffering under the realization that seminary was most definitely not what I had expected or hoped it would be. It was more about theology, academia, and social issues than it was about deepening one's relationship with God. The zeitgeist of the place had little reverence for God and not much regard for walking with Jesus Christ.

As a result, I had been attending the chapel services less and less. They were occasionally interesting or informative, but they in no way were feeding me spiritually. This was particularly true of the Eucharist services. Then a friend of mine suggested that I try going to a Eucharist service presided over by one of the deans late on Tuesday night.

After class on Tuesday night I walked over to the chapel. I found it dimly illuminated, with lit candles and icons prominently displayed. As I sat down and the service started, something within me fell silent and became attentive.

The presider processed in from the back with a crucifer, and the liturgy proceeded to unfold. As it did, I found myself drawn further into being truly present in the moment. Other thoughts and concerns fell away. The emotional baggage that I had walked through the doors with were carefully laid down. I was having, for the first time in a long time, a worshipful experience.

When the Eucharist reached the fraction, my world was turned on its head. The presider lifted the host high. My eyes followed it intently. A silence, so thick that you could almost chew it, hung heavy with expectation.

Then with one quick movement, in a heartbeat instant, the host was snapped in two.

Something happened. As that host fractured, something deep inside me fractured as well. As the audible sound of the fraction died away, I noticed that I had stopped breathing. I inhaled deeply, and life flooded my veins in what seemed like a new way.

The rest of the Eucharist followed on from there. I was enraptured in a wonderfully renewing and enriching worship experience. The fraction had been the fulcrum, the pivot point, in the service. The flow built up to it, and then new vistas became visible through that breaking open and breaking apart.

Appendix C

THE WEDDING VOWS

The breath marks that I have identified are not the only plausible ones. The richness of liturgies can often provide the semiotician with several possible directions to move in. The wedding ceremony is no exception.

The vows that a couple make can vary widely. As an example to follow, however, here are how the vows look in the BCP: "In the Name of God, I, *N.*, take you, *N.*, to be my wife, to have and to hold from this day forward, for better for worse, for richer for poorer, in sickness and in health, to love and to cherish, until we are parted by death. This is my solemn vow."[1] The couple vows to love and cherish each other, in the good times and the bad, until the end.

Previously we have considered the church as the body of Christ. This is not the only way to understand the church, however. It can also be thought of as the bride of Christ.[2]

If the church is the bride of Christ, then there is an intriguing implication for the vows in the wedding ceremony. The vows are being made by the church to the church. The church promises to love and cherish itself, for better for worse, for richer for poorer, until parted by death.

Every Christian marriage is, in effect, a renewal of the covenant that the church is making with itself before God. That covenant is that even in these poorer, worse times, the church is vowing to not give up on itself.

It is easy to get down on the church in twenty-first century America. It is easy to see the future as a time of increasing darkness rather than a time

---

1. Episcopal Church, *Book of Common Prayer*, 427.

2. Passages like 2 Corinthians 11:2, Ephesians 5:22–33, and Revelation 19:7–9 all help to sketch out this metaphor.

of growing light. Each wedding ceremony is a reminder, though, that the church is to love itself.

Also, and this is harder to face, we are to do this until we are parted by death. Until the earthly institution of the church dies, we love ourselves as the church and cherish ourselves. If you have ever seen a long-married, elderly couple walk through the dying process together, then this is what I am talking about. It is often not pretty, but it is a beautiful expression of love.

Our worship points us toward a way to face the future. With grace and tenderness for ourselves as the church, yet with a realism that, while the bride of Christ the church will never die, certain expressions of that, certain denominations even, almost certainly will.

Bibliography

Adams, William. *Shaped by Images: One Who Presides*. New York: Church Hymnal, 1995.

Alexander, J. Neil. *Celebrating Liturgical Time: Days, Weeks, and Seasons*. New York: Church, 2014.

Ancestry. "Wold Family History." https://www.ancestry.com/name-origin?surname=wold.

Anward, Jan. "Semiotics in Educational Research." *International Encyclopedia of Educational Research*, edited by Torsten Husén and T. Neville Postlethwaite, 9:5411–17. Oxford: Pergamon, 1994.

Athenagoras. "A Plea for the Christians." In *Fathers of the Second Century: Hermas, Tatian, Athenagoras, Theophilus, and Clement of Alexandria (Entire)*, edited by A. Roberts et al., translated by B. P. Pratten, 2:200–236. Buffalo, NY: Christian Literature, 1885.

Bacchiocchi, Samuele. *From Sabbath to Sunday: A Historical Investigation of the Rise of Sunday Observance in Early Christianity*. Rome: Pontifical Gregorian University Press, 1977.

Baker, Mike, et al. "Three Words. 70 Cases. The Tragic History of 'I Can't Breathe.'" *New York Times*, June 29, 2020.

Balthasar, Hans von. *Mysterium Paschale: The Mystery of Easter*. San Francisco: Ignatius, 2000.

Barrett, Mark. *The Wind, the Fountain, and the Fire: Scripture and the Renewal of the Christian Imagination: The 2020 Lent Book*. London: Bloomsbury Continuum, 2019.

Barry, John D., et al. *Faithlife Study Bible*. Bellingham, WA: Lexham, 2016.

———. *The Lexham Bible Dictionary*. Bellingham, WA: Lexham, 2016.

Basil of Caesarea. *De Spiritu Sancto*. https://www.newadvent.org/fathers/3203.htm.

Bauer, Walter, et al. *A Greek-English Lexicon of the New Testament and Other Early Christian Literature*. 3rd ed. Chicago: University of Chicago Press, 2000.

Bernard of Clairvaux. *St. Bernard's Sermons on the Canticle of Canticles*. Vol. 2. Translated by A Priest of Mount Melleray. Dublin: Browne and Nolan, 1920.

Bernardakis, D. N. *A Catechism*. Translated by C. D. Cobham. Nicosia: Cyprus Government Printing Office, 1903.

Binswanger, Ludwig. *Being in the World*. New York: Harper & Row, 1963.

Blue Corner Dive. "How to Relax; The Irony of a Breathe-Up in Freediving." https://www.bluecornerdive.com/blog/2019/4/8/how-to-relax-the-irony-of-a-breathe-up-in-freediving.

Boom, Jason Cronbach Van, and Pöder Thomas-Andreas. *Sign, Method, and the Sacred: New Directions in Semiotic Methodologies for the Study of Religion.* Berlin: de Gruyter, 2021.

Boussac, Paul, ed. *Encyclopedia of Semiotics.* Oxford: Oxford University Press, 1998.

Bower, Gordon, and Michal Clark. "Narrative Stories as Mediators for Serial Learning." *Psychonomic Science* 15 (1969) 181–82.

Bregman, Rutger. *Humankind: A Hopeful History.* New York: Little, Brown, and Company, 2020.

Brown, Brené. "Clear Is Kind. Unclear Is Unkind." *Brené Brown* (blog), October 15, 2018. https://brenebrown.com/articles/2018/10/15/clear-is-kind-unclear-is-unkind.

Burge, Ryan. "The Death of the Episcopal Church Is Near." *Religion in Public*, July 6, 2021. https://religioninpublic.blog/2021/07/06/the-death-of-the-episcopal-church-is-near/.

Burton, Tara Isabella. *Strange Rites: New Religions for a Godless World.* New York: PublicAffairs, 2020.

Catholic Church. *Sacrosanctum Concilium.* https://www.vatican.va/archive/hist_councils/ii_vatican_council/documents/vat-ii_const_19631204_sacrosanctum-concilium_en.html.

———. *The Roman Missal.* 3rd ed. Washington, DC: United States Conference of Catholic Bishops, 2011. https://www.usccb.org/prayer-and-worship/the-mass/general-instruction-of-the-roman-missal.

Centers for Disease Control and Prevention. "Coronavirus Disease 2019 (COVID-19) 2021 Case Definition." https://ndc.services.cdc.gov/case-definitions/coronavirus-disease-2019-2021/.

Cicero. *The Letters of Cicero.* 4 vols. Translated by E. S. Shuckburgh. London: Bell and Sons, 1908–9.

Cole, R. W., et al. *Eerdmans Dictionary of the Bible.* Grand Rapids: Eerdmans, 2000.

Conzelmann, Hans. *History of Primitive Christianity.* Translated by J. Steely. Nashville: Abingdon, 1973.

Corrington, Robert S. "Regnant Signs: The Semiosis of Liturgy." *Semiotica* 117 (1997) 19–42.

COVID-19 Mental Disorders Collaborators. "Global Prevalence and Burden of Depressive and Anxiety Disorders in 204 Countries and Territories in 2020 Due to the COVID-19 Pandemic." *Lancet* 398 (2021) 1700–1712. https://doi.org/10.1016/S0140-6736(21)02143-7.

Cross, F. L., and E. A. Livingstone, eds. *The Oxford Dictionary of the Christian Church.* 3rd ed. Oxford: Oxford University Press, 2005.

"The Decree of the Holy, Great, Ecumenical Synod, the Second of Nice." In *Nicene and Post-Nicene Fathers, Series II*, edited by Philip Schaff and Henry Wace, translated by H. R. Percival, 14:1020–23. Grand Rapids: Eerdmans, 1989.

Di Berardino, Angelo, et al. *Encyclopedia of Ancient Christianity.* Vol. 2. Downers Grove, IL: IVP Academic, 2014.

Dix, Gregory. *The Shape of the Liturgy.* London: Dacre, 1954.

Dobschütz, Ernst von. *Christian Life in the Primitive Church.* Theological Translation Library 18. New York: Putnam's Sons, 1904.

Downing, Crystal. *Changing Signs of Truth: A Christian Introduction to the Semiotics of Communication.* Downers Grove, IL: IVP Academic, 2012.

Dyer, Wayne. "Go with the Love." *Dr. Wayne W. Dyer* (blog). https://www.drwaynedyer.com/blog/go-with-the-love/.

Earls, Aaron. "How Do Most Pastors Plan Their Sermons?" *Lifeway Research*, July 20, 2021. https://lifewayresearch.com/2021/07/20/how-do-most-pastors-plan-their-sermons/.

Eco, Umberto. *The Name of the Rose*. Boston: Houghton Mifflin Harcourt, 2014.

———. "Semiotics and the Philosophy of Language." In *Reading Eco: An Anthology*, edited by Rocco Capozzi, 1–13. Bloomington: Indiana University Press, 1997.

Elwell, Walter, ed. *Baker Encyclopedia of the Bible*. Grand Rapids: Baker, 1988.

The Episcopal Church. *The Book of Common Prayer and Administration of the Sacraments and Other Rites and Ceremonies of the Church: Together with the Psalter or Psalms of David according to the Use of the Episcopal Church*. New York: Seabury, 1979.

———. *Constitution & Canons Together with the Rules of Order for the Government of the Protestant Episcopal Church in the United States of America Otherwise Known as the Episcopal Church*. New York: Church, 2018.

———. *Enriching Our Worship 1: Morning and Evening Prayer, The Great Litany, The Holy Eucharist*. New York: Church, 1998.

———. *The Hymnal 1982*. New York: Church Hymnal, 1985.

———. *Wonder, Love, and Praise: A Supplement to The Hymnal 1982*. New York: Church Pension Fund, 1997.

ETH Zurich. "Exhaled Breath Carries a Molecular 'Breathprint' Unique to Each Individual." *ScienceDaily*, April 3, 2014. www.sciencedaily.com/releases/2013/04/130403200254.htm.

Ferguson, Sinclair B., et al., eds. *New Dictionary of Theology*. Downers Grove, IL: InterVarsity, 2000.

Freakstyle571. Review of "Learning to Breathe." *Sputnik Music*, May 18, 2006. https://www.sputnikmusic.com/review/6971/Switchfoot-Learning-To-Breathe/.

Freedman, David Noel, ed. *The Anchor Yale Bible Dictionary*. 6 vols. New York: Doubleday, 1992.

Geary, James. *I Is an Other: The Secret Life of Metaphor and How It Shapes the Way We See the World*. New York: HarperCollins, 2012.

Gerety, Rowan Moore. "Buying the Body of Christ." *Killing the Buddha*, January 3, 2012. https://killingthebuddha.com/mag/buying-the-body-of-christ/.

Giles, Richard. *Re-pitching the Tent: Re-ordering the Church Building for Worship and Mission*. Collegeville, MN: Liturgical, 2004.

Gray, Donald. "Hands and Hocus-Pocus: The Manual Acts in the Eucharistic Prayer." *Worship* 69 (1995) 306–13.

Gregory of Nyssa. *On the Soul and the Resurrection*. Translated by C. Roth. Crestwood, NY: St. Vladimir's Seminary Press, 1993.

Grey, Melissa-Kay. "The Breath Mark Guide." *Grey Flute* (blog), December 3, 2020. https://www.greyflute.com/blog/2020/12/3/the-breath-mark-guide.

Guardini, Romano. *The Spirit of the Liturgy*. Edmond, OK: Veritatis Splendor, 1918. Kindle.

Guinness World Records. "Deepest No-limit Freedive (Male)." https://www.guinnessworldrecords.com/world-records/673884-deepest-no-limit-freedive-male.

Han, Byung-Chul. *The Disappearance of Rituals: A Topology of the Present*. Translated by Daniel Steuer. Cambridge: Polity, 2020.

Hartmann, Ernest. "We Do Not Dream of the 3 R's: Implications for the Nature of Dreaming Mentation." *Dreaming* 10 (2000) 103–10. https://doi.org/10.1023/A:1009400805830.

Hatchett, Marion. *Commentary on the American Prayer Book.* New York: HarperOne, 1995.

Hefling, Charles, and Cynthia L. Shattuck, eds. *The Oxford Guide to the Book of Common Prayer: A Worldwide Survey.* Oxford: Oxford University Press, 2006.

Henderson, John, and Taylor Hayes. "Meaning-based Guidance of Attention in Scenes as Revealed by Meaning Maps." *Nature Human Behavior* 1 (2017) 743–47.

Holladay, Carl. *Acts: A Commentary.* New Testament Library. Louisville: Westminster John Knox, 2016.

Hughes, Graham. *Worship as Meaning a Liturgical Theology for Late Modernity.* Cambridge: Cambridge University Press, 2003.

Irvine, Christopher. *The Use of Symbols in Worship.* Alcuin Liturgy Guides. London: SPCK, 2007.

Johns Hopkins Medicine. "Vital Signs (Body Temperature, Pulse Rate, Respiration Rate, Blood Pressure)." https://www.hopkinsmedicine.org/health/conditions-and-diseases/vital-signs-body-temperature-pulse-rate-respiration-rate-blood-pressure.

John Hopkins School of Medicine's Interactive Respiratory Physiology. "Dead Space." https://oac.med.jhmi.edu/res_phys/Encyclopedia/DeadSpace/DeadSpace.html.

John of Damascus. *On the Divine Images.* Edited by P. Argarate. New York: St. Vladimir's Seminary Press, 1980.

John Paul II. *Ut Unum Sint: On Commitment to Ecumenism.* Vatican City: Holy See, 1995.

Jones, Rory. "NFL Sees Average Viewership Grow 10% to 17.1m during Regular Season." *SportsPro*, January 13, 2022. https://www.sportspromedia.com/news/nfl-tv-ratings-2021-regular-season-viewership/.

Juergens, Sylvester. *The Roman Catholic Daily Missal, 1962: With Kyriale in Gregorian Notation.* Kansas City, MO: Angelus, 2004.

Justin Martyr. *The First Apology, The Second Apology, Dialogue with Trypho, Exhortation to the Greeks, Discourse to the Greeks, The Monarchy or The Rule of God.* Translated by T. B. Falls. Fathers of the Church Patristic Series 6. Washington, DC: Catholic University of America Press, 1948.

Kennedy, John F. "Commencement Address at American University, Washington D.C., June 10, 1963." *John F. Kennedy Library,* https://www.jfklibrary.org/archives/other-resources/john-f-kennedy-speeches/american-university-19630610.

Kingsley, Emily Perl. "Welcome to Holland." https://www.emilyperlkingsley.com/welcome-to-holland.

Klotz, Greg. "'Oh, Worship the King': Understanding Culture and Semiotics in Christian Worship." *Missio Apostolica* 23 (2015) 293–307.

Koester, Anne Y., and Barbara Seale, eds. *Vision: The Scholarly Contributions of Mark Searle to Liturgical Renewal.* Collegeville, MN: Liturgical, 2004.

Komonchak, J. A., et al. *The New Dictionary of Theology.* Collegeville, MN: Liturgical, 2000.

Kubicki, Judith. "Recognizing the Presence of Christ in the Liturgical Assembly." *Theological Studies* 65 (2004) 817–37.

Lakoff, George, and Mark Johnson. *Metaphors We Live By*. Chicago: University of Chicago Press, 2003.

Lee, Jeffrey, and Dent Davidson. *Gathered for God*. Church's Teachings for a Changing World 8. New York: Church, 2018.

Liddell, Henry George, et al. *A Lexicon: Abridged from Liddell and Scott's Greek-English Lexicon*. Sheridan, WY: Franklin Classics, 2019.

Litchfield, Peter. "A Brief Overview of the Chemistry of Respiration and the Breathing Heart Wave." https://www.aipro.info/wp/wp-content/uploads/2017/08/200.pdf.

Lukken, Gerard. "Betekenislagen van het kerkgebouw: een benadering vanuit de recente tensieve semiotiek." *Yearbook for Liturgy Research* 24 (2008) 117–38.

———. "Semiotics and the Study of Liturgy." *Studia Liturgica* 17 (1987) 108–17.

Lukken, Gerard, and Mark Searle. *Semiotics and Church Architecture: Applying the Semiotics of A. J. Greimas and the Paris School to the Analysis of Church Buildings*. Kampen: Kok Pharos, 1993.

Lukken, Gerard, et al.. *Per Visibilia Ad Invisibilia: Anthropological, Theological, and Semiotic Studies on the Liturgy and the Sacraments*. Kampen: Kok Pharos, 1995.

Maguire, Gregory. *A Lion among Men*. New York: Morrow, 2008.

Malina, Bruce. *Timothy: Paul's Closest Associate*. Collegeville, MN: Liturgical, 2007.

Malina, Bruce, and R. L. Rohrbaugh. *Social-Science Commentary on the Synoptic Gospels*. 2nd ed. Minneapolis: Fortress, 2003.

Malloy, Patrick. *Celebrating the Eucharist a Practical Ceremonial Guide for Clergy and Other Liturgical Ministers*. New York: Church, 2007.

Mangum, Douglas. *The Lexham Glossary of Theology*. Bellingham, WA: Lexham, 2014.

Martin, Ralph. *Worship in the Early Church*. Rev. ed. Grand Rapids: Eerdmans, 1974.

Martin, W. J., et al. *New Bible Dictionary*. 3rd ed. Downers Grove, IL: InterVarsity, 1996.

McGann, Mary. *The Meal That Reconnects: Eucharistic Eating and the Global Food Crisis*. Collegeville, MN: Liturgical Academic, 2020.

Melville, Herman. *Moby Dick*. Copenhagen: Titan Read, 2015. Kindle.

Michno, Dennis. *A Priest's Handbook: The Ceremonies of the Church*. Harrisburg, PA: Morehouse, 1998.

Mitchell, Leonel, and Ruth A. Meyers. *Praying Shapes Believing: A Theological Commentary on The Book of Common Prayer*. New York: Seabury, 2016.

Murphy, Agnes. *Melba: A Biography*. Glasgow: Good, 2021. Kindle.

NBC Sports Group Press Box. "NBC Sports' Coverage of Super Bowl LVI Averages Total Audience Delivery of 112.3 Million Viewers, Reaches 167 Million Viewers on Unprecedented Day in Sports Media History." https://nbcsportsgrouppressbox. com/2022/02/15/nbc-sports-coverage-of-super-bowl-lvi-averages-total-audience-delivery-of-112-3-million-viewers-reaches-167-million-viewers-on-unprecedented-day-in-sports-media-history/.

Negev, Avraham. *The Archaeological Encyclopedia of the Holy Land*. 3rd ed. New York: Prentice Hall, 1990.

Nouwen, Henri. *Behold the Beauty of the Lord: Praying with Icons*. Notre Dame: Ave Maria, 2007.

O'Brien, William. "The Eucharistic Species in Light of Peirce's Sign Theory." *Theological Studies* 75 (2014) 74–93.

O'Loughlin, Thomas. "Liturgical Evolution and the Fallacy of the Continuing Consequence." *Worship* 83 (2009) 312–23.

OnMusic Dictionary. "Breath Mark." https://dictionary.onmusic.org/terms/508-breath _mark.

Parker, Priya. *The Art of Gathering: How We Meet and Why It Matters*. New York: Riverhead, 2018. Kindle.

Patterson, Stephen. *The Forgotten Creed: Christianity's Original Struggle against Bigotry, Slavery, and Sexism*. New York: Oxford University Press, 2018.

Pilch, John. *A Cultural Handbook to the Bible*. Grand Rapids; Eerdmans, 2012.

Plato II of Moscow. *The Great Catechism of the Holy Catholic, Apostolic, and Orthodox Church*. Translated by J. T. Seccombe. London: Simpkin, Marshall, & Co, 1867.

Quasten, J., and J. Plumpe, eds. *The Didache, The Epistle of Barnabas, The Epistles and the Martyrdom of St. Polycarp, The Fragments of Papias, and The Epistle to Diognetus*. Translated by J. Kleist. 6th ed. Mahwah, NJ: Newman, 1948.

Quattrone, Aldo, et al. "Neurobiology of Placebo Effect in Parkinson's Disease: What We Have Learned and Where We Are Going." *Movement Disorders* 33 (2018) 1213–27.

Radcliffe, Timothy. *Alive in God: A Christian Imagination*. London: Bloombury Continuum, 2019.

Ratzinger, Joseph. *Pilgrim Fellowship of Faith: The Church as Communion*. San Francisco: Ignatius, 2005.

———. *The Spirit of the Liturgy*. Translated by J. Saward. San Francisco: Ignatius, 2000.

Rimbaud, Arthur. "The Seer Leeter #1." https://rimbaudanalysis.wordpress.com/letters/.

Ritchie, Hannah, and Max Roser. "Urbanization." *Our World in Data*. https:// ourworldindata.org/urbanization#number-of-people-living-in-urban-areas.

Rossano, Matt. "The Ritual Origins of Humanity." In *Interdisziplinäre Anthropologie*, edited by G. Hartung and M. Herrgen, 3–25. Wiesbaden: Springer VS, 2015.

Santayan, George. *The Life of Reason*. Vol. 1. London: Archibald Constable & Co., 1906.

Saussure, Ferdinand de. *Course in General Linguistics*. Edited by Perry Meisel and Haun Saussy. Translated by Wade Baskin. New York: Columbia University Press, 2011.

Schillebeeckx, Edward. *The Eucharist*. Translated by N. D. Smith. London: Sheed & Ward, 1968.

Schmich, Mary. "Advice, Like Youth, Probably Just Wasted on the Young." *Chicago Tribune*, June 1, 1997. https://www.chicagotribune.com/columns/chi-schmich-sunscreen-column-column.html.

Scruton, Roger. *I Drink Therefore I Am: A Philosopher's Guide to Wine*. London: Continuum, 2019.

Shakespeare, William. *The Merchant of* Venice. Edited by Barbara A. Mowat and Paul Werstine. Folger Shakespeare Library. New York: Simon & Schuster Paperbacks, 2009.

———. *The Tragedy of Romeo and Juliet*. Edited by Barbara A. Mowat and Paul Werstine. Folger Shakespeare Library. New York: Simon & Schuster, 2004.

Shklovsky, Viktor, ed. *Viktor Shklovsky: A Reader*. Translated by Alexander Berlina. New York: Bloomsbury Academic, 2017.

Short, T. L. *Peirce's Theory of Signs*. Cambridge: Cambridge University Press, 2009.

Siedentop, Larry. *Inventing the Individual: The Origins of Western Liberalism*. Cambridge: Belknap, 2018.

Simmons, Annette. *The Story Factor: Inspiration, Influence, and Persuasion through the Art of Storytelling*. New York: Basic, 2019.

Smith, Gregory. "About Three-in-Ten U.S. Adults Are Now Religiously Unaffiliated." *Pew Research Center*, December 14, 2021. https://www.pewforum.org/2021/12/14/about-three-in-ten-u-s-adults-are-now-religiously-unaffiliated/.

Soanes, Catherine, and Angus Stevenson. *Oxford Concise English Dictionary*. 11th ed. Oxford: Oxford University Press, 2004.

Sullivan, Karen. *Mixed Metaphors: Their Use and Abuse*. New York: Bloomsbury Academic, 2019.

Swanson, James. *Dictionary of Biblical Languages with Semantic Domains: Hebrew (Old Testament)*. Faithlife, 1997.

Sweet, Leonard. *Giving Blood: A Fresh Paradigm for Preaching*. Grand Rapids: Zondervan, 2014.

———. *Strong in the Broken Places: A Theological Reverie on the Ministry of George Everett Ross*. Akron, OH: University of Akron Press, 1995.

———. *The Well-Played Life: Why Pleasing God Doesn't Have to Be Such Hard Work*. Carol Stream, IL: Tyndale Momentum, 2014.

Sweet, Leonard, and Mark Chironna. *Rings of Fire: Walking in Faith through a Volcanic Future*. Colorado Springs: NavPress, 2019.

Sweet, Leonard, and Frank Viola. *Jesus: A Theography*. Nashville: Nelson, 2012.

———. *Jesus Speaks: Learning to Recognize and Respond to the Lord's Voice*. Nashville: Nelson, 2016.

Tayag, Yasmin. "Can You Read in Your Dreams? Science Reveals Why Most People Can't." *Inverse*, November 16, 2017. https://www.inverse.com/science/can-you-read-in-your-dreams.

Taylor, Steve. "Why Does Time Seem to Pass at Different Speeds?" *Psychology Today*, July 3, 2017. https://www.psychologytoday.com/us/blog/out-the-darkness/201107/why-does-time-seem-pass-different-speeds.

Tovey, Phillip. *Inculturation of Christian Worship: Exploring the Eucharist*. Burlington, VT: Ashgate, 2004.

Turner, Victor. *The Ritual Process: Structure and Anti-structure*. New York: Routledge, 2017.

Turrell, James. *Celebrating the Rites of Initiation: A Practical Ceremonial Guide for Clergy and Other Liturgical Ministers*. New York: Church, 2013.

Twal, Waleed, et al. "Yogic Breathing When Compared to Attention Control Reduces the Levels of Pro-inflammatory Biomarkers in Saliva: A Pilot Randomized Controlled Trial." *BMC Complement Altern Med.* 16 (2016). doi: 10.1186/s12906-016-1286-7.

van Rheede van Oudtshoorn, Andre. "Symbolising Salvation: A Semiotic Analysis of the Church as a Transformative Communication System in the World." *Verbum et Ecclesia* 36 (2015) 1–7.

Warren, Rick. *The Purpose Driven Church: Growth without Compromising Your Message & Mission*. Grand Rapids: Zondervan, 1995.

Weil, Louis. *Liturgical Sense: The Logic of Rite*. New York: Seabury, 2013.

Westminster Assembly. *The Westminster Confession of Faith: Edinburgh Edition*. Philadelphia: Young, 1851.

Whitney, William Dwight, and Benjamin Eli Smith, eds. *Century Dictionary*. http://www.global-language.com/century/.

Wilbricht, Stephen Sullivan. "Mark Searle's Vision for 'Pastoral Liturgical Studies': Liturgy as 'Rehearsal of Christian Attitudes.'" STD diss., Catholic University of America, 2010.

William of Ockham. *Quaestiones et decisiones in quattuor libros Sententiarum Petri Lombardi [Questions and Decisions in the Four Sentences of Peter Lombard]*. Lyon: Trechsel, 1495.

Williamson, Hugh. *The Great Prayer: Concerning the Canon of the Mass*. Leominster: Gracewing, 2009.

Witthoff, David. *The Lexham Cultural Ontology Glossary*. Bellingham, WA: Lexham, 2014.

WorldVision. "Global Hunger Facts." https://30hourfamine.worldvision.org/index.cfm?fuseaction=cms.page&id=3852.

www.ingramcontent.com/pod-product-compliance
Lightning Source LLC
Chambersburg PA
CBHW070918150426
42812CB00048B/997